Classical Music for Everybody

A Companion to Good Listening

Dhun H. Sethna

Foreword by Zubin Mehta

The Fitzwilliam Press

100 Monterey Lane, Sierra Madre, CA 91024

Published by:
The Fitzwilliam Press,
100 Monterey Lane, Sierra Madre, CA 91024
(818) 355 0622

Library of Congress Cataloging in Publication Data

Sethna, Dhun H, 1948-
    Classical Music for Everybody: A Companion to Good Listening / Dhun H Sethna
    p.   cm.
    Includes bibliographical references and indexes
    ISBN 0-9644103-3-8: $16.95

96-83154
CIP

To
my wife Virginia,
Jonathan and Judith
and Diana

and to
Ernst Krenek
(1900-1991)
Scholar, Composer and Friend

"And our hearts were fulfilled with the music he made with us,
Made with our hands and our lips while he stayed with us,"
-Algernon Charles Swinburne

iii

A Table of Contents

Acknowledgments vii
Foreword by Zubin Mehta ix
Prelude xi
How to Use this Book xv

Part I : How to Listen to Classical Music

1. The Sound of Music 3
2. The String Choir 15
3. The Wood Winds Choir 27
4. The Brass Choir 33
5. Musical Forms 41

Part II: The Timetables of Music

6. The Baroque World 63
7. The Classical Style 81
8. The Romantic Period 117
9. Impressionism 133

Part III: The Varieties of Musical Experience

10. The Sea 145
11. Death the Leveler 157
12. To Hell and Back 165
13. Faust 171
14. The Supernatural 179
15. The Human Condition 185
16. Struggling Heights: The Fight for Freedom 207
17. The Human Comedy 219
18. The Enchanted World 231
19. Myth and Legend 237
20. Shakespeare 243

An Appendix

A. Postlude 255
B. Bibliography 256
Index 259

Acknowledgments

This book has been put together from a large number of secondary sources which are liberally referenced in the text, and listed together to form the Bibliography.

Many colleagues, friends and strangers have given a largess of ideas, and an abundance of their time to review and comment on the manuscript at its varying stages, and to all of them that are unnamed I am much indebted. To write a foreword to any book is one of life's harder tasks, and to Maestro Zubin Mehta my heartfelt thanks for his kindness and generosity. My sincere gratitude also to Mr. G. Grant Gifford for his continued belief in my work and to Sharon Bise for her patience with my wearisome phone-calls, to Dr Charles Lee and my comrades-in-arms Myles E Lee MD and Tim Denton MD for their thoughtful suggestions that greatly improved the literary content of the manuscript, to William C Stivelman MD whose insight into recorded performances is legendary and who continues to make me hear new things in works that I thought I knew well, to Ann Heavey for her usual exuberant generosity in giving me her time and help, to Gladys Krenek, Frances Heifetz and Dady Kapadia for their support, and to Maestra Lucinda Carver, Ms Carole Stone, *Dean* David Swanzy and Professor Robert Greenberg for reaching out to help a stranger. Tom and Marilyn Ross of *About Books Inc.* magically transformed the manuscript into its present format, and to Gaelyn Larrick and Shannon Bodie of *Lightbourne Images* goes the credit for the magnificent cover. Thanks, too, to Virgie, Jonathan and Judy for the happiness of the past twenty years. The author absolves all but himself for errors of omission or commission that may remain in the book.

Foreword

At first sight there may appear to be no great necessity for yet another introduction to classical music for the lay-person. But as soon as one gets into this book, it becomes clear that it is different. The pleasures derived from almost any music lie hidden somewhere in the listener's past, and my pleasures with music I can certainly trace back to an early period of my childhood. In the beginning there is a sense of the Beautiful, a delight in the manifold sounds and forms and sentiments. But music that simply sings of the beauty before us, with however vivid a truth of the description of the sights and sounds, has failed to reach its very being and its substantial significance. For, quite independent of the passion with which it intoxicates the heart, or the truth by which it satisfies the mind, lies an indeterminate something else. And it is this something that Dhun Sethna's book challenges the beginner to reach out and examine, through its charming collection of little notes assembled from many sources. Music is spiritual nourishment; it cannot be reduced to a mere gushing forth of images separated from intelligence. It does not satiate, it only makes man more hungry, and therein lies its divine grandeur.

The music presented here is rich in experience, charged with passion, ready to take on Nature and Life, pleasure and pain, the thinker and the dreamer. Often, in moments of self-adoration, it forgets the world outside and becomes spellbound by its inner view, a sort of radiant inner glow, the phantoms of its Mind. At times the listener will feel comfortable with the music, rewarded by a vague but deep sense of contentment. But rational language, with its ready-made associations and worn-out meanings, is cut out to express the common-place. To strike at the heart and spirit through forbidden ways, composers have had to struggle to free themselves from rational language and its logical laws to create, in sound, a new language that is one with the music itself. Therefore, at other times, listeners may feel awkward as bits of the music begin to act strangely, when they start to leave the old ways to explore something that was never felt before.

For the lay music lover, this work serves as a magic solvent of the walls of a concert hall, rendering them transparent so that a vast audience might better benefit from the delights, and the illumination, that they conserve. The house of music has endless windows, any of which can be fashioned to open on the spreading field of the human scene by the pressure of an individual will and vision. And this book looks out of some of the windows and describes the view, and suggests what it tells.

Zubin Mehta
Los Angeles, 1997

"Alas for those who never sing,
But die with all their music in them"
— Oliver Wendell Holmes

Prelude

This book is an introduction for those who want to listen to what is colloquially called *classical music*, but have not the slightest idea of where to start. There are many today who would like to enjoy the good music that is so freely available on compact disc (CD), but who still believe that classical music is difficult and complex, and can only be appreciated after deep and serious analysis. *Classical Music for Everybody: A Companion to Good Listening* dispels this myth. Its purpose is to make such music more enjoyable and accessible to those who want to listen to it, and would like to know how to do so. It is assumed that the reader has had no formal musical training or any previous experience with musical design, analysis or nomenclature. There are no musical symbols or notations in this book. Nor are the subtleties of harmonic change or tonality, or of structural detail, discussed here. Indeed, this work is written with the conviction that little technical knowledge is necessary to begin an enjoyment of music through the senses and imagination. The only requirement is to come to the music with an open mind and a willing ear, and be prepared to use sympathetically all of one's faculties.

Music can be enjoyed without reading books about it; the taste for it is often innate. But natural abilities need definition, and it is the refinement of such natural abilities that is the task of this book. It does not intend to allow music to be a pretty amusement, or a mere narcotic to affect one in a passive state. Rather, its aim is to make the listening of music an exploration to discover the life in the music and to feel its spell and, perhaps, to reveal new insights to the listener about oneself and the human spirit. Where there is beautiful expression, we are told, there must be nobility of the prompting thought.

In simple language, this music companion gives the novice music lover the necessary background to understand and enjoy the great music of the ages. Every piece of music is a special kind of communication with a listener whose mind is operating not with impersonal aesthetic principles, but with personal sensitivities, perceptions and tastes. Such a communication will impress different minds differently, so that the *Listening Notes* in this book can, at best, only suggest images and lines of thought that will give the music lover a point of departure for his or her own imaginative flight. In other words, there is no single interpretation of any musical work.

Furthermore, no description of a passage of music can replace the actual sound of the passage; indeed, what a composer says in sound cannot be told in words. Herein lies one of the difficulties of writing about music, namely, the limitation of using words to communicate what words cannot communicate. This constraint, on the one hand, makes the same description applicable to many very different compositions and, on the other, makes it vexing to attempt to fit a program to any work simply because so many could be fitted.

The early chapters in this book introduce, in simple terms, the basic vocabulary of music. However, any schooling in music is of value only to allow one to respond more fully to its end, which is to communicate the varieties of human experiences. The larger part of this book, therefore, is a collection of musical pieces that reflect the broad human themes that have recurred over and over in the music of every age; the common themes of life and living that have been given their most intense and memorable expression in the sound of music. Perhaps the only end of music may well have been to enable one better to enjoy life, or better to endure it.

The selection of works for inclusion in a lay-person's book such as this has not been easy. Many favorites have been omitted, nor has every composer been represented. Many composers appear more than once in different contexts, and works of equal importance have not always received equal treatment. No list of musical pieces can please everyone, and this book is full of omissions. Vocal music and opera, for example, have for the most part been left out; they have earned books in their own right.

The compositions, however, *have* been chosen to give listeners a broad overview of the virtually infinite variety of recorded music. All the pieces are self-sufficient outside their original dramatic context and capable of striking up a life of their own in the general experience of the listener. Another consideration has been that they should be available readily and inexpensively on CD, so that they can be played as often as may be necessary to understand and appreciate them. It is often only after repeated listening that a composition suddenly comes alive and begins to make a definite though indefinable impression. And it is precisely such a moment that marks the beginning of an understanding of the music, and the opening of a new world of experience as rich and stimulating as any of the best.

This book is the outcome of syntopical reading and listening whereby many sources have been read, and many recorded performances listened to, as they relate to one another and to the musical piece about which they all revolve. From this a description of the piece has been constructed. The key ideas of more than a score of music masters have been quoted directly, or transcribed in summary, in the text. This book is, therefore, a distillation of that which has already been written in different places over a vast expanse of time. There is no new ground broken in its pages. In a sense, then, the references here assembled, and quoted from, are the very heart of the popular music appreciation tradition, and in these pages the best minds tell their thoughts, feelings and impressions, often in their own words. Most of these sources have been admitted in the references, and to them a debt is acknowledged at the outset.

In a way, the music offered here carries on a long talk, a great conversation, with the listener rather than present a formal introduction to classical music. The tone is informal, and this book does not have to be read from its beginning. The music lover may choose a specific topic, a culture, a century, or a particular composer. The problem will not be variety: no matter which chapter is selected, readers can look forward to a conversation with some of the liveliest composers the world has produced. The *Listening Notes* will point them out - the listeners must make friends by themselves.

"Good people all, of every sort,
Give ear unto my song"
— Oliver Goldsmith

How to Use this Book

Of all the arts, music is the only one that requires an intermediary for its projection from creator to observer. All recorded versions of the same musical work are, however, not the same. On the one hand, there is no definitive single recording on CD of any musical composition. On the other, a bad performance can be a very discouraging experience. Browsing through a large music store today is like setting out on a voyage without charts, and without a point of departure or an appointed destination. An unprecedented explosion of the classical music repertoire on CD, a vast range of bargain-priced good quality CDs, and the remarkable transfer to CD of the classic performances from the middle decades of this century offer a breadth of musical experience on CDs that is far beyond that possible from live performances.

For this reason, every musical *Listening Note,* or *Exhibit,* in this book is followed by a recommended inexpensive CD, indicated as "$", which evokes the mood of the piece as described in the *Listening Notes*. A mid-priced ($$) version is proposed when no budget CD has been found to convey satisfactorily the described listening experience. Sometimes, an exceptionally good performance is shown as a full-priced ($$$) alternative. The full-priced CDs, therefore, represent recorded performances whose magical quality make them a special treasure that is uniquely valuable.

As there are over 90 *Listening Notes* in this manual, the acquisition of even a basic CD collection can become an expensive proposition. The reader is advised to buy only one CD at a time from whatever arouses one's interest in the *Listening Notes*. A particular composer can be selected and his music more fully understood, or a certain mood or feeling can be explored to see how different composers have approached the same theme in their music. Whatever the approach, each piece should be heard several times before moving on to the next. This book, therefore, should be a base from which to journey forth into the music, return, and venture out again.

Complementing the *Listening Notes* are the references at the end of each chapter. These references form the core of the *Listening Notes*, and they have a singular purpose, which is to cite the authority for the statements in the text which may be in the form of summaries as well as direct quotations. The references are the heart of each chapter. Just as the *Listening Notes* are intended to help the readers to listen and think about a musical recording, the references are designed to direct them to the original sources for a greater discussion of a particular piece. The references are arranged in the order in which they appear in the text, and the authors and their works are collected together in the *Bibliography*. Many of these references are out of print, but are easily available at large public libraries. For this reason, the *Listening Notes* may well be an invaluable proxy for getting the flavor of the ideas and feelings expressed by these great authorities.

An extraordinary recording must be complemented by an outstanding sound system that reproduces the music as close to a live performance as allowed by one's budget. Shop around for the equipment with a couple of CDs in hand, and play the *same* music on each system. Try, for example, a symphony and a piano sonata. The technical "stats" of a system, no matter how impressive, are of value only if they allow it to respond more fully to its end, which is to produce a life-like sound. Two systems that do produce an outstanding sound for their price, unfortunately, cannot be examined at the shops. For budgets around $350, look at the *Bose* Acoustic Wave Radio if you can; any CD player can be attached to it. For those who can afford $1000, try out the more powerful *Bose* Acoustic Wave Music System with a built-in CD player. Both can be had on trial from *Bose* (1-800-898-BOSE).

List of Listening Notes by Topic

Page

The Sound of Music
1. Ravel: Bolero 3
2. Berlioz: The Roman Carnival Overture 10

The String Choir
3. Mozart: A Little Night Music (Eine kleine nachtmusik) 16
4. Mendelssohn: Violin Concerto in E minor 18
5. Berlioz: Harold in Italy 20
6. Saint-Saens: The Swan (Carnival of Animals) 22
7. Schubert: Symphony No. 8 (Unfinished) 23

The Wood Winds Choir
8. Tchaikovsky: Dance of the Flutes (Nutcracker suite) 27
9. Dvorak: *Largo* (Symphony No. 9: From the New World) 28
10. Beethoven: *Allegro ma non troppo* (Symphony No. 4) 30
11. Tchaikovsky: *Andantino in moda di canzona* (Symphony No. 4) . . 31

The Brass Choir
12. Mussorgsky: Pictures at an Exhibition 33
13. Holst: Mars (The Planets) 37

Musical Forms
14. Gregorian Chant 42
15. Beethoven: *Allegretto* (Symphony No. 7) 45
16. Bach: Fugue in G minor ("The Little") 48
17. Haydn: *Andante* (Symphony No. 94: Surprise) 49
18. Beethoven: *Rondo* (Piano sonata in C major: Waldstein) 51
19. Mozart: Symphony No. 40 55

The Baroque World

20. Vivaldi: Spring (The Four Seasons) 65
21. Bach: Brandenburg concerto No. 2. 67
22. Bach: Brandenburg concerto No. 5. 69
23. Bach: Concerto for violin and orchestra in E major. 70
24. Bach: Orchestral suite No. 2 73
25. Handel: Royal Fireworks Music 75
26. Bach: Mass in B minor 76

The Classical Style

27. Beethoven: Symphony No. 5 85
28. Beethoven: Symphony No. 6 (Pastoral) 90
29. Brahms: Symphony No. 1 95
30. Brahms: Symphony No. 4. 99
31. Mozart: Piano Concerto No. 21 (Elvira Madigan) 102
32. Schubert: Piano Quintet in A major (Trout) 106
33. Beethoven: Trio for Piano, violin and cello (Archduke) 109
34. Haydn: String Quartet No. 3 Op. 76 (Emperor). 112

The Romantic Period

35. Smetana: The Moldau (Ma Vlast) 118
36. Berlioz: Symphonie fantastique 121
37. Strauss: Ein Heldenleben (A Hero's Life) 123
38. Berlioz: The Corsair, Overture 126
39. Liszt: Hungarian Rhapsody No. 2 127
40. Mendelssohn: Symphony No. 4 (Italian) 128
41. Chopin: Polonaise Op. 53 130

Impressionism

42. Debussy: Prelude a l'apres -midi d'un faune 134
43. Falla: Nights in the Gardens of Spain 135
44. Respighi: The Fountains of Rome 137

The Sea

45. Debussy: La Mer (The Sea) 146
46. Debussy: Sirenes (Nocturnes) 149
47. Mendelssohn: Fingal's Cave. 150
48. Rimsky-Korsakov: The Sea and the Ship of Sinbad (Scheherzade) 151
49. Wagner: The Flying Dutchman, Overture 153

Death the Leveler

50. Beethoven: Funeral March (Symphony No. 3: *Eroica*) 158
51. Strauss: Death and Transfiguration 159
52. Berlioz: March to the Gallows (Symphonie fantastique) 161
53. Mahler: *Andante-Adagio* (Symphony No. 10) 162

54. Berg: *Allegro-Adagio* (Concerto for Violin and Orchestra) 163

To Hell and Back
55. Sibelius: The Swan of Tuonela 166
56. Liszt: Inferno (Dante Symphony) 166
57. Tchaikovsky: Francesca de Rimini, Overture fantasia 168

Faust
58. Liszt: A Faust Symphony 172
59. Liszt: Mephisto Waltz No. 1 (The Dance at the Village Inn) 175
60. Berlioz: Damnation of Faust, Excerpts 176
61. Wagner: Faust Overture 177

The Supernatural
62. Saint-Saens: Danse Macabre 180
63. Mussorgsky: A Night on Bald Mountain 181
64. Schubert: Der Erlkonig (The Erlking) 182
65. Berlioz: Dream of the Witches Sabbath (Symphonie fantastique) 183

The Human Condition
66. Liszt: Les Preludes 186
67. Beethoven: Symphony No. 3 (*Eroica*) 188
68. Tchaikovsky: Symphony No. 4 192
69. Brahms: Tragic Overture 195
70. Liszt: Tasso: Lamento e Trionfo (Tasso's Lament and Triumph) 197
71. Beethoven: Symphony No. 9 (Choral) 199

Struggling Heights: The Fight for Freedom
72. Tchaikovsky: 1812 Overture 208
73. Beethoven: Egmont, Overture 210
74. Sibelius: Finlandia 211
75. Weber: Der Freischutz, Overture 212
76. Berlioz: Rakoczy March 214
77. Rossini: William Tell, Overture 215

The Human Comedy
78. Haydn: *Finale, Presto-Adagio* (Symphony No. 44: Farewell) . . . 219
79. Strauss: Till Eulenspiegel 221
80. Wagner: A Siegfried Idyll 224
81. Strauss: Don Quixote 225

The Enchanted World
82. Dukas: The Sorcerer's Apprentice 231
83. Mendelssohn: A Midsummer Night's Dream, Overture 232
84. Weber: Oberon, Overture 234

Myth and Legend

85. Wagner: Prelude, Act I, Lohengrin 238
86. Wagner: The Ride of the Valkyries (Die Walkure) 239
87. Saint-Saens: Omphales Spinning Wheel (Le Rouet D'Omphale) 240
88. Beethoven: The Creatures of Prometheus, Overture 241

Shakespeare

89. Berlioz: Le Roi Lear (King Lear) 244
90. Tchaikovsky: Romeo and Juliet, Overture fantasia 245
91. Nicolai: The Merry Wives of Windsor, Overture 247
92. Berlioz: Romeo and Juliet, Excerpts 247
93. Tchaikovsky: Hamlet, Overture fantasia 250

List of Listening Notes by Composer

Exhibit No.

Johann Sebastian Bach

Brandenburg concerto No. 2 21
Brandenburg concerto No. 5 22
Concerto for violin and orchestra in E major 23
Fugue in G minor (*"The Little"*} 16
Mass in B minor 26
Orchestral suite No. 2 24

Ludwig van Beethoven

Overture, Creatures of Prometheus 88
Overture, Egmont 73
Piano sonata in C major (*Waldstein*) : *Rondo* 18
Symphony No. 3 (*Eroica*) 50, 67
Symphony No. 4: *Allegro ma non troppo* 10
Symphony No. 5 27
Symphony No. 6 (*Pastoral*) 28
Symphony No. 7: *Allegretto* 15
Symphony No. 9 (Choral) 71
Trio for piano, violin and cello (Archduke) 33

Alban Berg

Concerto for violin and orchestra: *Allegro-adagio* 54

Hector Berlioz

Damnation of Faust: Excerpts 60
Harold in Italy 05
Overture, The Corsair 38
Overture, King Lear 89

Rakoczy March 76
Roman carnival overture 02
Romeo and Juliet: Love scene; Queen Mab scherzo 92
Symphonie fantastique 36,52, 65

Johannes Brahms
Symphony No. 1 29
Symphony No. 4 30
Tragic overture 69

Frederic Chopin
Polonaise Op. 53 41

Claude Debussy
The Sea (*La Mer*) 45
Prelude to the Afternoon of the Faun 42
Nocturnes: *Sirenes* 46

Paul Dukas
The Sorcerer's Apprentice 82

Antonin Dvorak
Symphony No. 9 (*From the New World*) : *Largo* 09

Manual de Falla
Nights in the Gardens of Spain 43

Gregorian Chant
Chant. 14

George Frederic Handel
Royal Fireworks Music 25

Franz Josef Haydn
String Quartet No. 3, Op 76 (*Emperor*) 34
Symphony No. 44 (*Farewell*): Finale, Presto-Adagio. 78
Symphony No. 94 (Surprise): *Andante* 17

Gustav Holst
The Planets: *Mars* 13

Franz Liszt
Dante Symphony: *Inferno* 56
A Faust Symphony 58
Hungarian Rhapsody No. 2 39

Les Preludes 66
Mephisto Waltz No. 1 (The Dance at the Village Inn) 59
Tasso: Lamento e Trionfo (Tasso's lament and triumph) 70

Gustav Mahler
Symphony No. 10: *Andante-Adagio* 53

Felix Mendelssohn
Fingal's Cave (Overture, The Hebrides) 47
Overture, A Midsummer Night's Dream 83
Symphony No. 4 (*Italian*) 40
Violin concerto in E minor 04

Wolfgang Amadeus Mozart
A Little Night Music (*Eine kleine Nachtmusik*) 03
Piano concerto No. 21 (Elvira Madigan) 31
Symphony No. 40 19

Modeste Mussorgsky
A Night on Bald Mountain 63
Pictures at an Exhibition 12

Otto Nicolai
Overture, The Merry Wives of Windsor 91

Maurice Ravel
Bolero 01

Ottorino Respighi
The Fountains of Rome 44

Nicolai Rimski-Korsakov
Scheherzade: *The Sea and the Ship of Sinbad* 48

Gioacchino Rossini
Overture, William Tell 77

Camille Saint-Saens
Carnival of Animals: The Swan 06
Danse Macabre 62
Le Rouet d'Omphale (Omphale's Spinning Wheel) 87

Franz Schubert
Der Erlkonig (The Erlking) 64
Symphony No. 8 (Unfinished) 07

Piano Quintet in A major (Trout) 32

Jan Sibelius
Finlandia 74
The Swan of Tuonela 55

Bedrich Smetana
Ma Vlast: The Moldau 35

Richard Strauss
Death and Transfiguration 51
Don Quixote 81
Ein Heldenleben (A Hero's Life) 37
Till Eulenspiegel 79

Antonio Vivaldi
The Four Seasons: Spring 20

Peter Ilyich Tchaikovsky
1812 Overture 72
Francesca de Rimini: Overture fantasia 57
Hamlet: Overture fantasia 93
Nutcracker suite: Dance of the Flutes 08
Romeo and Juliet: Overture fantasia 90
Symphony No. 4 . . . . 68, 11

Richard Wagner
Die Walkure: The Ride of the Valkyries 86
Faust Overture 61
The Flying Dutchman: Overture 49
Lohengrin: Prelude, Act I 85
A Siegfrid Idyll 80

Carl Maria von Weber
Overture, Der Freischutz 75
Overture, Oberon 84

Part 1

How to Listen
to
Classical Music

"The man that hath no music in himself,
Nor is not mov'd with concord of sweet sounds...
Let no such man be trusted."
— William Shakespeare

1   The Sound of Music

Exhibit 1   Ravel: Bolero[1]

The French composer Maurice Ravel (1875-1937) became an in-
stantaneous American national hero when this extraordinary and gigantic
masterpiece of orchestration was introduced in New York City in 1929.
It was called a sensation, a minor miracle, a "bombshell". It was also a
unique experiment. More than any other work, this music, which is not
truly a bolero, illustrated how a whole composition may be built upon
the foundation of a single, purposeful and hypnotic rhythm which was
repeated relentlessly for nearly twenty minutes. The melody that was
used was a very old one that had been sung for centuries in certain provinces of Spain. It, too, was repeated persistently and forcefully with a
mounting excitement. Decades later, it is still impossible to convey, except through the music itself, the power and fascination of the cumulative
effects of this one, very long, crescendo of rhythm and melody.

The music begins to the military beating of a drum, played so softly
that it is only a whispered suggestion of the rhythm and the melody that
follows. The theme itself, reminiscent of an exotic Arabian night, is in
two distinct parts. The first part is introduced quietly by a solo flute,
sultry and intimate, and repeated by a solo clarinet. The second part of
the theme follows, and is unveiled by a solo bassoon and then repeated
by the clarinet. The wind instruments now take up this curious and wayward tune: First the bassoon, clarinet and the oboe, then the flute again,
followed by a muted trumpet and a saxophone. As the melody grows in
color, and the volume rises in a crescendo with the addition of more

3

instruments, the music exceeds the possibilities of the solo instruments. The tune is therefore picked up and repeated by groups of instruments to create novel and brilliant qualities of tone.

First comes the group of a piccolo, horn and the bells of a chiming celesta; then a combination of oboes, English horn and clarinets. Now the instruments are used in pairs, contrasting yet blending with one another. The tune never becomes monotonous, but the invariable rhythm creates an aching wearisomeness which is precisely the effect desired. The melody moves to the strings where it is divided and harmonized among them, and is then pitched against the similarly divided and harmonized wood winds. And all the time underneath, the maddening persistent rhythm moves on, enforced not only by the drums, but also by a plucking of the strings and the dissonant clusters of tones by a harp.

The whole orchestra now sways to the wicked rhythm. The volume rises, and just when a forceful finale seems inevitable, suddenly the melody changes ever so slightly in its tone, most noticeable in the violins and the wood winds. The music picks up power and spirals upwards, the sounds become more vibrant, the brass enters the fray and, finally, to the course bray of the trombones, the music propels forward and ends in a single, mountainous, demonic orgy of orchestral tone.

- Bolero; CHOPIN: Les Sylphides; DELIBES: Coppelia: Suite; GOUNOD: Faust, Excerpts, OFFENBACH Gaite Parisienne: Excerpts; TCHAIKOVSKY: Sleeping Beauty (suite)
    DG Double 437 404-2 (2) BPO, Karajan $
- Bolero; (i) Daphnis et Chloe: suite No. 2; Ma Mere L'Oye (suite); Valses nobles et sentimentales
    Naxos Dig. 8.550173 (i) Slovak Phil Ch.; Slovak RSO (Bratislava), Kenneth Jean $

What an exhilarating experience! We have just listened to one of the most well-known pieces in orchestral music, one that has become even better known over the last decade as the music in the movie "10".

For many of us who grew up enjoying rock'n'roll, pop or jazz, classical music still remains perplexing. Often, it seems like an abstract series of sounds having little connection with reality. Some of this pessimism may have been perpetuated by the well-meaning efforts of many who, by more commonly investigating "how it is done" rather than "what is being done", have unintentionally distracted the mind of the beginning listener from the sheer beauty and poetic enjoyment of it as a work of art. To look at such music exclusively through a technical analysis of its depth of modulation, the nobility of its form, or the fullness of its harmony is like looking at the Gothic cathedrals of Europe for the problems they solve in engineering.[2]

Fortunately, as Mark Twain has put it, classical music is "better than it sounds." Good music is a personal interpretation of experience, shaped and endowed with meaning, ordered by a particular intelligence and a particular sensitivity. The approach used in this book is to make the music itself create the taste by which it is judged, and allow the music to be appreciated by the listeners by having the listeners recognize themselves in the music. The task is made simpler because one of the marvelous things about this music is that it has many faces, and can be appreciated both intellectually and emotionally. Like poetry and painting it is modeled on life and, like all great art, its essence lies in the way it reveals the true feeling of the human condition and the human spirit, and the secrets of their inner world that long accumulate and ferment before they come surging up to the surface. This book challenges the listeners to reach out and examine the music, and then re-examine themselves, so that it becomes a joint effort to make sense of life—a shared world created through sound, to be imagined, explored and interpreted.

As an appreciation and expression of individual experiences, classical music does not always reflect life as it is lived and acted, but commonly as it is "recollected." It is life seen in the mode of contemplation, recreated into a new kind of life under the power of a new kind of drive through the activity of re-collecting, combining, amplifying and animating it to get it into an organic order.[3] From whatever embryo the sounds begin— an event, an emotion, a character, a scene, an idea—their themes seldom exist in isolation. They spread and proliferate, their consciousness swarms with physical and emotional impressions and associations that jostle and fertilize each other in the creative process. Sounds and memories become inextricably entwined into a medium in which both meaning and matter marry, and visions and revisions play their parts.

Some of the music introduced in this book suggests no transcendental quality of inspiration, no flint to kindle its flame; just a compulsive quiet energy that holds its steady flow. Much of it, however, seems to burst from a lifetime of standing out in thunderstorms and being struck repeatedly by lightning, from a capricious energy outside the purely conscious faculties that cannot be commanded but comes and goes, leaving only an impotent will at its withdrawal.[4] When material conditions have been hard, when life has been bitter and worn, when opportunity has been starved and happiness driven away, then the human spirit seems to have been forced back upon itself, and expression has sought refuge in

5

the more intimate recesses of musical articulation. Music, like running water, has the power to change misery into melancholy. Both, through their smooth, unceasing flow, pour over the soul the anodyne of forgetfulness and peace.[5]

It is within this more extended domain, through its relationship with the ways and manners of society and the life of an epoch, through the griefs and joys of humanity and the individual, that classical music is introduced in these pages. No formula can define or hold it. It is presented at once as an expression of the affectation and princely pride of the royal courts, and as the lyric expression of revolutionaries. It is heard as an art of faith and defiance during the Reformation, and as an art of the *salon* in the age of elegance. It is the voice of the democratic societies of the future and the voice of the aristocratic societies of the past.[6] It is the writing of princes and peasants, scholars and scoundrels, rationalists and madmen. It is the offspring of meditation and sorrow, of exultation and frivolity. Some have called it architecture in motion, others see it as poetical psychology; to one man it is a well-defined art, to another a purely spiritual expression.[7] It is an ever-welling stream of sound and song with plenty of haunting tunes and vigorous rhythms suggesting, on the one hand, a morning in May or a bustling town square and, on the other, the subtle soul of a decadent society or a jubilant celebration of life. It is this variety of experiences and spirit, this magical blend of intellect, emotion and poetry, that the present work seeks to capture, to take the beginner by the hand, by the ear and the imagination through the process of turning sound into meaning or into images, and thereby get more out of the music and, perhaps, out of life itself.

The music presented here has been arranged in arbitrary categories for the purpose of stimulating the novice music lover to explore the compositions. The arrangement is simply a convenience for grouping pieces that have something in common, and to allow the listener to appreciate simple distinctions in music that have a common bond. To pursue these adventures in good music, the reader is urged to go right ahead and browse through the *Listening Notes* in the other chapters. Let the voices of the orchestra sing their songs, let the music tell its tales from the heart. And at some later stage when the mind has been ripened, return to this chapter to read the scant introduction that follows, and pick up the basic vocabulary that formally describes the sound of music. This capsule guide, like the others in the later sections on musical genres and forms, is simplistic and approximate, and is intended to provide only the slightest coaching on the subjects.

＊　　＊　　＊　　＊　　＊　　＊

In its simplest sense, music has been defined as sound over time.[8] It is a performance in sound; it is something *made* with sound whereby the best sounds are arranged in their best order. In music, successive sounds follow one another, sometimes continuously, and sometimes with short spaces of silence in between. Hence, one fundamental characteristic of the sound of music is its horizontal progression over **time**: Sounds must follow one another to make music. In other words, specific sounds that are organized to occur in specific sequences, or in specific time relationships, make up a piece of music. If music can be expressed on a graph, then time must clearly be one coordinate, and it must be the horizontal one.[9] Every sound that makes music must have a certain position on the horizontal axis in relation to the sound before it, and the one after it. If you have understood this simple idea , then we're off to a sound start!

Some sounds may be made higher or lower than others; they may be more shrill or somewhat deeper. Some sounds, like a whistle, are high-pitched and others, like a thud, are low-pitched. In fact, every sound, no matter what it is, has its own intrinsic **pitch**. And we can make music when sounds of specific pitches are directed to follow each other over time. It appears, therefore, that in our graph, every sound must also have its own pitch. Pitch, from low to high, is the other essential component of each sound on the graph, and it forms its vertical coordinate.[10] Music, therefore, in its most primeval condition, must have the dimension of time and the property of pitch. When different sounds, or the points on our graph, are joined together by a line, then that line is the sound of music!

We can influence any sequence of sounds of different pitches to make better music by applying a few additional strategies. For example, we can adjust the duration of each sound, as the one follows the other, to create a certain systematic beat or **rhythm** (Greek: flowing). Rhythm is one of the most primitive elements in music and the one with an almost universal appeal. It is better heard than described; it is what makes you tap your feet or clap your hands to the music. That rhythm is intrinsic to music becomes apparent from the musician's game of tapping out a rhythmic pattern, and then having someone guess the piece of music. Rhythm is an inherent characteristic of music and, on our graph, it is a feature of its time dimension, or the horizontal axis. Musical notes, and the way they are arranged, are the formal ways of expressing "measured sound" on our graph. Sometimes, rhythms are made not only by sounds of various lengths but also by sounds alternating with short silences, and these can have a hypnotic or an electrifying effect.

A series of sounds can be made to follow each other at a slow speed or can be briskly abbreviated, as in a fast tune. The speed at which music moves, or its **tempo**, has been qualitatively expressed in Italian terms as follows:[11]

Presto	very fast
Allegro	fast
Allegretto	somewhat fast
Moderato	moderately paced
Andante	walking
Lento	somewhat slow
Adagio	slow
Largo	very slow
Grave	half dead!

Sounds can be manipulated even further. Any sound can be made loud or soft. The degree of loudness or softness of a sound in a musical piece is called its **dynamics** (Greek: *dynamis*, power). From the whisper of a single voice to the martial blast of a score of trumpets, music is capable of innumerable gradations of loudness or softness with each creating a different emotional effect. Sorrow or joy, mystery, triumph and introspection have each called for its appropriate dynamic scheme. To allow communication, the vocabulary of music has expressed the dynamics of sound qualitatively, also in Italian terms:[12]

forte, fortissimo	loud, very loud
mezzo forte, mezzo piano	medium loud, medium soft
piano, pianissimo	soft, very soft

Sounds that are successively growing louder are called crescendo, while those that are getting softer in sequence are decrescendo (*diminuendo*). After each musical climax, there is usually a relaxing of emotional intensity before the music gradually builds up to the next.

A variety of **tones** can be introduced to color our music by playing different instruments. Every musical instrument emanates a characteristic sound, often well recognized, called its tone or **timbre**. It is the property of tone that allows you to recognize the sound of a piano or a trumpet even without seeing the instrument. Many tones have been consistently associated with certain emotions, or have been used to produce specific orchestral effects. The oboe, for example, has a serene and tearful tone, and many a spectacular entrance in music has been announced to the loud flourish of the trombones.

A series of sounds with specific tones, set in a meaningful pattern over time, makes for a good strong tune or **melody**. Put another way, a melody is nothing else but a series of tones of different pitches arranged in a rhythmic pattern. But it is a conscious arrangement, with a planned beginning, middle part, and an ending. Melody is what we remember and what we whistle or hum. A single tone tells us little. It is when one tone leads to another, and still another, when each takes on a definite relation to the pattern as a whole, that a melody is born. Tones can be made to rise or fall to impart an effect that far transcends the meaning of words. Melody is the most expressive part of music; if rhythm is the heartbeat of music, then melody is its soul.

Finally, there is one last way in which we can manipulate sound, and that is through harmony. Harmony is the combination of two or more sounds at one time. Clusters of tones, called chords, when agreeably sounded and heard in combination form **harmony**. Three or more tones when combined together produce a **chord**. Various chords, or tone clusters, put together from distinct musical instruments can have distinctive personalities of their own. They can be sweetly harmonious giving an effect of tranquillity and fulfillment, or they can be harshly dissonant and restless. Some chords can be sensuous and caressing, and still others can be grim and foreboding. Often, instead of being played together, chords can be *arpeggiated* (Italian: *arpeggiare*, to play on a harp) whereby their individual tones are sounded quickly in succession like the strings of a harp.

Unlike pitch and tone which are inherent characteristics of a sound, harmony is an intellectual conception. It is man's deliberate creation, although harmony can fortuitously exist in nature. Harmony richens and colors a melody, adding to it support and a third dimension. It serves as the backbone for a tune. Harmony may even reinforce a tune's rhythm: It has been described as the "um-pah-pah" that the left hand sounds on a piano while the right hand plays the tune. Even when we whistle or sing a tune, we may "hear" its harmonic background—the "um-pah-pah"—in our imagination. If melody be the soul of music and rhythm its heartbeat, then harmony makes up its body, its substance.[13]

So there you have it! If you've got rhythm, harmony, a melody and different tone colors, you are ready to make music. The smallest group of sounds that have a germ of a musical idea is called a **figure**; two or more figures that are connected are called a **motive**.[14] Motives unite to form a **phrase**, and music is nothing else but a series of balancing phrases which stand to each other in the relation of question and answer to create a complete thought. Series of thoughts put together form a **movement**. A musical idea, or its fragment, which is repeated or developed during the course of a composition is called a **subject** or **theme**. A composition may also have an introduction, and an ending called a *coda* (Italian: tail).

The first *Listening Note (Bolero)* was chosen to illustrate the importance and power of **rhythm** in a musical piece. It is also an excellent example to show the wide variety of **instrumental color** that can be evoked by a modern symphony orchestra and, as such, it is a good introduction to the instruments of an orchestra. The **single tune** itself is easy to follow and, with this music, even a novice listener can learn how to follow a melody, which is the main musical theme, through a movement, and track its development in the composition. The listener should play the first piece (*Bolero*) again, just for fun. This time, try to identify the instrumental tones as the theme is taken up, first by the different instruments alone, then by groups of instruments, and finally by the whole orchestra.

Our second example (*The Roman Carnival Overture*) has **two** very distinct **melodies**: The music opens with a dashing *Saltarello*, a wild Italian dance, followed by a lovely tune which is the main theme of the movement. These two subjects are then developed skillfully into a work of great dramatic effectiveness. Identify the two themes and follow them through the music; see how the one predominates and then recedes to the background to give the stage to the other, only to come to the fore again. This music is ideal to demonstrate one of the important elements of good listening: In any piece of music, identify the theme and then follow the theme and its transformations carefully.

Exhibit 2 Berlioz: The Roman Carnival Overture

The opera *Benevuto Cellini* by Hector Berlioz (1803-1869) was a resounding failure at its *premiere* performance. The audience, we are told, hissed at it with admirable energy and unanimity. Determined to salvage what he could from the wreckage, the young and hot-headed composer drew up the tenor's main aria from Act I and the irresistible *Saltarello* dance that opens Act II, and blended them together into what became an immediate success, the "immense and terrifying" *Le Carnaval Romaine.*

This overture is a single movement that opens with a very brief, fiery and energetic rhythm given out by the violins, to which the wood winds and then the brass respond briefly to set a carnival mood. This is the wild *Saltarello* theme that forms the introduction to the overture, and ushers in a haunting tune, the second theme, that is chanted mournfully by a solo English horn. The melody is taken up by the violas, then by the violas and cellos, followed by the violins with a rhythmic accompaniment by the brass. Interwoven with this romantic song (the second theme) are fragments of the first theme, (the *Saltarello* dance passage), played by the wood winds and brass, and also the percussion instruments. Presently, swooping scales are heard on the wood winds to herald in the main part of the overture.

The dashing dance figure of the first theme is announced again by the muted violins, initially in a light passage, but then bursting out very loud. Rapid repeated tones of the brass also bring in the second theme, the familiar song of the horn. Now begins a development of the two themes, with a loud argumentative chorus by the entire orchestra over which the persistent and loud reiterations of the violin stand out. The music suddenly softens, the *Saltarello* seems to fade away in the distance, and the haunting horn melody is picked up by the bassoons and then by the trombones, while the second violins echo the throbbing rhythm of the dance theme in the background. But this is a mere feint; the dance returns, wilder than ever, to end in a long crescendo.

The *finale* begins with the haunting horn melody, first heard in the lower strings, then again by the trombones. Soon the tempo changes, and the strings begin the *Saltarello* again. The dance returns with an impetuous rhythm at a rushing pace to dominate the music in a glorious melee of dazzling orchestral colors, full of the gay and bustling scenes of the carnival. The music grows in swiftness and excitement, and is urged onwards to end in a powerful and brilliant climax with blazing brass and dashing strings.

- Overtures: Le Carnaval romaine, Op 9; Le Roi Lear, Op 4; Harold en Italie, Op 16
  Sony MPK mono 47679-2 . William Primrose, Viola, RPO, Sir Thomas Beecham $$

- Overtures: Le Carnaval romaine; Le Corsaire; Symphonie fantastique; Harold en Italie; Symphonie funebre et triomphale
  Ph Duo. 442 290-2 (2) Nobuko Imai; John Aldis Ch. LSO, Sir Colin Davis $

- Overtures: Le Carnaval romaine; Beatrice en Benedict; Benevuto Cellini; Le Corsaire; Romeo et Juliette: Queen Mab scherzo; Les Troyens: Royal hunt and storm; SAINT-SAENS: Le rouet d'Omphale
  RCA 9026 61400-2 Boston SO, Munch $$

---

[1] Rudel, Anthony, *Classical Music Top 40* (Simon & Schuster, Fireside Books, NY, 1995). The *Bolero* is analyzed in great detail, line by line, in Rudel's book

[2] Tovey, Donald Francis, *Concertos and Choral Works* (Reprinted, Oxford University Press, NY, 1989)

[3] Drew, Elizabeth, *Poetry, A Modern Guide to its Understanding and Enjoyment* (Laurel Editions; Dell Publishing Co., NY, 1959)

[4] Ewen, David, *Romain Rolland's Essays on Music* (Dover Publications, NY, 1959)

[5] Maurois, Andre, *Ariel: The Life of Shelley* (D. Appleton & Co., NY, 1929)

[6] Ewen, David, *Romain Rolland's Essays on Music*

[7] *Ibid*

[8] Kerman, Joseph, *Listen* (Worth Publishers, NY, 1972)

[9] *Ibid*

[10] *Ibid*

[11] Hurwitz, David, *Beethoven or Bust* (Anchor Books, NY, 1992)

[12] *Ibid*

[13] Stringham, Edwin, *Listening to Music Creatively* (Prentice Hall, NY, 1946)

[14] Hamilton, Clarence, *Music Appreciation* (Oliver Ditson Co., Boston, 1920)

Musical Instruments

Instruments provide the tone color in music. Every instrument produces a characteristic sound which identifies a property called tone or **timbre** that is characteristic for each instrument. It is also an important property of the human voice. Good listening requires an awareness of the separate tonal characteristics of different instruments, and an appreciation of how instruments, alone and in combination, have been used to state the meaning behind a musical idea or to express a certain mood or feeling. An overriding reason for trying to hear as much as possible in a musical work is that the composer does assign every note carefully and with great deliberation, and intends for *everything* to be heard. Aside from enjoying the sheer beauty of music itself, a greater pleasure can be derived if a melody is identified from its surrounding and supportive elements, and then followed from one orchestral section to another, or from one instrument to another, through its variations and peregrinations.

The credit for standardizing the musical instruments into the physical form and balance of a symphony orchestra goes to Franz Josef Haydn (1732-1809) who, for thirty years, was employed as resident composer and conductor at the palace of Prince Esterhazy near Vienna. Basing his work on some earlier experiments carried out by others at the ducal court at Mannheim, he used the Prince's private band of players as a laboratory to explore the proper balance between instruments. Haydn considered each instrument's tone to be a distinct contribution to the eloquence of the orchestra as a whole. And having a whole orchestra at his disposal, he could no sooner conceive a novel instrumental tonal effect than he was able to try it out. It was from his trials with musical symmetry and balance that our modern ideas evolved about the symphony orchestra. It was he who divided the instruments into four main instrumental families or choirs: The strings, wood winds, brass and percussion. Each family, in turn, was made up of a related group of four principal instruments, every one

13

of which had its own identifying tone color that stood out by itself. Such an orchestral division opened a new world of musical expression: The strings, for example, could now alternate with the wood winds for special dialogue effects instead of always combining with them as they had done before. Indeed, it is the blending of tones from various instrumental combinations that accounts for the infinite variety of music.

A few of the customary smaller unions of different instruments are the trio (three instruments) and the string quartet (four strings); a symphony orchestra, on the other hand, permits the most interesting tone assortment with instrumental combinations.

"It is sweet to dance to violins
When Love and Life are fair:"
— Oscar Wilde

2   The String Choir

The **string section** is the foundation of an orchestra. The four main types of stringed instruments are the violin, viola, violoncello (or cello, for short), and the double bass. The sound that each produces corresponds to one of the four basic human voices in a chorus: Soprano, alto, tenor and bass.

The sounds from a violin are amply familiar: They can dance and mock and flirt like Columbine or sigh and glow like Juliet. A violin is capable of light-hearted gaiety, empty-headed brilliance, or a soulful discourse on things of mighty import.[1] The viola produces a heavier, very emotional and gravely expressive sound. The sonority of a cello is more sober, like the voice of a friend bringing comfort; indeed, the cello has been called the eloquent amorist and imposing rhapsodist of the orchestra. The function of the double bass has been to supply a firm foundation for the entire string section.

The string section when played *pizzicato* (plucked) can evoke a variety of emotional moods. It can suggest the ominous and restless pacing of some giant, incredible beast lurking in impenetrable shadows (as in Beethoven: Symphony No. 5, third movement, see *Exhibit* 27). Or it can evoke a cavernous gloom as if to mark the departure of loved ones (for example, Schubert: Symphony No. 8, *Unfinished*, second movement, see *Exhibit* 7). And the *same* device has been used to mirror a gaiety that is nothing less than exuberant (as in Tchaikovsky: Symphony No. 4, third movement, see *Exhibit* 68).

There is no better way of appreciating the tone color of the various strings, or, for that matter, of any of the other instruments than to hear them sing their own songs. The *Listening Notes* (*Exhibits*) that follow in this section have been chosen to demonstrate the tonal characteristics of the entire string choir, and then the unique tone colors of each string instrument.

Exhibit 3 Mozart: Eine Kleine Nachtmusik

This elegant and delicate serenade ("A little night music") of Wolfgang Amadeus Mozart (1756-1791) is the most familiar example of an **orchestral string section** in action. Unlike the usual serenades that have five separate movements, this composition is made up of only four compact and intimate movements; it is believed that an additional movement, a minuet, has been lost. The serenade was written for first and second violins, violas, cellos and double basses; in its modern version, however, the body of instruments is usually enlarged with additional players on each part. Its four movements provide a good idea of the varied possibilities of a string choir, ranging from an introspective rendering of sentiment to a light and fleeting celerity of which no other instruments in the orchestra are capable.

Imagine a Sunday garden *fete* in the spring or early summer in eighteenth century Vienna. The beauty, nobility and talent of this grand city are here assembled, enjoying the freshly scented air and sunshine as they promenade along the green walks or sit luxuriously in the shade. Somewhere, among the trees, an orchestra is erected and, as the first sound of music rises delicately in the air, all conversation is suspended, the assembled sit quietly, and the promenaders pause to cluster around the musicians. On such a charming evening, with such airs and graces, originated the refined elegance and voluptuousness of this serenade. The music was meant to delight the senses, and should be listen to with this in mind.

The first movement is brisk, gay and march-like with a definite air of warmth and festivity. The musicians have started their cheerful task. The melody opens directly and is played loudly and with much gusto by all strings in unison. A second melody by the violins replies promptly, softer and with much daintiness to provide a contrast to the boisterous good humor of the first.[2] Note that the sounds of the first tune grow progressively louder (*crescendo*) in volume, whereas the second tune contrasts gracefully by becoming progressively softer in volume. Play this opening section again until the two melodies are well placed in your mind. Perhaps you should try to whistle or hum these two catchy tunes.

Now comes a series of alternations between the two tunes: The energetic assertions of the former and the quiet pleas for calm by the latter.[3] The music gives a feeling of being propelled forward with a potential energy like a coiled spring. Try to follow these themes as they course through the movement, whole or in part, or even altered. At times a melody may appear lost as you wander with it through its peregrinations but, just when you feel that it is getting completely mislaid, it reappears with all the fanfare of its original form. The entire point of these excursions is to maintain the tension between the two tunes. There is also a sprightly third theme, often called the "closing theme", which brings the exposition to a close; it is a whispering, chuckling fragment for the first violin, adorned with many trills and decorations which make it light and gay and altogether charming.[4] Once all three themes are exposed, they are not musically developed or manipulated in any serious fashion. The melodies are repeated unaltered in the second half of this movement but now in a different key. Although they are the same tunes, they somehow seem like an altogether new experience.

The second short movement, labeled a *Romance*, is appropriately slow and tenderly lyrical. There are no specific issues to concentrate on here. Just lie back and let the music waft around you. There is an air of grace and elegance throughout. The mood is definitely more personal, but the sentiment never gets any deeper than the intimacy of a song that is appropriate for a charming summer evening. A dialogue between the first violin and cello, supported by a fixed design of repeated tone clusters (chords) by the second violin and viola, can be recognized in the middle section.[5]

The minuet of the third movement is bright and forthright. It is followed by the traditional trio (violin, viola, cello) which provides a more feminine contrast to the music, as if the gentlemen had stepped aside and had permitted the ladies to grace the floor.[6] The first section of the minuet proper is now recalled (*minuetto da capo*) to end the movement.

The *finale* is a bustling gay piece with a jolly sprightly melody which, once heard, is hard to forget. The movement is in a *rondo* form so that the melody is merrily repeated a number of times with only slight variation, with each reappearance being separated by lively music. A second, more flowing melody provides some contrasting diversion. The movement ends in an assertive climax.

17

What a wonderful way, aristocratic and refined yet summery and colorful, to end an enchanting evening!

- Serenades Nos. 1; 7 (Haffner); 9 (Posthorn); 13 (*Eine Kleine Nachtmusik*), Serenata notturna, K 239
    Decca Double 444 458-2 (2), V. Mozart Ens., Boskovsky. $

Exhibit 4 Mendelssohn: Violin Concerto in E minor

After hearing this most popular of concertos for **solo violin,** a critic told Felix Mendelssohn-Bartholdy (1809-1847) that there was something exquisitely feminine about the piece: If Beethoven had made the heroically masculine Adam of violin concertos, then surely this was its mated Eve.[7] Profound it certainly is not, but this work has maintained a pure lyrical beauty, characteristic of the Romantic spirit of its time, which has never failed to enchant the listener.

Mendelssohn follows a new precedent that had been set by Beethoven, which was to dispense with the traditional orchestral introduction that usually led in the solo instrument. He also omits the traditional orchestral linkages that were used to connect the movements. Instead, the solo instrument itself opens the first movement, very fast and impassioned, by immediately announcing the first theme. It begins as a dreamy rather than a passionate melody, but it soon assumes a more ardent character. The tune continues with a consummate rhythm, expanding through brilliant passage work, and is eventually caught and restated by the full orchestra. Presently, the orchestra thins out, and a second contrasting melody, serene and tranquil, introduced by the violins and oboes, is picked up by the solo violin. An impassioned musical episode follows in which the solo violin soars, playing up and down the strings, poised for a moment on the highest note, then descending softly to linger on the lowest note while the clarinets hum the tune, softly and peacefully, along with the flutes. The accompaniment ceases, and the solo violin once again develops this second theme.

Now the first theme returns with a warm and gladsome mind, first fragmentarily on the violins and oboes, and then on the solo violin where it is lavishly developed leading to a brilliant dialogue between the solo and the orchestra. The orchestra soon becomes silent, giving the stage to the violin which continues its magic fantasy flights with skillful rapid runs and showy swoops, never once stopping to catch a breath, teetering brilliantly at times as if it were at the top of a slide, until a loud trill tells a gasping and bedazzled orchestra to come in again to a fast and loud ending. But forthright the theme is brought back in softly by the violins and the wood winds, the solo instrument meanwhile being preoccupied with playing a series of tripping, rapidly successive notes. Both the first and second themes are now recapitulated, the movement gathers momentum, and ends in an orchestral climax accompanied by a brilliant outburst by the solo violin.

The second movement begins at once after the first; indeed, the two are actually linked together without interruption by a long tone by the bassoon. A lovely lyrical tune, the same poignant simple melody of the first theme, unfolds slowly, filled with breadth and dignified expression.[8] Here is music of such serenity and calm that it seems to come from another world, a place of peace, beauty and tranquillity. A contrasting theme, introduced by the orchestra, recalls the more impassioned mood of the first movement. The first theme is now repeated, then the music goes through a brief moment of anxiety in which the solo violin performs a series of semi-quavering figures; but this passes, and the movement ends peacefully.

A short violin interlude connects the second with the joyous final movement. A courtly flourish of horns, bassoons and drums, interrupted four times by swishes in the solo violin, opens the *finale*. Now the first theme reappears in the solo violin embellished with faery-like accompaniments by the wood winds. A sprightly conversation ensues between the solo violin and the wood winds with the strings plucking the tones here and there until, with an upward sweep from the violin, the entire orchestra announces the second theme which carries on a cheeky and vivacious exchange with the first.[9] The music becomes impetuous, full of dash and verve, gay and animated in the best capricious vein, to end in a brilliant close with the second theme.

- Violin concerto in E minor, Op 64; TCHAIKOVSKY: Concerto
    Naxos Dig. 8.550153. Nishizaki, Slovak PO, Jean $

- Violin concerto in E minor, Op 64; TCHAIKOVSKY: Concerto
    DG 419 067-2. Milstein, VPO. Abbado $$

- (i) Violin concerto in E minor, (ii) Symphony No 4 (Italian); Overtures: The
    Hebrides (Fingal's Cave); A Midsummer Night's Dream; Ruy Blas; BRUCH:
    Concerto No. 1
    EMI Seraphim CEDB 68524-2 (2) LSO with (i) Menuhin, cond. Fruhbeck de
    Burgos (ii) Previn $

- "Favorite violin concertos" (with (i) Concg. O;(ii) New Philh O; (iii) Sir Colin
    Davis; (iv) Bernard Haitink; (v) Jan Krenz); BEETHOVEN: (i;iii) Concerto in D;
    (i;iv) Romance No. 2 in F;— BRAHMS: (ii;iii) Concerto in D. (ii;v)
    MENDELSSOHN: Concerto in E min. —TCHAIKOVSKY: Concerto in D
    Ph. Duo 442 287-2 (2) Grumiaux, Arthur $

Exhibit 5 Berlioz: Harold in Italy

Hector Berlioz (1803-1869) first met the famous violinist Paganini in 1833. Although some have reason to doubt his recollections, Berlioz states in his published *Memoires* that Paganini approached him to commission a virtuoso viola solo that could display his talents on a wonderful new viola, an admirable Stradivarius, that he had recently acquired. A flattered Berlioz went to work at once to plan a piece where the solo viola would be combined with an orchestra, but always keeping the solo instrument in first place. The initial version met with Paganini's disapproval when he saw the number of orchestral episodes usurping his solo time. The commission fell through, but Berlioz resolved to proceed alone and write a series of scenes for orchestra where the solo viola would serve as a sort of a principal character, a melancholy dreamer in the style of Lord Byron's *Childe Harold*. Thus was born, says Berlioz, a new symphony in four movements (*The Harold Symphony*) with the title *Harold in Italy*.

But there is no trace in Berlioz's music of any of the famous passages in *Childe Harold's Pilgrimage*. There is nothing Byronic about this music. Although the central character of the work purports to be *Childe Harold*, the true hero is, of course, Berlioz himself. And in this music he recreates his own pilgrimage of earlier years when he had wandered, carefree and happy, in the Abruzzi mountains near Rome. The part of Harold is played by a viola soloist who, in true Romantic form, stands far from the orchestral crowd, lost in his musings. This symphony is presented here because of the unique role given to the **viola** in this music.

The music opens with Harold in the mountains, surveying the view as he reflects upon his past experiences of sadness, happiness and joy. A melancholy opening, arising from the depths of the orchestra, leads to a minor version of the theme announced by the wood winds. Presently, the solo viola enters dramatically to represent Harold himself, accompanied by a harp and two clarinets. The theme (or *idee fixe* as Berlioz called it) is played twice over, the second time as quietly as possible. This delightful melody is soon restated gorgeously by the full orchestra with the wood winds echoing the strings at a distance. The resemblance of this tune to the main theme of Beethoven's seventh symphony has not gone unnoticed!

As the theme dies away, there follows a group of lively musical figures upon which the viola intervenes somberly. There is a sudden break-off, and then a second theme is cheerfully announced by the solo viola which then carries on a dialogue with the orchestra. Fragments and variants of the *idee fixe* reappear to represent Harold's straying thoughts. Somewhere, the theme is developed and echoed by the wood winds with a displaced rhythm. The music flows magnificently towards the end of the movement when Harold reintroduces himself, with the tune beginning very expressively in the double basses and then taken up gradually by the rest of the orchestra.

The second movement describes the march of the pilgrims singing their evening prayer. After some mysterious clusters of tones, a hymn-like melody is chanted by the strings, softly at first, then getting progressively louder as the pilgrims approach and then recede away. A picturesque effect of distant monastery bells is suggested by a high pitched flute, oboe and harp and then by the horns and harp. Harold, whose presence is conveyed by the solo viola, contemplates the approaching pilgrims. The *idee fixe,* at one point, accompanies a solemn little chorale heard high in the air as the footsteps of the pilgrims retreat in an unbroken march that is represented by the plucked basses. The march finally dies away to the sound of distant bells and retreating footsteps in a musical ending of fantastic length and originality.

A serenade of an Abruzzi brigand to his mistress forms the third movement. Armed with mountain pipes, guitar and *musette*, he sallies forth to place himself under his beloved's window. After some lovely rustic piping on a piccolo and oboe against the drone of bagpipes, the serenade begins, stated by a plaintive English horn, in a tempo that is twice as slow. Presently, Harold appears to contemplate the scene, and the solo viola becomes more lively as the serenade continues independently to come to a close. Then the lively piping is resumed, and the viola enters again, but this time to play the slow serenade while the *idee fixe* hovers airily, played in bell-like tones by the flute and harp, until the music fades away.[10]

The brigands' orgy begins fast and fierce with a wild and brilliant *tarantella*-like dance in the fourth movement. Its violent strains are interrupted as Harold recalls, through the viola, the things that have recently passed, such as the melancholy main theme, the pilgrim's march and the brigand's serenade. But these are opposed and suppressed by the orgy theme. Harold's own past happiness is not so easily ousted.[11] Whatever may have induced Harold to join the lot of the brigands, it is a moment of genuine pathos when he parts with his very identity in the last broken reminiscences of the *idea fixe* that is now played faintly by the clarinets, echoed by sobs, as it dies away.[12]

Sardonic laughter is now heard, growing to exultant cries as the orgy resumes. This musical material is traversed twice when suddenly it is interrupted. From the distance arises the chant of the pilgrims, not a reminiscence but the real sound—pathetic pleas of mercy as the brigands respond with fiendish laughter! Harold listens with a palpitating and breaking heart. He can endure this ruthless life no further, and he leaves this world to have the brigands continue their orgies without him.

- Harold en Italie; Symphonie fantastique; Overtures: Le Carnaval romaine; Le Corsaire; Symphonie funebre et triomphale
   Ph Duo. 442 290-2 (2) Nobuko Imai; John Aldis Ch. LSO, Sir Colin Davis $

- Harold en Italie; Overtures: Le Roi Lear, Op 4; Le Carnaval romain, Op 9
   Sony MPK mono 47679-2. William Primrose, Viola; RPO, Sir Thomas Beecham $$

Exhibit 6 Saint-Saens: The Swan in Carnival of Animals

Nowhere else did Camille Saint-Saens (1835-1921) show such engaging humor as in this imaginative fantasy of zoological impressions for orchestra that he composed for a Mardi Gras concert. Melodies from Offenbach, Berlioz, Mendelssohn and Rossini are freely borrowed and interpolated in this music to provide witty, satiric and tender characterizations of the different animals. But of all the pleasing moments in this charming score, none has been so popular as the deservedly famous melody for **solo cello** that represents the *Swan*.

The short cello solo is associated with two pianos, one of which provides a continuous accompaniment whereas the other only interposes at intervals. The elegance, grace and calm of a swan gliding serenely is imagined picturesquely by the cello. The mood is enchanting, the music slow and sustained, and the movement closes gently to the sound of the pianos.

- (i) Carnival of Animals; Danse macabre, Op 40; Suite algerienne, Op 60: Marche militaires francaise; Samson et Dalila: Bacchanale. (ii; iii) Symphony No 3 in C min. Op 78.
   Sony SBY 47655-2 (i) Entremont, Gaby Casadesus, Regis Pasquier, Yan-Pascal Tortelier, Cause, Yo Yo Ma, Lauridon, Marion, Arrignon, Cals, Cerutti; (ii) Phd. O Ormandy, (iii) with E. Power Biggs $$

Exhibit 7 # Schubert: Symphony No. 8 in B minor (Unfinished)

It has been said that the music of Franz Schubert (1797-1828) was the product of his genius and his miseries. Indeed, what he had composed in his greatest distress, when he had felt most betrayed by fate in his brief life, was that which has seemed best to the world. Few people have been able to escape the spell of the tragic Unfinished symphony, so called because this masterpiece has only two movements.

The twenty six year old composer had presented the score to the Styrian Music Society of Graz in 1823 when he was elected a honorary member. Why the symphony, which was not his last work, was never completed, and why the Society's director kept the score private for thirty seven years after the composer's death, will always remain unanswered. Some have speculated that the many resemblances to Beethoven's second symphony might have made Schubert fear an accusation of plagiarism. And yet the incomplete state is as exquisitely perfect in finish, and as ineffably charming, as the incomplete Venus de Milo. Music can go no further; in language of inexpressible beauty it communicates an intensity of passionate emotion and a degree of sacred exaltation that is a completely satisfying and expressive experience.[13] A haunting melody in the second movement for which this work is famous has been claimed to be one of the purest melodies in existence. Indeed, it has been said of this music that the closer one listens to it, the more distantly one hears it. This piece is presented here because the opening movement is an example of how well the deep and gruff **double bass** can project a lyrical melancholic tune.

The first movement opens with an air of gloomy and brooding sadness expressed by the cellos and double bass. It is a mysterious prophetic utterance which foreshadows the actual melody. Listen to the double bass: First comes a quivering in the strings, and somewhere within the rhythmic bass, like the restless pacing of some giant creature, an indefinable tune is hovering.[14] Presently, like a royal figure sweeping in after his noble precursors, the pensive tone of an oboe and a more robust clarinet begin the real idyllic melody. The song emerges high and clear in its soft sadness, urged by insistent rhythms from the violins, but still preserving the prevailing tone of delicacy and lightness. The full orchestra interrupts the song dramatically with crashing clusters of tone. Try to remember these shattering chords because later they will be used to provide, temporarily, a striking contrast to the main musical theme. Fragments of the melody now reappear—a horn and bassoon enter with one voice; one note lingers, changing color as it fades away to usher in again the iridescent accompaniment of the violins.[15] The melody is developed with more striking orchestral interjections to an increasingly powerful, expressive and tragic intensity. The orchestral clashes recur, but now they seem not to be dramatic interruptions but are quite a real part of the music.

A new, sweet and charming melody, perhaps representing a dream or a memory, is presently introduced by the cellos, and delicately echoed by the violins with full romantic poetry. This is the unforgettably moving song of the cellos, perhaps one of the most beautiful melodies ever written. And with it, the music is set firmly on its way. A marvelous succession of tunes, with an array of variations, flows in an uninterrupted and wandering stream, sometimes faint with moments of sadness and pain, sometimes loud and powerful and utterly ecstatic. The melody is repeated with gentle persistence and an almost pious stubbornness to close this section in a poignant mood.

Quick, tragic-sounding, loud interjections from the bassoons, horns and trombone, that immediately get softer, set the stage for a change in mood. This is the music of mourning, expressing the loss of something that, perhaps, may not even have existed, perhaps the loss of something passionately desired yet never achieved. The tension starts to emerge slowly, beginning softly with the cellos and basses, after which the violins take over with a bassoon. The music becomes progressively louder. One can almost feel the irreducible and insoluble passion and the pain as a struggle sets in and accelerates in a series of peaks and short explosions. It is heightened by a continuous agonized and agonizing shivering from the basses and cellos, only to die down just as swiftly. The brass now joins the fray and, to the blaring sustained notes by the trombones, the music bursts into a forceful climax.

A haunting duet by a flute and oboe provides a brief respite, but the stress and conflict builds up again hysterically, led by the strings and wood winds. Once again the music seems to momentarily run out of energy, and once again the cellos return with fragments of the opening melody. But this time it is joined fiercely by the violins, clarinets, bassoons and oboes to build up into an overwhelmingly tragic and emotionally draining peak that is accentuated by a forceful rumbling by the timpani. The orchestra is spent and exhausted following this epic climax. Three loud distinct chords, like sudden howls aroused by a personal loss, change the mood, and a tremulous music fades softly and slowly away into emptiness and silence to end the movement.

The second movement is in five sections, with similar musical material being played in alternating sections. The mood of the music changes as the second movement begins with the same melodious double bass of the opening, once again presaging a new melody. This gracious tune is played wistfully by the horns and bassoons with the strings answering in unison over a plucking bass, the latter seeming almost like the sounds of the footsteps of an impending and uncertain destiny.[16] Full orchestral interruptions intervene between this pensive question-and-answer-type melodic conversation of the wood winds. The vision is rudely broken at its loveliest by loud and angry crashes whereby all sense of connection with the past is lost, only to reappear as a noisy whisper in the bass.

A second section begins with a melody which is played intensely by a clarinet and flute, with a string accompaniment whose weak beats are strongly accented to give a dance-like rhythm. The music surges forward, clothed in a beauty that snatches away the breath, and seems to arrest momentarily the incessant pulsation of life.[17] This tune is extended by the full orchestra, and then developed expressively by the strings. The heavy footfalls of destiny seem to draw closer and closer, becoming stronger and more positive. The gentle plaint of the flutes and clarinets rises over and over again, and one begins to feel in the music a certain attitude of resignation and acquiescence.[18]

The scene glides quietly into the third section with a return of the first melody on the wood winds, complete with the ominous progression of the plucking basses. This is developed through both its gentle and wild phases with new and surprising musical phrases. The two following sections (four and five) are a repetition of the preceding two (two and three) respectively. The movement ends abruptly in a lingering silence.

- Symphony No. 8 in B minor (unfinished)—MENDELSSOHN: Symphony No. 4 (Italian)
  DG Dig. 445 514-2 . Philh. O, Sinopoli $$

- Symphony No. 8 in B minor (unfinished); 9 in C (Great)
  DG 439 475-2. BPO, Karl Boehm $

[1] McKinney, Howard, & Anderson, WR, *Discovering Music* (American Book Co., NY., 1934)
[2] Stringham, Edwin, *Listening to Music Creatively* (Prentice Hall, NY., 1946)
[3] Hurwitz, David, *Beethoven or Bust* (Anchor Books, Doubleday, NY., 1992)
[4] Downes, Edward, *Guide to Symphonic Music* (Walker & Co., NY., 1981)
[5] Moore, Douglas, *From Madrigal to Modern Music* (W W Norton, NY., 1942)
[6] Downes, Edward, *Guide to Symphonic Music*
[7] *Ibid*
[8] Stringham, Edwin, *Listening to Music Creatively*

[9]   *Ibid*
[10]   *Ibid*
[11]   *Ibid*
[12]   *Ibid*
[13]   O'Connell, Charles, *The Victor Book of the Symphony* (Simon & Schuster, NY., 1935)
[14]   Goepp, Phillip, *Great Works of Music* (Garden City Publishing Company, NY., 1913)
[15]   O'Connell, Charles, *The Victor Book of the Symphony*
[16]   *Ibid*
[17]   *Ibid*
[18]   *Ibid*

"To dance to flutes, to dance to lutes
Is delicate and rare:"
— Oscar Wilde

3 The Wood Winds Choir

The four principal wood winds are the flute, oboe, clarinet and bassoon. They are called wind instruments because they are blown with the breath; a number of them, however, are no longer made out of wood. Since their tone is so much more striking, they are used in a musical piece for shorter periods than the strings. A flute is the most agile and versatile, and can be played faster than any of the other wood winds. It exudes a cool, fluid or feathery tone. In contrast, an oboe has a serene, pastoral sweetness, sometimes even a plaintive sound. The clarinet is usually crystal clear and brilliant, almost as agile as the flute, but it can also be used with dramatic effect to clad a tune in haunting apparels. A bassoon, in its lowest tones, supplies a deep, bass voice.

Each of the four principal wood winds has a related family member. The flute is related to the piccolo, the oboe to the English horn, the clarinet to the bass clarinet, and the bassoon to the double bassoon. Much has been said of the English horn; it has been called "the romantic poet of the tonal world which, like the evening star, can bid the west wind sleep on the lake and wash the dark with silver."[1]

Exhibit 8 Tchaikovsky: Danse des Mirlitons from The Nutcracker Suite

A poor little girl who has received a plain old nutcracker as a Christmas gift dreams that it has turned into a handsome prince. Together they fly away to the court of the Sugar-Plum Fairy, where all the flowers and toys dance to celebrate the romance of the little girl and her Prince Charming. Out of this simple story by E.T.A. Hoffmann comes this charming ballet music with its exotic rhythms, captivating melodies and a perennial vitality. Peter Ilyich Tchaikovsky (1840-1893) himself conducted the premiere performance in St. Petersburg in 1892. This well-known selection is presented here to demonstrate the bird-like agility and brilliance of the **flute**.

A brief introduction by the plucking of violas, cellos and double bass, and the sparkling airy tune, pensive but gay, takes off, played by three flutes and a piano. After a slow melody sung by the horn, the tune is repeated again. The middle section sports the famous robust passage with a rising and falling gentle swell played by a muted trumpet against a background of brass and percussion that is taken up presently by the whole orchestra. The flutes resume the exquisite fairy-like tune again, more strongly supported now, and the music rises to a climax to close the dance.

- Nutcracker suite; Sleeping Beauty: suite; Swan Lake: suite
  DG 429 097-2; BPO, Rostropovich $$

Exhibit 9 Dvorak: Largo from Symphony No. 9² "From the New World"

Antonin Dvorak (1841-1904) came to America from his native Bohemia in 1892, and he composed this symphony during a retreat to the little Czech colony of Spillville in Iowa. Inspired by the chants of the American Indian and the plantation songs of the American Black, he modeled his melodies after the idiom of the native American music that he had heard, blending them with Bohemian folk tunes and mannerisms. The violent racial controversy that this music sparked has long since been forgotten, but the symphony remains, vitally imaginative and alive, flush with beauty and poetry and personal utterances of genuine poignancy.

The slow second movement (*Largo*) is one of the most appealing and best-known pieces of symphonic music. It has been said that Dvorak was especially influenced by the Indian burial scene in Longfellow's *Song of Hiawatha* when he composed this movement. It is rich with the mellowness and religious feeling of the Negro Spiritual that is eloquently expressed by an **English Horn** (*cor anglais*), and this musical piece is presented here as an example of what is probably the most beautiful melody for the horn.

The slow movement opens with mysterious tonal clusters, thrice repeated, solemnly struck by brass and bassoons, and which progressively gets brighter and louder with each new chord. Muted strings now strike softly, and gently usher in a languishing melody played by the English horn with the still muted strings supplying a lovely accompaniment. The reedy yearning quality of the horn brings out to the full the poignant wistfulness of the tune.[3] The ideas that flow from it are not readily definable: Some have compared it to the brooding tenderness of a Bohemian lullaby, others to the vast awesome loneliness of a night on the prairie; indeed, one may fancy in it whatever may grip the imagination of the listener! A clarinet breaks in, rich and quiet, then a bassoon intervenes for an equally brief space and, as the horn fades away, the clarinet alone continues its echo.

Now the tearful oboes moan, then the flutes, clarinets and bassoons. Presently, a single sustained chord from the brass sounds one brief outburst of emphatic passion before the violins and cello softly unfold the melody. There is a feeling of terrible loneliness, a sense of an intense peace. The horn emerges again to sing its slowly winding song, mournful and holy, and in its song it dies off slowly, allowing the clarinet to complete the phrase.

A pastoral serenity clothes the air as the flute and oboe start a new trill to a tremulous accompaniment by the strings. As the music proceeds, the horn's song echoes distantly in the wood winds, followed by a dreamy intoning by the horns themselves. As they fade away, a new melody is picked up, sadder yet more vigorous than before, first by the clarinets, then by the flutes and oboes, set to a dismal march plucked by the basses. The tune is renewed by the violins more fiercely, and to this the flutes respond with cool caressing tones like soothing fingers.

Suddenly, the dreary clouds seem to part and the sun comes dazzling through the leaves! The oboe launches a cheery melody, a trilling flute merrily takes over, the lively violins follow, the pace quickens, and the whole orchestra trembles with excitement. But the happiness is short-lived. A resounding blast cuts through the jubilation, and the brass responds loudly with the rumbling timpani. As the anxiety subsides, the soothing horn emerges again with its soulful song, followed by the muted strings and violas. A solo violin and solo cello echo the theme, the strings and then the wood winds rise slowly and fade, then rise again to meander on and dissolve softly into the low tonal chords of the basses.

- Symphonies Nos 7, 8, (ii) 9 (New World); (I) Symphonic variations Op. 78
  Ph Duo 438 347 (2). (i) LSO (ii) Concg O, Sir Colin Davis $

- (i) Symphony No. 9 in E min. (From the New World); SMETANA: Moldau
  London 417678-2 VPO, Kertesz $

- Symphony No. 9 in E min. (From the New World) —SMETANA: Bartered Bride
  overture; —WEINBERGER: Schwanda polka and fugue
  RCA 09026 62587. Chicago SO. Fritz Reiner $$

Exhibit 10 Beethoven: Allegro ma non troppo from Symphony No. 4

About the time that he was writing his fourth symphony, Beethoven was in love with the Countess Theresa von Brunswick who seems to have reciprocated his sentiments. This has been used to explain the gay mood that prevails in this music. There is something pretty and light in its movements, and whatever may lie behind its history, it sounds happy and ingratiating and complacent. But it is hardly the kind of expression one would expect from a Beethoven who is successful in love.

The symphony was dedicated to a Count who had paid the composer a handsome fee to write a new symphony for him. The story goes that Beethoven had intended the fifth symphony for the assignment. But pressed by perennial pecuniary problems, he had been compelled to sell this work prematurely, and therefore he committed the fourth symphony to this patron. This musical piece is presented here because of the **bassoon solo** in its fourth movement.

The fourth movement is an outpouring of pure joyous laughter; it is perhaps one of Beethoven's merriest conclusions. But those who think the finale too light may well have missed a true understanding of this piece. Some have claimed that to do full justice to the boldness and power that underlie all the grace and humor of this fourth movement may well need a lifetime of study.[4] For, it has been said, this *finale* represents Beethoven's first and full mature mastery of the true inwardness of his great predecessors Haydn and Mozart, a discovery that hitherto had seemed inaccessible to him.

The first and second violins open the music in a frolicking perpetual-motion rhythm evoked by whirling figures that set the pace and establish the brisk rhythm. The strings run along in sequences of musical fragments until at last a real tune comes along. The main theme now passes to a scurrying solo bassoon which appears comical because, at this pace, it is very difficult to play this instrument gently as instructed! Little wisps of melody and musical fragments in the wood winds emerge briefly, and as quickly subside in this symphonic whirl. As the garrulous strings keep running indefinitely on their old musical motive, a loud single note breaks in as if to say: This really must stop! The music briefly pauses after a roll on the kettledrums, then gathers momentum again.

But the discussion is never very serious. A rollicking dance and the whirling figures return, the melodies skip again in another round until, quite needlessly, they join in together and dance to a fierce climax. There is again a lull, then the basses steadily hum the little tune and the violins sing a tuneful answer. After another pause, the theme deliberately slows its pace and stops once more. The wood winds sing four more notes to a halt, then the strings do the same. Then all the orchestra joins in boisterously in a big festive noise, and the speed scampers down to close the music.

- Symphony No. 4; Symphony No. 6 (Pastoral)
   Sony SMK 64462, Columbia SO, Walter $$

- Symphonies 1-2; 4-5.
   DGG Double 439 681-2 (2) VPO, Karl Boehm. $

Exhibit 11 Tchaikovsky: Andantino in moda di canzona from Symphony No. 4

"No one of my orchestral pieces was the result of such labor, and on no one have I worked with so much love and with such devotion." Thus spoke Peter Ilyich Tchaikovsky (1840-1893) of his favorite fourth symphony. It was composed for his loyal confidante and patroness Mme. von Meck who had helped the sorrowing composer through many bleak periods. He wrote to her, "How glad I am that this is *our* work." The slow second movement is presented here as an example of the mournful quality of the **oboe**.

The second movement, explained Tchaikovsky in his program notes, shows another phase of sadness. Here is the melancholy feeling that enwraps one when one sits at night alone in the house, exhausted by work, mourning the past, but without the courage to start anew. One thinks about the sad moments gone by and the glad hours so irrevocably lost. And all this is so far away, all so sad, and yet so sweet to muse over.

The music of this movement flows in the slow and measured style of a song. The main melody begins in the plaintive chant of an oboe accompanied by the plucking of strings. Here is music for reminiscence, passivity

31

and melancholy. But there is also a certain vitality in this sweet lament which is picked up by the strings. The mood becomes more cheerful as the violins sweep upwards, and the melody grows stronger in its sonority and emphasis as the other strings join in. Presently the violas take up the strain, adorned by gay little decorative figures by the violins and the wood winds.[5]

The rhythm now lightens up in the strings and a lively tune, like a grotesque sort of dance, continues the optimistic mood until it begins to dominate the music. The melody is a low-pitched and lilting strain played by a bassoon and clarinet to the rhythm of the strings. Presently, the strings themselves sing the tune, with the wood winds lending an additional brighter spirit. But a sigh at the end of the melody recalls the sadness of the original lament.

Now the melody and rhythm colors the whole orchestra as more of the instrumental forces join in to participate in a splendid climax made magnificent by the horns, trumpets and the kettledrums. But the outburst of happiness is brief. The opening song returns again, weary but not too sad, illuminated with flashes of brightness by a flute. The movement comes to a serene close.

- Symphonies Nos. (i) 2 (Little Russian); (ii) 4 in F min
  DG 429 527-2 (i) New Philh. O, (ii) VPO, Abbado $

- Symphonies Nos 4-6
  Ph Duo 438 335-2 (2). LSO, Markevitch $

---

1   McKinney, Howard, & Anderson, WR, *Discovering Music* (American Book Co., NY., 1934)
2   Rudel, Anthony, *Classical Music Top 40* (Simon & Schuster, Fireside Book, NY, 1995) The *Largo* from Dvorak's ninth symphony is analyzed in detail, line by line, in Rudel's book
3   Stringham, Edwin, *Listening to Music Creatively* (Prentice Hall, NY, 1946)
4   Tovey, Donald Francis, *Symphonies and other Orchestral Works* (Oxford University Press, NY, reprinted 1990)
5   O'Connell, Charles, *The Victor Book of the Symphony* (Simon & Schuster, NY, 1935)

"Hark! the shrill trumpet sounds, to horse, away,
My soul's in arms, and eager for the fray."
— Colley Cibber

4   The Brass Choir

It is the brass choir that provides the patches of blazing color, the thunderous and stirring martial effects of triumph in music; indeed, we are told, the very walls of Jericho came tumbling down before their sound. In the brass section, the sound of trumpets is well known: Its sharp imperious tone is an indispensable element of heroic climaxes. The French horn airs a lovely round tone and, when played loud, takes on a brassy and majestic quality. The trombone, too, possesses a noble and ornate sound that is even rounder and larger than the horn. Moments of grandeur and solemnity in music are commonly announced to the sound of the trombones. The tuba functions as the bass support for the brass.

Exhibit 12   Mussorgsky: Pictures at an Exhibition[1]

In 1874, Modeste Mussorgsky (1839-1881) attended a posthumous exhibition of paintings by his close friend, the painter and architect Viktor Hartmann, that was held at the St. Petersburg Academy in honor of the artist's memory. As he walked, deeply moved, along the best canvases done in oil and watercolor, memories and melodies came flooding into his mind, almost of their own accord, and so fast that he could barely manage to put them all down on paper. The music was originally written for the piano, but was arranged for the orchestra decades later in 1929 by Maurice Ravel. In their orchestral guise, the "Pictures" breathed a new color and form that would have been impossible to realize on a piano. Indeed, nowhere before had music so brilliantly captured the earthy hu-

33

mor, or the gorgeous colors, or the somber atmosphere, or the grand majesty of pictorial images than in this imaginative requiem of ten musical pictures. They are presented here as an incredible example of the **brass choir**, both as solo instruments, and as members of a complete brass ensemble.

The music opens with the *Promenade*, in which the composer, portrayed by a trumpet, is strolling idly through the exhibition, uncertain where to begin, occasionally going to the right, then to the left, at times urged to go close to examine a picture. It is a joyous occasion, worthy of his friend's talents, but it is a joy tarnished by the sadness of his memory. The theme is played first by a solo trumpet, then the horns, trombones and the tuba join in to create an awesome mass of sound. It is a tune that is repeated in several guises throughout the work, usually serving as a bridge between the musical pictures. The entrance of the strings leads to a tremendous climax, and forthright the music wanes. But it is swiftly picked up again by the wood winds, and the movement ends abruptly in a splendid loud chorus played only by the brass.

The first picture of the Gnomes (*Gnomus*) is a musical portrait of a grotesque fellow, bandy-legged and deformed, jerking awkwardly as he drags himself along. The music opens in a wall of sound, with the lower strings and the wood winds blaring loudly in unison. The melody, too, seems jerking, with a start-and-stop quality just like the awkward and stumbling gait of a dwarf. It comes to an abrupt halt, and a new theme emerges, slow and heavy, played by the flutes, oboes and a xylophone. This is the mysterious and creepy picture of the gnome, realized by the wood winds, together with plucked violins and viola and muted brass. The sounds become discordant and louder, the bass drums pound out the limping ugly footsteps, and the wild music races to a frenzied crescendo. A loud clap brings the noises abruptly to a close, and then from the silence, the gnome theme re-emerges on a clarinet, backed by a hollow xylophone. Two harsh blares from the brass launch the music again to end in a fast and fierce climax.

The *Promenade* theme returns on the wood winds, slower and less vigorous than at the opening, as the pensive stroller moves along to the next painting.

A lonely troubadour, standing in the shadow of an old medieval castle (*Il vecchio castello*), sings sadly to his lady. A dark and nostalgic melody is introduced by a bassoon, and then a plaintive song pours forth, with a lovely string accompaniment, in the solo voice of an alto saxophone. The music rises and fades, and then slowly dissipates to end this image.

The *Promenade* theme returns, this time in the tones of a trumpet, the trombones and a tuba, to escort the listener to the next painting.

A brief passage by the plucked strings opens the scene at the *Tuileries* gardens where, so it seems, the dew-wreathed trees of Paris rise soft and lovely in the delicate spring morning. A masculine, bass-heavy *Promenade* theme contrasts strikingly with the pastel wood winds that evoke the lively play and petulant squabbles of the chattering and capricious Parisian children in the gardens. A triangle chimes in, and the happy and light melody returns on the wood winds to end abruptly.

The next watercolor picture, titled *Bydlo* (Polish ox-cart), must be hanging just adjacent, for there is no *Promenade* intermission. A solo tuba softly recreates the sound of the huge wooden wheels dragged cumbersomely by the stoic oxen. The cart's progress is followed by the full orchestra, ploddingly at first, but the mood lightens as a harp glides in with the violins and violas. The plodding grows perceptibly into a march, the march grows loud as other instruments join in, the snare-drums roll, and the music rises almost funereally to an overwhelming and thundering climax. The solo tuba resumes its sad, unhurried melody, and the cart rolls tiredly on to disappear at the horizon to the weak tones of a muted, distant horn.

Three flutes and two clarinets again usher in the *Promenade* theme briefly as the pensive promenader continues the stroll. Oboes and bassoons take over the tune, but the melody stops abruptly, and the music changes its mood to come to a close.

The next picture is a cheery dance of the unhatched chicks (*Ballet des poussins dans les coques*). Here is a charming ballet on a preposterous subject, as the little delicate creatures virtually pirouette lightly in their shells to the tender and delicate strains of the wood winds. The flutes and bassoons sing a duet, the violins trill like chirping birds, and a piccolo charmingly brings the image to an end.

Next comes a sympathetic caricature in oil of the rich Jew *Samuel Goldenberg* played luxuriously by massed strings and the wood winds against which a sort of gypsy tune, interjected nervously by the bleating tones of a muted solo trumpet, represents the poor and wheedling Jew *Schumyle*.

The shrill quarreling of French housewives as they bargain at the colorful market place in *Limoges* follows in the next vivid and animated picture introduced by a duet between the horns and the violins. The sounds are exhilarating, busy and wild, and ascend hysterically, with sudden silences, to a screeching conclusion.

The music changes startlingly from the bustle and life of the markets to the stark reality of death at the scene of the *Catacombs*. Terrifying blasts and echoes by the trombones, tuba and horns announce the tombs by lantern-light. A solo trumpet tries to sing a less somber note, but it is overwhelmed by the deeper brass. A much transformed *Promenade* theme arises in a solemn and sacred guise in the mournful wood winds, as hushed and tremulous strings converse creepily "with the dead, in the language of the dead (*Cum mortuis in lingua mortua*)." It is almost as if the creative soul of the dead Hartmann has invoked the skulls to glow again softly! Ascending scales in the harp let in the light of day as an oboe and clarinet start to brighten the mood, and the promenader is swiftly transported, without pause, to a land of fantasy in the next picture.

Here is a *Hut on Fowl's Legs*! Look again, and it is the Russian folklore's bogey witch, Baba Yaga, on a glowing hot mortar, rowing with a pestle through the air to collect some human bones to pound to a powder. This is music rich in folk tunes, played to a bizarre and malignant rhythm by the trombones and tuba. The music starts and stops, seeming to build up momentum, and then charges unrelentlessly like one possessed. But the orchestra soon exhausts itself, and the instruments fade out, one by one, until only a solo trumpet remains. Now begins a babel of ghoulish music, complete with trembling cellos and basses, burping tubas, and tinkling celestas, xylophones and harps. The wood winds blast in after a transient eerie silence, the trumpets blare, violins screech, the music grows fast and fierce, culminating in a series of volatile demonic outbursts to end the picture on an abrupt high note.

The final painting is one of Hartmann's triumph as an architect, the design of *The Great Gate of Kiev*, capped by a cupola in the shape of a Russian helmet. The music explodes loud and full, with blaring brass and crashing cymbals, in a melody reminiscent of the *Promenade* tune. Here is the artist's grand masterpiece, standing proud and tall in an apotheosis of the *Promenade* theme. The music is interrupted suddenly, and from this silence emerges a hymn-like tune played softly by the clarinets and bassoons. But the brass soon takes over, and charges into an exhilarating and fresh musical passage until the next abrupt silence. A calm interlude prevails briefly as the clarinets and bassoons sing quietly to the cherubic tones of the flutes. Presently, the lower strings seem to become restless and awaken, a heavy plodding rhythm begins in tense opposition, the wood winds start to intervene and, all at once, the melody bursts out again, brighter and more splendid than before, proudly displaying itself to the world. The full orchestra acknowledges its splendor with a powerful explosion, and a loud reprise of the tune is unfolded luxuriously so all can bask in its glory. A sudden silence, and then the whole orchestra blares out the song once more, the instruments joining in one by one, to peak into a loud explosion. Undeterred, the loud music seems determined to outdo even itself in its intensity. Pealing bells seem to fling their wild harmonies from the stately Byzantine turrets, and the powerful and splendid music rises spaciously to a cosmic intensity as sonorous brass and tolling percussion joyfully reach a deafening climax. Here is a fitting musical portrait worthy of the memory of a great Russian artist and friend.

- (i) Night on the bald mountain (ii) Pictures at an exhibition (orch. Ravel); RCA 09026 61958-2. Chicago SO, Fritz Reiner $$

Exhibit 13 Holst: Mars, from The Planets[2]

When the English composer Gustav Holst (1874-1934) completed this Impressionistic masterpiece in the early decades of this century, nothing so radical had existed in English music. It was as if the music drew its inspiration from the unearthly and the unaccountable, not merely from the raw and inscrutable forces that govern nature and outer space, but from the primeval mysticism and pagan mythology that had given birth to our own ancient civilizations. Therefore, it comes as no surprise to learn that, for many years, Holst had immersed himself in the lore of Hindu philosophy and Sanskrit texts. He had become a skilled interpreter of horoscopes, and he was the first to point out that it was the astrological characteristics of each planet, rather than any mythological associations, that he meant to express in this music. The first tone-picture of this seven-movement suite, *Mars, the Bringer of Wars,* was composed when the cataclysm of the first Great War was well under way. It has been said that many a shaken war veteran experienced in this music the feelings of one who "knew what it was all about."

The music opens with a barbaric rhythm hammered out by the strings, harps and the timpani, softly at first, but then becoming angry and relentless. A war theme is announced by the bassoons, contrabassoons and the horns, and it rises in volume as the other wood winds join in, prophesying an imminent horrifying conflict. The violins soar, the music roars and, to the incessant pounding of the drums, it erupts into a volcanic climax.

Presently, the swelling tones of an organ are heard, and then the march resumes, established by the strings to a pompous accompaniment by a solo tuba and trumpets.[3] The violins begin a joyful melody, but it is short-lived: a horrible orchestral blast shatters the song and, to the distant roll of a snaredrum, the bassoons, contrabassoons and strings glide in again. The volume grows louder as the other instruments join in, and deafening blasts from the brass instruments explode into the fray like the clash of Titans. The music intensifies in force and volume, the organ swells powerfully above the orchestra, overwhelming the rhythmic hammering of the drums that soon ceases. The tension rises, and the whole wall of sound explodes, once again, into an overwhelming conflagration.[4]

There is a lull, and then the strings emerge slowly, joined by the wood winds to break into a rapid tempo of sustained clusters of tone on the horns. The music becomes fast and fierce, explosive blasts, heavy and dissonant, break into the action, the brass blares out a metallic fanfare, the pace becomes frenzied until, completely exhausted, the movement ends in a final overpowering climax.

- The Planets (suite), Op 32; ELGAR: Enigma variations
  DG 439 446-2, Boston SO, Steinberg $

- (i) The Planets; (ii) The Perfect Fool (suite)
  Decca 433 620-2 (i) LAPO, Mehta; (ii) LPO, Boult $

---

1   Rudel, Anthony, *Classical Music Top 40* (Simon & Schuster, Fireside Book, NY, 1995). The "Pictures" are analyzed in detail, line by line, in Rudel's book from which the present description is put together. See also O'Connell, Charles, *The Victor Book of the Symphony* (Simon & Schuster, NY, 1935)

2   Rudel, Anthony, *Classical Music Top 40*. *The Planets* is also discussed in detailed, line by line, in Rudel's book

3   *Ibid*

4   *Ibid*

The Percussion Section

The percussion section is a mixed bag. Percussion instruments are used predominantly to sharpen rhythmic effects and add color to other instruments, or heighten the sense of tension in a musical climax. In general, the less the percussion are used, the greater is their effectiveness during the required moments. The percussion group distinguishes between those instruments that produce a noise at a fixed pitch such as the tambourines, castanets, triangles and cymbals, and those which may be tuned to a desired pitch such as the kettledrums, *glockenspiel*, celesta, xylophone and the bells which may be selected for a definite pitch. The kettledrums with their ability to emulate everything from a distant, effervescent rumble to an overpowering and resounding noise, the clashing cymbals, and the bass drum are the common percussion instruments.

"Music alone with sudden charms can bind
The wand'ring sense, and calm the troubled mind."
— William Congreve

5 Musical Forms

Form is to music what a plot is to a story: It is the order in which things happen. It is the way in which the separate parts of a musical composition which are alike, and those parts which are not alike, are arranged, and the way they make up the pattern or form of the individual piece. Just as a knowledge of the simple rules of architecture allow a better appreciation of a splendid building, so also a knowledge of musical form permits a better appreciation of a beautiful melody or musical phrase, and a truer understanding of a composer's intended expression of idea or mood. The discussions below are simplistic and approximate and are intended to provide only the slightest introductions to the subjects.[1]

Monophony

In the beginning was the voice. The human voice was the foundation of all music; it was the first musical instrument and still remains the most expressive and versatile. The voice is so characteristic that a person may be identified on the phone just by the sound of his or her voice. Apart from dance music, most of the music that was written before the year 1600 was for the voice, and was meant to be sung without any instrumental accompaniment. Such music, when composed between the years 600 to 1100 (The Middle Ages), was invariably woven from a texture called monophonic music or **monophony** ("one voice").

Monophonic music found its highest function in the music of the Church, as expressed in the Gregorian Chants. The earliest chants were, most likely, an accented mode of speech. Each syllable of a Latin text was sung in a steady, balanced, single voice with perhaps a change of pitch, either up or down, at the end of a line. At any moment, only a single note was heard, strong and expressive, and it never lost its devout, somewhat austere, feeling. In any span of time, only a *single* melody, with its unique rhythm and tone color was present, without accompaniments of any kind. Its beauty lay, and still does, in the balanced rise and fall of the lines.

Exhibit 14 Gregorian Chant

Of all the ceremonies in human society, those concerned with religious worship have remained the most profound.[2] The Christian Church has always distinguished between private worship and the liturgy, with the latter being a formal worship enacted by a community coming together to offer thanks to God. The center-piece of the Christian communal world was the **Mass** (Latin: *Ite missa est,* Go, you are dismissed). This ritual enactment of the Last Supper was designed to impress the ordinary person about the assurance and splendor of the spiritual world in contrast to the miseries and uncertainties of everyday existence. A Mass could celebrate a feast day, a saint's birthday, a funeral (*requiem mass*) or a universal event such as Easter or Christmas. The text of the Mass was in Latin which, having open and clear vowels, was particularly well suited for chanting. In a Low Mass, all the words were spoken, but a High Mass (*missa solemnis*) required many sections to be sung. The human voice, with its deep expressiveness and versatility, became the obvious instrument to praise the glory of God in the song of His Church.

The sections of a *missa solemnis* were grouped into the Ordinary, or unchanged portion, in which the text for the Mass was the same for all occasions, and the Proper, or changing part, where additional text was chosen to suit the event that was being celebrated. The five parts that made up the Ordinary of a Mass were the *Kyrie* (Lord have Mercy) sung three times by the congregation, *Gloria* (Glory to God in the highest) based on the song of the angels at the birth of Christ, *Credo* or a statement of faith (beginning with "I believe in one God"), *Sanctus Benedictus* (Holy, holy, holy), and the *Agnus Dei* which was a prayer petitioning for mercy and peace ("Lamb of God, who takest away the sins of the world"). In a *requiem* Mass, the *Gloria* and the *Credo* were omitted, and other hymns and prayers including the *Dies irae* (Day of Wrath) were added.

The Ordinary divisions of a Mass, that occurred in every Mass, were the ones that were initially set to music. Such music could then be played at any time whenever that particular text was used. It is this group of five texts of the Ordinary that has been set to music, over the centuries, by the great composers.

The five sections that were added to the Ordinary to form the Proper alternated with the five parts of the Ordinary. The first of these five additions was a musical introduction or *Introit* that opened the Mass, and preceded the *Kyrie*, and announced the particular occasion that was being celebrated on that day in the Mass. The next addition was the *Gradual* which followed the *Gloria*, and was originally sung from the step (*gradus*) of a pulpit as the epistle was being moved from one side of the alter to the other. The *Alleluia* (a hymn of praise or verses from the Bible) was added to follow the *Gradual*; the *Offertory* (offering of bread and wine at the altar to God) followed the *Credo*; and the *Communion* (partaking of the consecrated brcad and wine) was added to follow the *Agnes Dei* and end the Mass.

The earliest song of the church was the chant (plainchant or plainsong), commonly known as the **Gregorian Chant** after Pope Gregory I (590-604). Here, the music of the entire Mass consisted of a single, repetitively chanted line, trance-like and deeply mystical, devoid of any instrumental accompaniment. Instruments were considered to be too distracting and empty, and popular melodies too heretical in their content, to be allowed in communal worship.[3] Only the unadorned human voice with a single-minded focus of attention could be worthy enough to become a medium between heaven and earth. Sometimes, soloist and congregation would alternate; sometimes, the congregation was divided to sing alternate verses and then come together.[4] Over time, the chant developed into a very sophisticated form of free rhythm.

The plainchant was not intended to represent actual men praying in an act of worship. Rather, the sorrow of the Christ, the soul tormented and longing for union with God and salvation were the spiritual issues evoked, and the chant was devoted solely to the mystery of God. The music had about it a strange quality of otherworldliness and timelessness. It appealed to what was highest in the soul, and its beauty and nobility came from the fact that it borrowed little from the world of senses.

• Gregorian Chant
  Ph Dig 416 808-2, Choralschola der Weiner Hofburgkapelle, P. Hubert Dopf
  SJ. $$

On the first day of Christmas there are three different masses celebrated by the Catholic Church—the first on the eve of Christmas (the Vigil), the second early in the morning, and the third before midday. This recording includes all the parts of the Ordinary and Proper sung at the third Mass with the exception of the *Credo*. The *Introit, Gradual, Alleluia* and *Offertory* from the Vigil are also sung. The full Latin text of the Mass is printed in the program notes.

Polyphony and Homophony

The musical genre between 1100 and 1500 typically involved a combining of two or more equally important voices or melodies with contrasting rhythms and pitches. In those days, the music notes were called "points". An early experiment in the music of this period was to match one "point" of a soprano in a choir, for example, against the corresponding point, or note, of an alto, tenor or bass voice. Such a musical texture became known as *punctus contra punctum* or *point counter point (contrapunctal).*[5] **Counterpoint,** therefore, became a process that allowed several voices or melodies, or their parts, to be combined simultaneously. It allowed an expression of a variety of illustrations of the same idea, but with a peculiar reinforcement that was manifested by the simultaneous and harmonious beauty of their union.

Put simply, when two or more melodies are sung or played simultaneously, the music is called **polyphony** ("many voices") or counterpoint. In its simplest form, called imitative polyphony, only one and the same melody is sung, but at staggered time intervals by the different voices. For example, first one voice such as a high-pitched one begins the song, then another, and then a third, perhaps low-pitched, voice enters at staggered intervals to sing the same melody. In such a situation, polyphony occurs when two, or all three, voices are singing together, but each would be, at any given moment, in a different phrase of the *same* melody. On the other hand, in the more common non-imitative type of polyphony, the voices are singing *different* melodies at the same time.

In the early years of instrumental music, instruments were treated as though they were a substitute for the voices. In fact, a piece of music was likely to have a notation "For voyce or viols." It therefore comes as no surprise to learn that instrumental music from the high Middle Ages was polyphonic (contrapunctal) in style, taking its character from the vocal Church music of the time. In their instrumental versions, the same or different melodies were played by different instruments at the same time, or in staggered sequence. The instruments were chosen to suit the meaning of the melody and to create a specific effect or mood. Music can be considered to be contrapuntal when a musical theme is flipped from one combination of instruments to another, or from one solo instrument to another, interweaving it all the while with other thematic material.

44

In contrast to monophony and polyphony is another musical texture called **homophony,** or harmonic music. Here, there is only one main melody, but it is combined with other clusters of tone (chords) that are not complete melodies, and serve merely to accompany or decorate the main melody. A singer accompanying herself on a guitar would be a common example of homophonic music whereby the singer sings the main melody and the strummed guitar provides the accompanying decorative chords. In some instances, the distinctions between homophony and polyphony can become unclear. In simple terms, if only one melody stands out, the texture is homophonic. If the accompaniment begins to attract equal attention, the music has shifted into polyphony.

Polyphonic music requires that a listener must be able to hear the separate strands of a melody simultaneously. The importance of the melody in any piece of polyphony or homophony cannot be overemphasized. It is the key to the art of listening to such music. Whatever the quality of the main melody considered alone, the listener must never lose sight of its function in a composition. It should be followed like a continuous thread that leads the listener through a piece from its beginning to its end. It may even help to hum or whistle the theme every time it appears in a composition as the work is being performed. This would allow the listener to hang on to the melodic line without being distracted by the decorative and elaborate secondary materials that frequently accompany a melody. It is vital that the melody be separated from everything that surrounds it. The melody may even disappear momentarily, only to return again more powerfully.

There are many examples of polyphonic music presented in the *Exhibits* in the music of the Baroque era. The following *Exhibit* (Beethoven: *Allegretto* from *Symphony No 7*) is an example of varied texture in which polyphony and homophony are both represented.

Exhibit 15 Beethoven: Allegretto from Symphony No. 7

Something very astonishing happened when the virtually deaf Beethoven (1770-1827) conducted the first performance of his seventh symphony in Vienna in a benefit concert held for the Austrian and Bavarian soldiers who had been wounded in the Napoleonic Wars. The second slow movement was such a success that it was encored repeatedly, a compliment that hitherto had not been accorded to slow movements. Indeed, its popularity grew not only at the expense of the rest of the symphony, but also at that of his other works; music directors began to insert this piece into Beethoven's Eight Symphony to help popularize that symphony![6] This well-known slow movement is presented here as an example of varied musical texture in which both polyphony and homophony are manifest. After the first theme, a second and a third melody are staggered in, with a switch from a melancholy to a sunnier mood in a different rhythm.

The entire movement is based on a slow march rhythm. It begins with a soft sustained chord in the wood winds, and then the quiet rhythmic pulse of the lower strings—the violas, cellos and basses—commences. It is full of poignant elegiac feeling, more a somber broken heartbeat than a melody, and it pervades the entire theme and the set of variations that follow.[7] A lovely second melody soon appears, at first as a counter-melody in the violas and cellos, but afterwards destined to dominate the orchestra. The second melody abandons the solemn vein with an expression of pure lyrical feeling, directed more to earthly human and mortal issues instead of eternal truth. The rhythms of the two themes—one persistent and strongly marked, the other fluent and flexible as a stream—are oddly contradictory, and yet they seem to fit together perfectly.[8] The lyric song being over, the mournful hymn returns alone, but sung with greater freedom and lightness.

A third and equally beautiful theme is presently introduced by the clarinets and bassoons, and momentarily irradiates the sadness that permeates the movement as a whole.[9] And all along, the old rhythmic pulse sounds softly at the bottom of the orchestra. A progressively softening series of tones by the violins, with pauses in between them, recalls the first theme, which is then taken up by the wood winds.

The strings now start another new melody, the rhythm of which is derived from the introductory theme. The main theme, first announced by a clarinet, is restated by the horns and bassoons, accompanied by the strings, with the opening rhythm being always audible in the basses. As the climax dies down, fragments of the theme are whispered from one part of the orchestra to another, and the movement ends in an echoing sigh, as of a dying soul, in the violins.[10]

- Symphony No. 5; 7
  DG Dig. 447 400-2, Vienna Philh, Carlos Kleiber $$

- Symphonies 6, 7, 8; Overtures: Leonora No 3; Fidelio
  DG Double 437 928-2 (2) VPO, Karl Boehm $

The Fugue[11]

A particular form of polyphonic music that reached its maturity in the baroque era is the fugal form or the **fugue** (Latin: *fuga,* flight), so called because it concerns the musical exploration, or flight, of a single musical theme.[12] Most fugues are written for three or four voices, i.e. soprano, alto, tenor or bass, of which one voice always predominates. The musical instruments are chosen to reflect these voices. Moreover, to allow a proper appreciation of the voices, no more than three of the voices are kept active at any one time. The main melody, or theme of a fugue, is called its subject, and it contains the essence of the music. The subject is invariably short and has a definite personality that is easily recognized. It establishes not only the rhythmic and tonal pattern, but also sets the mood and character for the entire composition.

All fugues begin with a well defined musical form called an exposition where the fugue subject, or its main melody, is clearly presented (exposed), alone and without accompaniment, by any one of the voices (V1). The subject is then repeated by each one of the remaining voices in a sequence. In this chronology, the alternating voices such as V2 and V4 are referred to as "answers" to the subject.

The first voice does not stop when the second voice enters with the subject. Rather, it continues as a counter melody. The second voice, likewise, continues to add a counter melody to the musical piece when the subject is taken over by the third voice, and so on. Hence the subject is repeated, voice by voice, until all the voices have joined in. The successive entrance of the voices may sometimes give an effect of a crescendo and a feeling of growing excitement caused by the persistent repetition of rhythms, and this effect can beat upon one's emotions. After each voice has demonstrated the melody and a counter melody, it becomes free to continue on its way in the exposition in an unrestricted fashion as a free voice. The exposition is said to come to an end when each of the voices of a fugue has sung the melody once.

A diagrammatic representation of the exposition of a fugue would be as follows:[13]

V1	Subject	Counter-subject	Free-form	
V2 (answer)		Subject	Counter-subject	Free-form
V3			Subject	Counter-subject, etc.

Following the exposition, a fragment of the melody or counter melody is isolated and altered in a variety of ingenious ways. This portion of the fugue is called an episode, and its purpose is partly to act as a showcase to display a composer's skills and, in part, to divert attention temporarily from the main melody so as to better prepare the stage for its reentrance. And reenter it does, after the first episode, but in a different fashion, either shortened or lengthened, sung louder or more quietly, alone or augmented by additional melodies. The subject of a fugue, therefore, must be one that can be isolated and repeated to form the basis of the episodes. Usually a fugue consists of a series of episodes that alternate with statements of the fugue subject which, in turn, are returned clothed in new garments. The fugue ends in a final dramatic flourish of the subject, invariably in a *stretto* form in which the separate parts enter so closely, one after another, that an impression is created of toppling voices.

Exhibit 16 Bach: Fugue in G Minor ("The Little")

To Johann Sebastian Bach (1685-1750), the fugue was as natural a musical form to use in his greatest works as the German language. He had learned to express in fugue all the emotions that have ever been worthily expressed in music. Lamentation, jubilee, coquetry, adoration—fugue came amiss to none of these in his hands.[14] Like his other works, he gave the world a definitive summary of all that had come to pass in this field, and in his two comprehensive masterpieces, *The Art of Fugue* and *The Well Tempered Clavier,* he spun wonderful webs of exquisitely beautiful fugal traceries in sound, quite beyond all ordinary human talent.

The *Little Fugue* of Bach is so called to distinguish it from a longer and complex fugue in the same key. It was composed for the organ, but has been transcribed for the orchestra. It progresses in one continuous sweep through a series of climaxes, with various instruments and choirs of the orchestra putting forth their versions of the theme in contrasting tones.

The jaunty subject is introduced by an oboe, and the music takes off! It is a solid-sounding melody that forms the basis for the rest of the composition. It is written for four voices, and every choir of the orchestra makes its comment on the theme. On the entrance of the cellos, and then again of the basses, the key changes to the major mode, but the answering voice leads back to the original form. From this point, the music grows rapidly in intensity and power until the whole orchestra joins in to end in a thundering climax.

- The Art of fugue, BWV 1080; A Musical Offering, BWV 1079
  Ph Duo 442 556-2 (2) ASMF, Marriner $

Theme and Variations

The meaning of the very old musical form called **Theme with Variations** is self evident. William Byrd (?1543-1623) is said to have been the first composer to have used this form. It became very popular after his time as a means of displaying the talents of composers in manipulating their material. The musical ideas are looked at from first one side and then another, examined in this or that aspect, in order that one may find in just what circumstances they differ from each other.

The theme must be a whole tune rather than a small portion of it, and it can be repeated as often as required but each time in a different manner. It is generally short and clearly defined to allow the listener to hear it in its simplest version. This allows the variations to be better appreciated. Furthermore, a simple theme can be made more subject to variations. The initial variations usually stay close to the theme, with only slight embellishments that reveal either a new glimpse or character of the theme, or set a new mood. Considerable liberties, however, may be taken in melody, rhythm, harmony or counterpoint towards the end of a composition to display the abilities of the composer. The original theme is usually restated unadorned at the very end of the musical piece.

It is important that the listener be conscious of the beginning of each new variation so that the piece can be split up in the listener's mind just as it was in the composer's mind. The musical *Exhibit* that follows is an example of a popular tune that has been set to variations.

Exhibit 17 Haydn: Andante from Symphony No. 94 (Surprise)

Tradition has it that Prince Nicholas of Esterhazy was accustomed to take a nap at the frequent concerts that his resident composer Franz Josef Haydn (1732-1809) gave at his master's splendid court.[15] This offended the composer, who therefore proceeded to plan a joke on the Prince. He set to work on the composition of this symphony, in the second slow movement (*Andante*) of which—after a passage calculated to soothe the Prince to slumber—he inserted a sudden *Bang!* to awaken the Prince with such a start that he might even fall from his chair! But this story is

49

probably pure fantasy. Others have said that this work, which forms part of the London Symphonies, was planned to present the English audience with something new and brilliant in the *Andante* so that the composer would not be outdone by his star pupil, Ignatz Pleyel, who was also debuting in London at the same time.[16] The effect was electrifying. The public encored the second movement, and even Pleyel complimented his master on this idea. The modern listener should be forewarned that the "surprise" appears so gently in the kettledrums that one is almost certain to miss it if one is not expecting its occurrence.

The movement opens with the theme played with much energy by the flutes and bassoons. It is a simple melody of great charm based on a familiar Croatian folk-song, reminiscent of the lullaby *"Twinkle Twinkle Little Star."* This first fragment of eight measures is immediately repeated, very softly, and at the end of this quiet repetition comes, in a spirit of playfulness, the infamous *Paukenschlag (Bang!)*. The melody returns, and the theme is then repeated with many happy variations by different combinations of instruments.

The first of these variations follows immediately. The tune sounds, at first, almost exactly as it did earlier when played by the second violins and violas, but by the end of its second round, the first violins add another gracefully flowing and delectable melody. The addition of this new melody is the most interesting feature of this variation.

The second variation is in a different mode, and very loud and bold whereas, before, it had been dainty and modest in character. It ends very softly, getting progressively more quiet, embellished with little musical figures that lead into the next section.

Here the original melody is repeated in quick succession, first by the oboes, then the violins. After the second repetition, the tune is taken up by the strings and, as in the first variation, a new and lovely melody is added by the oboes and flutes.

The final variation opens directly, without introduction, with the whole orchestra playing in a gay and boisterous mood. The main theme is again presented in the original, played very loudly by the wood winds and brass but, this time, it is so profusely embellished with ornamental decorations by the violins and violas with such vivid chordal accompaniments, that the melody itself becomes almost unrecognizable. The theme is further varied by strikingly abrupt changes in volume, ranging from loud to soft, that end in a brilliant climax. The original theme returns, echoed tenderly with soft chordal accompaniments, and moves along through many fascinating changes in tonal colors. The music ends with a fresh and dainty, almost poetic, repetition of the opening fragments of the main theme.

- Symphonies Nos. 93-98
  EMI mono CMS7 64389-2 (2), RPO, Sir Thomas Beecham $$

- Symphonies No. 94 in G (Surprise); 83 in G minor (Hen); 101 in D (Clock)
  Naxos Dig.8.550139, Capella Istropolitana, Barry Wordsworth $

- Symphonies Nos 93 in D; 94 in G (Surprise); 97 in C; 99 in E flat; 100 in G (London); 101 in D (Clock)
  Ph. Duo Analogue/Dig, 442 614-2 (2). Concg. O, Sir Colin Davis $

Rondo

The musical form called the **rondo** probably derives from the style of some old folk songs where the principal theme was sung in unison by a simple chorus consisting of a number of persons, and this alternated with solos of the theme sung by only one of the performers. The music invariably came around again to the melody that was announced at the beginning. It is a most primitive and unsophisticated method of presenting musical ideas, almost as if the idea were being beaten into the mind through iteration and reiteration.

So it is with the classical rondo form in which the principal subject (A), usually written in a light and free style, returns at least three times in alternation with the solo parts that are called episodes. The principal theme may be varied, and may show different versions with each return, which makes for a new interest in this music despite the repetitions. The solos provide a necessary digression to make the whole piece both balanced and contrasted. A rondo form may be represented as

A1   B   A2   C   A3   D,   and so on,
where B, C and D are the episodes.

Exhibit 18   Beethoven: Rondo from Piano
Sonata in C Major (Waldstein)

For Ludwig van Beethoven (1770-1827), the newly introduced pianoforte was to become a fully realized medium for his artistic expression. But it was with the *Waldstein* sonata that he cast into this genre of music that extended design, and the nobility and grandeur of spirit, that was to mark his greatest piano sonatas, and raise the whole standard of pianoforte music to a loftier height. Here is the Beethoven of fiery tempers and restless spirit, challenging God and defying the universe. But it is also an exuberant and high-spirited Beethoven that is heard in the *Rondo* that forms the conclusion of this musical piece. Count Waldstein, to whom this sonata is dedicated, was a Bohemian nobleman and patron who had lived much of his time in Vienna.

The principal subject of the rondo is lighthearted and fluent, made up of short symmetrically paired phrases. It is played three times: first in its barest form, next as a soft, almost dreamy vision, and finally in all its full and brilliant glory. The first episode that contrasts with the main rondo theme has no strong melodies of its own; rather, it concentrates more on exploring different aspects of pianistic technique. The rondo theme returns and is played in its entirety; the episode that follows is similar to the preceding one, but soon moves into a section in which fragments of the main theme reappear, blended together into a soft ethereal air. Once more the rondo theme returns with feeling, once more it is repeated with vigor. The music is brilliant, and becomes progressively more dazzling to reach a spectacular virtuoso intensity with broad sweeps softening tenderly to a pause, only to take off again eruptively to new and demonic heights.

- Piano Sonatas Nos. 21 in C (Waldstein); 23 in F (Appassionata); 26 in E flat (Les Adieux)
    DG 419 162-2, Emil Gilels $$$

- Piano Sonatas Nos, 8 (Pathetique); 14 (Moonlight); 15 (Pastoral); 17 (Tempest); 21 (Waldstein); 23 (Appassionata); 26 (Les Adieux)
    Ph. Duo 438 730-2, Alfred Brendel $

The Sonata Form[17]

Perhaps the greatest glory of all classical music was the development of the **sonata form**. Whereas polyphony and the fugue had reached a pinnacle only after a long period of experimentation covering many centuries, the sonata form was not only established within a relatively brief span of time, but was also perfected during this period into a level of artistic fulfillment that has remained unsurpassed in the annals of music. Indeed, between its first tentative stirrings and its mature expression in the later works of Haydn and Mozart, less than half a century had elapsed.

The sonata form was traditionally conceived as a blueprint to give structure to a single movement within a musical composition. Since it was the normally prescribed form for the first movement of a composition, be it a symphony or a string quartet, and since the first movement was normally in a quick (*allegro*) tempo, it was also referred to as the *sonata-allegro* form. However, this was such a satisfactory musical form that it was also usurped by some composers for certain other movements.

Put simply, the sonata form can be understood from two perspectives: An overview of its structure (thematic aspects), and the aspect of its function (harmonic aspects).[18]

The structure of the sonata form, when reduced to a ground-plan, is disarmingly simple. It is divided into three parts, and since each division starts with the same, or almost the same, musical idea, they are usually sufficiently clearly demarcated to allow even a novice listener to identify them. Just as one is introduced to the main characters in the first part of a play, so, too, in the first part of the sonata form, called the *exposition,* the main musical ideas and tunes are presented, or exposed, for the listener. The *exposition* contains the first theme that is stated either directly or after a brief introduction, then follows a transitional bridge passage leading to a contrasting second theme that is usually quieter and more lyrical than the first. The first theme is generally a simple tune, and this is a prerequisite because its simplicity enables it to be subjected to further development.

The next section, which usually follows without a pause, is called the *development* because in it some of the themes are further developed. It usually involves picking up one or more fragments or themes from the exposition and turning them over in new and unsuspected ways, working them out and savoring them under different circumstances, and seeing how far they will go—ideally to a point where the material seems to be used up, and the original tunes can barely be recognized.[19] Development is a demonstration of a composer's ability to use the themes in different and musically satisfying ways. The first theme is always subject to development; often the second is also developed, or a new theme may be introduced at this juncture. The varieties and horizons of development are limited only by the imagination and the capabilities of the composer. The development section, in essence, is a huge canvas that allows the highest type of creative effort. Herein lies the importance of the development section, and the popularity of the sonata form.

The *recapitulation* is the final section and, as its name implies, it is thematically identical to the exposition, so that the movement ends with a thorough affirmation of the main theme. The recapitulation should carry with it a true sense of homecoming.

The functional, or harmonic, characteristics of the sonata form are less simple. As mentioned in Chapter 1, the sound produced by a musical instrument is called its tone, and every instrument has its characteristic tone that allows it to be identified. Certain tones have been selected and arranged in families or groups called *keys*, in which one tone assumes greater importance than the others.[20] This important note in a group, around which the others revolve and to which they ultimately gravitate, is called the *Tonic*. In other words, a key is a group of related tones with a common center or Tonic.[21] The tonic is also called the *Home* note.

Within each group, the tones are arranged in a sequence, beginning with the home note. The fifth note in the sequence is called the *Dominant*; although it is located five notes up from the tonic, it is the one that has been considered to be the closest to home, and therefore to be as significant as the home key itself. And since all notes intuitively gravitate towards the tonic, the dominant also naturally gravitates to the tonic. Western music recognizes twelve such keys that come in two flavors, much like the white and black keys of a piano: Vanilla (Major), which is plain and fundamental but generally happy sounding, and chocolate (Minor), which is definitely sadder and more mysterious in character, and adds the richness and the decadence to music.[22]

The process of passing from one key to another in music is called *modulation*, and modulation, and the musical tensions generated by it, is the essence of the classical sonata form. The first theme in the exposition is ordinarily played in the tonic or home key. The answering second theme, (and all subsequent themes), is contrasted not only in mood but also in key, and is usually built on the dominant key. It is designed to express the dominant harmony almost as fully as the first theme expresses the tonic. This is intentional: Since conflict and contrast are the essence of drama, one cannot very well mix the two contrasting themes of an exposition without creating a sense of struggle or drama. The pitting of the dominant against the tonic sets the stage for a potentially challenging psychological and dramatic tension during the development.

Having outlined and contrasted the fundamental structure of a key in the opening statements (*exposition*), its tonal implications are now explored in the *development*. The commonest maneuver is to allow the music to modulate and actually arrive at a new and foreign key. A new key gives the same music a new location, and makes it heard from a different perspective.[23] The new key may have many, or few, notes in common with the original key. The more notes there are in common, the more the music will sound like, and tend to stay close to, home. The fewer notes the new key has in common with the old, the farther away from home, and the more daring, are the explorations.

54

The development, therefore, gives an opportunity for working freely with materials already announced. The themes, or their fragments, may be made to wander through a series of new keys, taking on a wealth of additional meanings during their peregrinations, but always with subtle intimations of an inevitable return home. Eventually, just when the point is reached that a theme has gallivanted astray too far, and the tension has become unbearable, and the listener is getting lost in the harmonic by-ways, the original theme is made to return to the home key. It is as if a character (theme or musical fragments) sets out from home, has a series of adventures, and finally returns home changed by his or her experiences.[24] Along the way there are many sidetracks, and routes leading in from other points.

The *recapitulation*, in a sense, is a sort of psychological climax of the sonata form, just as the climax of many a long journey is the return home.[25] The tension has abated. Indeed, all themes are played in the recapitulation section in the home key, even the subsidiary ones which, in the exposition, were presented in the dominant key. And, just in case some may not have the homecoming fixed in mind, the last chords of a recapitulation may hammer out the main theme in the home key in full volume, over and over, until it becomes transparently clear that all is well and the end is secure.[26] Commonly, a coda is tacked on at the end of the movement. Its purpose is to create a sense of apotheosis: the material is seen for the last time, and in a new light.[27]

And there you have the whole secret of the sonata form. Tonal drama and thematic contrasts—these are the essence of the sonata form. Let us now understand the workings of the sonata form together, and listen to the first movement of a charming symphony to hear the effects of a change of key on the music. The *Exhibit* presented here (Mozart: *Symphony No. 40*) is rather unusual in that even the second and fourth movements are in the sonata form.

Exhibit 19 Mozart: Symphony No. 40

It has been said of Wolfgang Amadeus Mozart (1756-1791) that people will not believe that his music can be powerful because it is so beautiful. Mozart's whole musical language was a happy one of joy and comedy; he was even blamed for using it in his *Requiem!* But this does not imply that he could not rise to an opportunity for tragedy.[28] In fact, the present symphony, his penultimate one, has been compared to all manner of tragedies. It must have required a heart of fire and a brain of ice to compose three such emotionally different symphonies, including the present one, in the brief space of two months. Yet, Mozart wrote his three last and greatest ones over the course of a single summer. There is a breath of foreboding in this work, a grave and somber feeling as meets the waning days of the year, when the face of nature has changed from summer pride to autumnal brooding.[29] The original score was cast without clarinets, but this was rectified when the instrument became available, and its mellow tones were used to replace the acid sounds of the oboe.

The first movement of this symphony is in the sonata form. Over a soft, impassioned accompaniment by the violas, the violins state directly the first theme, sounding like a babbling brook in early spring, which is repeated after sharp chords from the whole orchestra. It is a delicate and dainty tune, not a sweeping or flowing melody but more a collection of musical fragments, with each fragment being made up of a cluster of three-note groups that create a restless and pulsating sense of forward movement.[30] After a short transition passage, a graceful second theme unfolds between the violins and the wood winds. It is different in mood and style to the first, reflecting a sweetness and a faint sadness reminiscent of the complexity of life. Another transition-like passage follows in which fragments of the first theme are interspersed, played alternately by a clarinet and a bassoon, to wrap up the exposition.

The development is limited to the first theme; indeed, the magnificent dramatic life of the whole first movement is lived in the spirit of the first theme only. The first half of the first theme is played three times, each in a new key; then as the lower strings play the melody in yet another key, the violins begin a more intense counter melody. Finally, the theme is fragmented, with the first few notes tossed back and forth between the flute, clarinet and violins, at times in a shout, at times in a whisper, then repeated again with further fragmentation in new additional keys.[31] The wistful dialogue between the violins and the wood winds seems to give a dogmatic and pugnacious quality to a graceful tune that otherwise seems to be better fitted for lighter retorts: more, perhaps, for just singing a simple song.

The first theme returns in the violins in the recapitulation, with the bassoons adding a few notes of contrast. The second theme, too, sings with an intense poignancy, also in the home key. The movement ends in an urgent coda, with fragments of the first theme passing from the violins to the violas, and then finally to the wood winds, mounting upwards to the heights of a dramatic tension.

The restless and pulsating undertones in the music continue into the slow second movement which is also in the sonata form. Six equal soundings of the same pitch, arising somewhere between the voices of the violins and the basses, describe a new main melody which steals in quietly. It seeks comfort, and seems to find it within itself. It is repeated by another instrument with a prophetic sternness that is instantly relieved by a light response from a second theme, a poignant chord, whose short beginning phrase is played twice by the strings.[32] After a brief discussion, the main melody is announced again with even greater solemnity. It grows ever more complex, more human, more pregnant with meaning, significant in its many voices, with its many phrases all singing to the same end.[33] There is minimal development of the first theme—just a pattern of coupled quick notes between the wood winds and the strings that conclude with a new short phrase that is repeated four times.[34] A short coda ends in a sharp, agonized climax.

A kind of Titan's dance, perfect in its heavy strange rhythm announced by the strings and the wood winds, rings in the bright humor of a *Minuet* in the third movement. Yet, its firmness creates a curiously austere mood. The *Trio* brings in a softer air, a tender, purely human delicacy, in which the strings and the wood winds seem to bow graciously to each other. After a brief colloquy between the cellos and the double basses and the upper wood winds, the *Trio* works up to a subtle climax. The minuet returns with its earnest stern urgency and thumping rhythm.

On the face of it, the *Finale* is pure playfulness. It is all a jolly wild revel of childlike joy, well earned after the profound and serious absorption of the earlier music. But it is a grim and hectic humor, perhaps even next door to tragedy.[35] A pompous eccentric striding about, as if terrible things were impending, seems to occur under the very noses that had witnessed the most impish dancing just moments earlier! A popular theme takes off lightly at first in the strings, but it is soon overwhelmed by the wild rushing figures in the violins, and then the whole orchestra joins in the fray. Not even the joyous second theme, played suave and smooth by the first violins, can hold back the dynamic drive and the wild and dizzy maze of sounds. For a moment, chaos seems loose in this curious and complex simulation of wild disorder. There is a quick, tragic climax, then the music simmers down to a lull. The movement ends in a joyous simplicity, but darkened by insistent, almost despairing, reiterations from the orchestra.

- Symphonies Nos. 40 in G minor ; 41 in C (Jupiter)
  DG Dig. 445 548-2, VPO, Bernstein $$

- Symphonies Nos. 36 in C (Linz); 38 in D (Prague); 39 in E flat; 40 in G minor ; 41 in C (Jupiter)
  Ph. Duo 438 332-2 (2), ASMF, Marriner $

[1] For scholarly discussions on musical form, style and genre, the readers are referred to Joseph Kerman's *Listen* (Worth), Joseph Machlis' *The Enjoyment of Music* (W W Norton), Robert Winter's *Music for our Time* (Wadsworth), Roger Kamien's *Music, An Appreciation* (McGraw Hill) and Kenneth Levy's *Music: A Listener's Introduction* (Harper Row).

[2] Stringham, Edwin, *Listening to Music Creatively* (Prentice Hall, NY, 1946)

[3] Le Mee, Katherine, *Chant* (Bell Tower, NY, 1994)

[4] *Ibid*

[5] Stringham, Edwin, *Listening to Music Creatively*

[6] Downes, Edward, *Guide to Symphonic Music* (Walker & Co, NY, 1981)

[7] *Ibid*

[8] O'Connell, Charles, *The Victor Book of the Symphony* (Simon & Schuster, NY, 1935)

[9] Newmarch, Rosa, *The Concert-Goer's Library of Descriptive Notes* (Oxford University Press, London, 1931)

[10] Downes, Edward, *Guide to Symphonic Music*

[11] Altschuler, Eric, *Bachanalia* (Little, Brown and Company, Boston, MA, 1994) Altschuler's erudite yet charming listening guide to Bach's *Well Tempered Clavier* is the single best work on the fugal form for the layperson.

[12] Copeland, Aaron, *What to Listen For in Music* (The New American Library, NY, 1959)

[13] *Ibid*

[14] Crompton, Louis (Ed.), *The Great Composers: Reviews and Bombardments by Bernard Shaw* (University of California Press, Los Angeles, 1978)

[15] Kinscella, Hazel Gertrude, *Music and Romance* (RCA Manufacturing Co. Inc, NY, 1941)

[16] Downes, Edward, *Guide to Symphonic Music*

[17] Hurwitz, David, *Beethoven or Bust* (Anchor Books, NY, 1992) The discussion of the sonata form in Hurwitz's book remains unsurpassed, and the reader is urged to acquire this excellent and inexpensive volume.

[18] Carter, Harman, *A Popular History of Music* (Dell Publishing Co, NY, 1956)

[19] *Ibid*

[20] Machlis, Joseph, *The Enjoyment of Music* (W W Norton, NY, 1984)

[21] *Ibid*

[22] Hurwitz, David, *Beethoven or Bust*

[23] *Ibid*

[24] *Ibid*

[25] Machlis, Joseph, *The Enjoyment of Music*

[26] Carter, Harman, *A Popular History of Music*

[27] Copeland, Aaron, *What to Listen for in Music*

[28] Tovey, Donald Francis, *Symphonies and other Orchestral Works* (Oxford University Press, NY, reprinted 1990)

[29] McKinney, H & Anderson, WR, *Discovering Music* (American Book Co, NY, 1934)

[30] Machlis, Joseph, *The Enjoyment of Music*

[31] *Ibid*

[32] Goepp, Philip, *Great Works of Music* (Garden City Publishing Co, NY, 1913)

[33] *Ibid*

[34] Machlis, Joseph, *The Enjoyment of Music*

[35] Downes, Edward, *Guide to Symphonic Music*

Part 2

The Timetables
of
Music

Music began its career, like man, by leaning on another.[1] Music in ancient Greece and Rome slavishly followed the meter of poetry. In the early Christian world, music was fostered jealously by the Church exclusively for worship, and the birth of musical form and structure was wrought over the Middle Ages within its cloisters. The first explorations in musical form began with the addition of a second human voice in the liturgy as a servile accompaniment to the single-voiced chant, with the second voice always keeping its unaltered and respectful distance. The possibilities of combining several voices, independent in melody yet interdependent in harmony, reached their highest levels of precision, dignity and elaboration over the next few centuries. But no matter how exalted or articulate its power, music could be used to express only those feelings that were sanctioned within the Faith, in the austere and somber musical forms of the Church school.

With the Renaissance came a sweeping wave of earthly feeling and expression, and a rebellion against the ubiquitous intellectual dominion of the Church. The rebirth of learning brought the beginnings of an instrumental music that could usurp the spoken words and stories. Initially, an organ took the place of the sacred voice. By the end of this era, music had virtually thrown away all her vocal supports and had learned to tread an independent course, speaking her message purely in her own language of instrumental tones unaided by words. However, even with the best intentions to be worldly, it seemed as if the Renaissance composer of pure instrumental music was glancing outdoors at the secular world only through the window of his study, rather than actually stomping through the fields with a firm foot.[2] The authoritative and ascetic stamp of the Church still hung sternly over his works: even dance moods remained overcast with the pale hue of meditation.[3]

The absolute novelty of this purely instrumental music required the making of an entirely new garb to allow it to venture out of the cloister without great awkwardness. There were no vocabularies or forms of expression for the new instrumental sounds. The first century of this pioneering phase was channeled into a constant and self-conscious search for, and emphasis on, the mere sound itself. Outside the Church, the Baroque composers dared to celebrate the woods and the flowers and fields of the earth, and the rustic dances of the summer. Their early works showed their reactionary spirit through the frivolity of their compositions. A pastoral element, the poetry of nature discovered anew, was unmistakable, as was the peculiar playfulness of their humor. Though the music rang with the clearest note of tonal serenity and certainty, there was little breath of philosophy or depth of feeling. The music expressed but a single idea at a time.

It was the attainment of the sonata form and the Classical style that marked a sudden spring of true poetic feeling into instrumental music. The free and irresponsible fancy that had danced earlier over the meadows and in the forests now turned to the lives of men, to the turmoil and triumph of strife and war, and eventually to the agony and the ecstasy of the human condition.

The following chapters unfold this story of music over time, from the Baroque world to the threshold of the modern era.

---

[1]   Goepp, Philip, *Great Works of Music* (Garden City Publishing Company, NJ, 1913)
[2]   *Ibid*
[3]   *Ibid*

"... some to the church repair,
Not for the doctrine, but the music there."
—Alexander Pope

6   The Baroque World

The word baroque, (Portuguese *barroco*: "a pearl distorted"), was originally applied with a sense of disapproval for the arts of the seventeenth century.
In contrast to the clarity, unity and proportion of the Renaissance, the baroque
style promoted a taste for over-elaborate extravagance with a lesser regularity
of form. On the one hand, it was driven by the Catholic Counter Reformation
through which it articulated an intense sacred devotion and emotional fervor.
On the other, it was patronized by the aristocratic wealthy who flaunted their
power through costly and elaborate architecture that was embellished with complex detail and sensual splendor. This intense devotion to detail found expression
in music in delicate instrumental patterns that were continually repeated and
imitated with lavish and intricate over-ornamentation and glorious bursts of
tonal color.

The music of the baroque era was characterized by a break with polyphony,
and by the development of new dynamic forms of vocal and instrumental music. The latter was spurred, in part, by rapid strides in instrument making which
reached unsurpassed levels of perfection with the violins crafted by the Amati,
Stradivari and Guarneri families. The harpsichord, too, reached new heights of
quality, and the organ became more flexible. Unlike the polyphony of the Renaissance, baroque music showed a singleness of purpose, with usually one
idea progressing insistently with irresistible forward motion. Baroque melodies had a style of their own. They were longer and more elaborately organized,
and were embellished with trills that often served to emphasize the accents of
the rhythm.[1]

The Baroque Concerto

The musical genre called a *concerto* signifies two or more instruments and/or voices that perform together (*in concert*). They might play together harmoniously in agreement, or be pitted against one another to provide contrast.[2] The principle of contrast between voices or instruments was so important in baroque music that a baroque concerto soon acquired a more specific connotation of exhibiting a contrast between dissimilar tonal bodies pitted against each other.[3]

The contrasting of voice and instruments in music goes back to the ancient Greeks. Initially, as with the troubadours and with medieval church music, the role of the instrument was mainly that of an accompaniment to a song or dance, or to a Mass. The voice was completely left out for the first time in a concerto relationship when Torelli published a concerto for two violins and bass. The instruments were considered to be partners, with an equal give-and-take between them in order to contrast, in various ways, their individual and collective musical tone qualities. The purely instrumental concerto, as it first evolved, was not a showpiece for a solo instrument. Its purpose was not to display the abilities of a solo instrument or instrumental groups, or the virtuosity of the soloist. Rather, the instruments were an inextricable part of the music, intermittently playing it in unison, and intermittently offering contrast to it.[4]

The large-scale baroque instrumental form of the seventeenth century that embodied the general principles of concerted (concerto) music was the **Concerto Grosso.** Instead of contrasting individual instruments, it contrasted a small *group* of solo instruments with the whole orchestra. The latter could be just a string choir with a harpsichord, or a larger band of instruments put together from the string, wood winds and brass families. Both, the smaller group of solo instruments and the orchestra itself, were assured an equal and undifferentiated participation in the development of the musical material. In the usual situation, the best regular members of the orchestra came forward to play the solos, and then sat right back to merge with the orchestra when their parts were done.[5]

In a *concerto grosso*, the orchestra was called the *tutti* (or the *ripieno*, meaning literally "full"), and the very small choir of instruments that came forward, from time to time, to play the solo parts was called the *concertino* or little concerto. The *concertino* could be a string trio such as two violins and a cello, or could be made up of any small combination of instruments that was pleasing to a composer. Such an interplay between two unequal groups of instruments opened the door to a whole category of musical effects. The *ripieno* was necessarily a heavier, louder, more deliberate body of sound while the *concertino* was lighter and softer with a delicate gossamer quality.[6] The continual shifting from the one to the other produced a fascinating chiaroscuro of color and movement, especially when the concertino was taken over by a flute, a harpsichord or a trumpet against an orchestra composed predominantly of strings. Clearly, the soil was ripe for an extension of the boundaries of instrumental technique and styles, and it came as no wonder that the *concerto grosso* form, with its splendid spectacular effect of a full orchestra as a background for a display of instruments, could not remain the exclusive domain of one instrument or fire the imagination of only one composer.

A baroque *concerto grosso* was made up of three or more movements which were standardized into a fast-slow-fast pattern: A bustling first movement, a song-like slow movement, and a gay *finale*. Each movement was a self contained musical piece, and a constituent member of a larger piece.[7] The first movement invariably employed a *ritornello* form (Italian: *ritorno*, return) in which an easily recognizable orchestral theme was played again and again as a key element of a *concerto grosso*. To break the monotony, the *ritornello* alternated with the solos which were made strikingly divergent. Hence, the *ritornello* functioned as the supports for the solo passages which could then take off in fantastic directions; the *ritornello* was always solidly there to bring the music back down to earth and restore the original feeling of the musical form.[8]

The end of the baroque era saw the demise of the *concerto grosso* form. It was abandoned in favor of a concerto in the classical style for the professional soloist and orchestra. The solo parts were intentionally made difficult to display the uninhibited showmanship and superior technique of the virtuoso player. Vivaldi and Bach, along with other baroque composers, also wrote solo concertos for their favorite instruments. The *concertino*, naturally, was now confined to a single type of instrument, and it admittedly was refined to allow a greater degree of virtuosity. However, these baroque **solo concertos** retained the principle of competing sonorities that was the hallmark of the *concerto grosso*: the solo instrument and orchestra remained equal partners in the music.

Exhibit 20 Vivaldi: Spring from The Four Seasons[9]

Spring is a *concerto grosso* with the violins making up the solo interludes. Like a typical *concerto grosso*, it is in three movements arranged in a fast-slow-fast pattern, with the first movement exhibiting the characteristic *ritornello*. The music was designed to portray the text of four sonnets that Antonio Vivaldi (1675-1741) had written, each describing one of the seasons of the year. In his original composition, each line of the sonnets was printed precisely over the music it was meant to represent, and further notes were added to the margins. This was the first attempt to transform a *concerto grosso* into a vehicle for the most explicit type of programatism.[10]

The first movement sets the mood briskly, and begins with a jaunty, fresh, spring-like tune played by the orchestra to the words "Spring has returned." The festivity of the season is expressed in a melody that has two phrases, each of which gets repeated. This is the introductory orchestral *tutti*, and everyone in the string orchestra plays it together with zest. Indeed, the music makes one feel that spring *has* returned! The orchestra is now interrupted by the first contrasting solo played by three violins that describe a happy song of the birds. Part of the opening orchestral *tutti* then returns, and this time it is interrupted by the next solo which is played by softly murmuring violins representing the sound of flowing water, a babbling brook, with fountains fanned by little Zephyrs. The subsequent solos, alternating with some part of the orchestra, are played to represent a tremulous storm complete with blackened skies, lightning flash and the roar of thunder, then more singing birds as the skies clear, and then a final solo left to the listener's imagination.[11] The orchestra concludes the first movement after the final solo.

The slow second movement is a musical picture of a lonely, warm, lazy day depicted by a slow-flowing, monotonous melody played by a solo violin. Amid the murmuring leaves and boughs a goatherd slumbers, while repeated notes by the violas, loud and abrupt, imitate the "arf-arf" barking of his trusty dog.[12] The entire movement is a single, slowly wandering melody with the barking of the dog continuing from beginning to end, and the whole musical piece forms a striking contrast to the first movement.

Festivity returns in the fast third movement as nymphs and shepherds dance to the lilting rustic tunes of a bagpipe underneath a brilliant sky. There are no alternating orchestral and solo sections here; the solo merrily shares the dance with the whole orchestra.

- The Four Seasons, Op.8/1-4; Concerto in G min. per l'orchestra di Dresda, RV 577.
  Ph. Dig. 422 065-2, Accardo and soloists with CO. $$

- The Four Seasons. Op.8/1-4;
  Argo 414486-2. Alan Loveday, ASMF, Marriner $$

Bach: The Brandenburg Concertos

Johann Sebastian Bach (1685-1750) was impressed by the provocative vitality of Vivaldi's music. Six of the *concerti grossi* published by Vivaldi were arranged by him for other instrumental compositions. In his characteristic fashion, he surveyed the field of the *concerto grosso* comprehensively, and expanded the principle of contrasted instrumental combinations to more systematic varieties than any of his predecessors. Like his other works, he provided the definitive summaries of all that had gone before in this field in his Brandenburg Concertos.

Research has it that these six concertos were composed over a span of four years by Bach during his productive employment at the court of the youthful Prince Leopold of Anhalt-Cothen. The energetic Leopold played the viola de gamba, violin and harpsichord quite well, and some parts of the concertos were probably designed to give him an outlet to display his talents. In response to a request for some of his compositions by a court visitor, the Margrave of Brandenburg, Bach neatly copied out *Six Concertos for Divers Instruments* and sent them to the Margrave with a beseeching note. They were dubbed "Brandenburg" when these handsome copies were rediscovered, decades later, in the Brandenburg archives.[13]

Exhibit 21   Bach: Brandenburg Concerto No. 2

The immense popularity of this piece, which is a *concerto grosso*, probably stems from its dazzling trumpet part which, together with the flute, oboe and violin, makes up the group of high-pitched instruments that are chosen for the solo parts. The flute originally used was a recorder, and the trumpet was a natural trumpet without valves that produced a powerful brilliant sound that cannot be duplicated by its modern counterpart. The strings and harpsichord form the accompanying orchestra. The whole work shows the alternations of the orchestra and solo that are characteristic of a *concerto grosso*.

The sheer clarity and simplicity of the first movement has deemed it to be a masterpiece.[14] The opening movement is virile and assertive, with a fine vigorous melody given out by all the instruments, with the trumpets trying to gain an edge over the others. It is characteristically baroque in its richness and in the uninterrupted flow of its stalwart rhythm. It sparkles, it trips and twines with an elastic step, rich with bright colors, like a moving chiasoscuro.[15] A sprightly violin, a bright-toned flute, and a tearful oboe play the theme in sequence, and then in unison with the massed sonority of the orchestral strings.

There is a good deal of humor in this music. A graceful little theme is presented by the solo violin with a sort of dancer's flourish and is promptly copied by the flute, from whom, in turn, the oboe learns the melody.[16] A trumpet enters with a clear and long-drawn note, and picks up the music with brilliant embellishments and fanciful configurations. Although the flute and oboe can follow the violin very nimbly, the trumpet is much more limited in the selection of notes it can play, and when it takes over the melody it has to be carefully tailored![17] Now the quartet appears, both in unison and in contrast, as intervening solos, duets, and trios, to make up the "solo" sections. The fine elastic rhythm continues energetically throughout to support the delicately balanced structure above it. Suddenly, there is a transient stop when all activity ceases, but the music resumes forthright with an exuberant joyous return to the main theme and, rising to a vigorous flourish, the movement closes.

The trumpet is uneasily silent in the slow second movement: The hitherto abundant jubilation is supplanted by a lovely song woven tenderly from strands provided by a trio of violin, oboe and flute. They enter, in turn, to trace a tender and soulful melody supported only by a sympathetic accompaniment by the harpsichord and the deeper strings of a cello. The mood is beautifully serene with an almost religious quality, ever moving along a quiet course. The music speaks for itself and needs no annotation.

The blinding high notes of a trumpet, played alone against the barest bones of a bass, launch the very fast and jovial last movement. An oboe joins in, and together they revel briefly in an exhilarating duet. Violin and flute follow in succession, and the four participate merrily and equally in a lively and luxurious conversation that moves propulsively forward. With extraordinary agility, they continue a vibrant four-voiced interchange, the trumpet and oboe pitched against the violin and flute. Each voice is crystal clear, each thread of tone shines independently in its own color, never quite imitating any other, but blending miraculously into a harmonious whole.[18] The main interest in the music remains with the four solo instruments and the supporting bass. The other instruments of the orchestra do not make their entrance until all the soloists have had their turn with the melody, and when they do arrive they are restricted to a simple accompaniment. The entire piece comes to a riveting finale to the awesome sound of the trumpet.

Exhibit 22   Bach: Brandenburg Concerto No. 5

The popular appeal of the fifth Concerto may well lie in the elaborate solo for harpsichord (piano) that is its most distinguishing feature. So overpowering is the harpsichord in this music, that this concerto has been commonly regarded as the first known concerto for solo harpsichord, and thus may well be the earliest ancestor of the piano concerto.

Bach was a brilliant performer upon this keyboard instrument, and it is most likely that he wrote this long solo piece to avail himself of an opportunity to exhibit his own virtuosity. The solo instruments in all three movements of this *concerto grosso* are the violin, flute and harpsichord.

The musical theme of the first movement opens at once in the strings, and is then taken up more powerfully by the entire orchestra to end in a loud flourish. This is the complete *ritornello*, whose initial fragments are returned frequently, later in the movement, to alternate with the solo sections. There are seven such fragmentary *ritonello* sections that hold the musical piece together. A variety of short graceful musical ideas, new themes, and imitative fragments are artfully blended between a flute and a violin in the initial solos. Occasionally, the orchestra functions as an accompaniment to the soloists as they weave their intricate musical web. The harpsichord gradually begins to dominate more and more in the solo sections, overshadowing the flute and violin, until finally it emerges alone in a gigantic solo to end in a powerful flourish. The complete opening theme is played again in its entirety by the orchestra to end the movement.

A melancholy and very emotional theme is introduced by a violin in the second slow movement, and is immediately taken up by a flute. This provides the much needed gentle relief after the loud and forceful first movement. The movement is scored exclusively for the solo instruments whose separate voices are intricately woven together. The string orchestra is dispensed with entirely to emphasize the special tonal colors of the solo group. An unusual feature here is that the right hand and left hand harpsichord parts are written as if for separate instruments, thus creating the impression of a quartet rather than a trio.

The brisk third movement, probably the finest of the three, is cast in a very fast compound rhythm (ONE two three *four* five six).[19] The musical subject is announced by a solo violin, and is immediately repeated by an instrumental sequence as follows: the solo flute, the harpsichord left hand, the harpsichord right hand, and finally the whole orchestra.[20] It is a light and merry melody with bright tunes played with an abandoned fleetness that is unusual for a concerto. The soloists and the tutti do not play contrasting material; a single theme pervades the entire piece. After a time, a song-like melody with a slower rhythm can be discerned, but more as little decorations to the whole music.[21]

- Brandenburg Concertos Nos. 1-6, BWV 1046/51; Orchestral Suites Nos. 1-4, BWV 1066/69
  EMI mono CHS7 640472 (3), Adolf Busch Chamber Players, Busch. $$

69

- Brandenburg concertos 2,4 and 5
    DG 415911. Munich Bach O. Richter $$

The first Brandenburg concerto is scored for hunting horns, oboes and bassoon against a string orchestra to which a *violino piccolo* has been added. Unlike the others, it has four movements. Solo episodes are excluded from the first movement, but are present in the second and third. The final movement is a minuet. Nos. 3 and 6 are scored entirely for strings. Each of the three solo portions of the third concerto are for three instruments apiece: three violins for the first solo, three violas for the second, and three cellos for the third. All nine strings plus a double bass and harpsichord form the tutti. The violins are excluded in the sixth concerto which therefore has a deep and sobering color. The solos are scored for *viole da bracchio, viole da gamba* and cello. A concertino of flutes and violin provide a less startling contrast to the string tutti in concerto No. 4.

Exhibit 23 Bach: Concerto for violin and orchestra in E major[22]

Bach supposedly wrote a number of solo concertos for violin during his employment at the court of Anhalt-Cothen, but only three have survived: one each in E major, A minor and G major. He was a fine violinist, and the influence of this instrument can be heard in virtually all of his works. The concerto in E major has the typical baroque fast-slow-fast movements. The violin appears to great advantage throughout, but the solo parts, while of considerable difficulty, are always an integral part of the musical idea, and are not calculated to dazzle the audience into an admiration of the performer's technical accomplishments.

Three heavy hammer strokes announce the first movement and its tuneful melody which is played by the whole orchestra. These first three notes form a sort of a motive which is taken up and unfolded by the solo instrument. The violin solos alternate with the orchestra, either in part or in entirety, as the music moves along. There is a passage of increasing difficulty for the soloist in the middle section where fragments of the main theme are developed, especially the three opening hammer strokes. Then the music surprisingly comes to a transient halt, followed at once by a short slow passage on the solo violin. The movement itself comes to a close with a repetition of the entire opening theme.

The plan of the second movement is somewhat unusual for a solo concerto in that the melody is played by the orchestra and does not appear at all on the solo violin. Instead, it serves as a point of departure for the violin to take off on its own rhapsodic and imaginative journeys. The movement begins with the main theme played immediately by a cello and harpsichord, and the strings join the melody when the former seem to require a breathing space. The melody, which is perhaps one of the most beautiful ever penned by Bach, has a haunting sadness depicting an intense but controlled grief. Its organization has an implicit feeling of crescendo which can be sensed, even though it is not quite properly realized.[23] The music seems to live completely in a timeless world of its own; it can blend with virtually any listener's particular personality, adding to it the coloration of any momentary mood. The solo violin enters this enchanting world with a long, sustained note, followed by melodic flights of exquisitely touching beauty.[24] In the middle section, the solo is supported by a very simple accompaniment by a violin and viola against which a cello plays the background theme in somber tones. The movement concludes as it began, with the solo violin silent, and the main theme played by the cello, bass and string accompaniment.

The last movement begins with a jovial, dance-like melody, high-spirited and tuneful, played by the whole orchestra. The exuberant melody is repeated five times and, in between, the solo violin plays virtuoso interludes, supported by a simple accompaniment. The solo sections become progressively more difficult, and the final interlude is twice the length of the others and is the most brilliant. This movement is a popular one and is easy to follow and listen to.

- BACH: Orchestral suites Nos 1-4, BWV 1066-9; The Violin concertos
  Philips Duo 446 533-2 (2) Henry Szernyg; Maurice Hasson; ASMF, Marriner $

The Baroque Overture

The other great baroque instrumental form was the orchestral accompaniment to the newly evolving baroque opera. The opera has always been a favorite market place for a virtuoso composer to display his wares. An **overture** (French: ouverture) initially had the sole function of announcing that a show was about to begin. Eventually, it became longer and more organized until it formed a full-scale composition in its own right. It was the most successful of the early attempts at a purely orchestral composition. Unlike the *concerto grosso* which had three separate movements, a baroque overture was usually a single movement in three parts. If the pattern of this movement was fast-slow-fast like a *concerto grosso*, then it was called an Italian overture or a *sinfonia*. A reverse pattern of slow-fast-slow, or only a dual slow-fast, in a single movement characterized the French overture that was developed at the court of Louis XIV.

The operatic overture matured rapidly at the royal palaces in France to blend with the brilliance and effervescence of Versailles. Its overwhelming character was modified to suit the practical requirements of court life in an age of elegance. The music needed to be simple in form with a popular tune, and it soon evolved to become a series of stately court dances, with a mix of different

71

types of rhythm and tunes to get a balanced assortment. Such an orchestral composition *was* initially called an overture, but the term was soon replaced, and this whole baroque dance sequence of the royal courts became known as a suite.

A **suite**, therefore, was an instrumental form of baroque music played in the same musical key, and made up of a number of dances. Often, it became a grab bag for a miscellaneous collection of dances usually with a preliminary movement, an overture, to introduce them. The dances, themselves, were of peasant stock and came from different countries. They were invariably arranged in pairs and, in such instances, it was usual to play the first, then the other, and then the first again in an A-B-A sequence. Each dance had a distinctive rhythm which made it easily identifiable, just as a polka or a waltz can be promptly recognized today. The form inevitably extended beyond the royal courts, and the suite was well suited, and commonly employed, to compose outdoor music for public occasions.

The most common sequence of dances for a suite was the A-C-S combination, involving an *allemande* (German, also called *balletto*), a *courante* (French) and a *sarabande* (Spanish), in that order. The *allemande* was a slow dance with simple, ordinary steps. The *courante*, on the other hand, had a quicker tempo with jumping movements, allowing a variety of steps limited only by the dancer's agility and fancy. The *sarabande* originated as a wild and lascivious country love dance which was initially viewed with alarm and indignation, and even officially suppressed at one time by the shocked upper social circles.[25] It was eventually tamed for the grand courts of Spain into a stately and refined step which found its way into the suite. To this was added the exuberant English jig ("*gigue*") with its triple rhythm, interposed either before or after the *courante*, with the *sarabande* retaining its position as the last dance. By 1700, the *sarabande* and the *gigue* had exchanged positions to allow a zippy final movement (A-C-S-G combination).

The development of an orchestral suite became complete with the addition of an introductory prelude (overture) and other optional dances. The latter, too, were of peasant origin from the French provinces, but were developed to an elegant refinement in the ballrooms at Versailles. The *bouree* from Auvergne was a lively folk dance ("bourrir" = to flap the wings) with a rapid and well marked rhythm in which the second beat was accented by stamping vigorously; it was usually accompanied by the bagpipes or a hurdy-gurdy. The *gavotte* came from the Pays de Gap in Dauphine and, most significant of the additions, was the *minuet* from Poiteau.

The reign of the baroque suite lasted a little over a century; by 1750, it had disappeared, leaving only vestiges of its former self in the divertimento and in the minuet of the classical symphony.

Exhibit 24 Bach: Orchestral Suite No. 2 for flute and orchestra[26]

The rich and ancient multinational musical heritage of peasant dances, with their vivid imagery of physical movement, is captured in the four orchestral suites of Bach, especially the second one for flute and strings. Here is the lighter side of Johann Sebastian Bach (1685-1750), recording for posterity the simple earthiness and charm of a vanished world.

The slow and stately first movement of the introductory three-movement overture (slow-fast-slow movements) with its variety of rich rhythms evokes, in the beginning, an image of elaborate and quiet opulence, of ornate statuary, and a plush majesty characteristic of the baroque royal courts. The music is slow and stately, and is adorned by intricate trills. It oscillates between a flute and the first violin which are pitched together against a mixed consort of second violins, violas, cellos and bass. Presently, the flute soars sweetly above the strings and harpsichord. This expression of grandeur blends imperceptibly into a fast, gay and round measure, perhaps expressing the joyous pleasures of a peasant life, introduced in quick succession by the violins, violas, cellos and bass. Soon, the melody is aired by a light-hearted and graceful flute solo played to a rough and rhythmic accompaniment by the strings. The brief overture concludes by returning to the slow and stately rhythm of the opening.

The suite of dances that follows begins with a *rondeau*, descended from the medieval poem-songs. Originally, the *rondeau* was a form of litany, a style of prayer, in which the celebrant intoned a variety of short verses to which the congregation answered with a uniform response.[27] The music, likewise, shows various couplets alternating with a beguiling chorus refrain, reminiscent of the traditional style of these poems. But there is nothing pious in this merry piece! A flute and the first violins intone the melody as a congregation of second violins, violas, cellos and bass respond.

Next comes a sad and sullen *sarabande*. A solo flute announces the melody, soft and reflecting, which is taken up leisurely by the strings and a harpsichord. The subdued tune is repeated, changing in ornamentation and design, and meanders sadly down to a lone and forlorn close.

Two sprightly *bourees* follow. Usually, a *bouree* should have two melodies in the same rhythm and of the same length. In this instance, one is twice as long as the other, but the first is repeated to even things up. The music is brisk and bouncy, with the flute and first violins overshadowing the choir of second violins, violas, cellos and bass. The second *bouree* sports a long flute solo rising above a softer accompaniment by the strings.

A stately Polonaise is next, reminiscent of the old Christmas carols of the Polish court. A solo flute expresses one of the most brilliant passages in this music, its glittering tone contrasted with the main melody in the cellos, bass and harpsichord. The baroque opulence evoked by this piece continues into an aristocratic *minuet,* with its dainty little steps that gave the dance its name. Images seem to flash by of vast luxuriant spaces, gilded cherubed ceilings and swirling drapery, as the flute and first violins sway ecstatically against the lower strings in a graceful and elegant dance.

To round off this generous dance experience is a happy and playful *badinerie*, full of merriment and mischief, quite free in form, with a frisky rhythm and a light-footed tune. Here is heart-warming music rich with the spirit of the dance, in which a relentless virtuoso flute solo rushes to a thrilling close.

The astute listener may detect a subtle historical continuity in this piece—each melody is an artful and delicate variation on the preceding dance, so that the music reaches all the way back chronologically to its medieval hierarchy.

- BACH: Orchestral suites Nos 1-4, BWV 1066-9; The Violin concertos
  Philips Duo 446 533-2 (2) Henry Szernyg; Maurice Hasson; ASMF, Marriner $

The dance sequence of the first Orchestral Suite opens with a courante, and the third Suite characteristically closes with a gigue. Gavottes abound in all Suites except the second, and the bouree is played in all four Suites. The Air which is the second movement of the third Suite was adapted for violin in the nineteenth century as the haunting *Air for the G String.*

Exhibit 25 Handel: Royal Fireworks Music[28]

Here is an example of an orchestral suite applied to a public musical spectacle. The War of the Austrian Succession had ended and, to celebrate King George's victory, George Frederic Handel (1685-1759) planned an extravagant demonstration of *son et lumiere* (sight and sound). To fulfill the expectations of a jubilant public, proud in this moment of triumph, a musical style with a strong popular appeal was necessary. The use of a suite for this occasion was therefore deemed appropriate. The music was written for a big war-like band of brass and winds made up of a total of sixty trumpets, French horns, oboes, bassoons and drums, and the whole event was blasted off to the roar of a hundred and one brass cannons and magnificent fireworks in London's Green Park. Handel wanted to add a large force of strings, but the king had emphatically said, "No fiddles!" The string components were eventually added to the music after the show, and they form an integral part of most modern versions of this piece.

The first 6 bars of the opening overture are monumental, rich and awesome enough to seize the attention of even the most non-musical spectator in the crowd of 12,000 that viewed the celebration. The opening bars are immediately repeated, and the gripping impact is sustained to a most dramatic effect by the contrasting of brass and wood winds— the trumpets, oboes, bassoons and horns—whose overlapping rhythms grow more dynamic and more complex. The rhythms keep changing, the energy builds up, and finally explodes in a splendidly invigorating climax.

Following this opening movement, the first dance is a popular and sprightly *bourree*. The next movement, titled *La Paix* (The Peace, in celebration of the Treaty of Aix-La-Chapelle), is a serenely flowing, peaceful melody reminiscent of baroque pastoral music, and lined by the golden sounds of the French horns. The rejoicing (*La Rejouissance*) continues in a brisk, martial marching tone in the following movement, affording a striking contrast to the preceding peace, and reminding the audience of the military nature of the occasion. A pair of majestic but simple minuets, originally performed only by the oboes and bassoons, conclude the suite. The music is repeated several times over, with the movements being repeated using different combinations of instruments.

- Music for the Royal Fireworks (original wind scoring)—Holst: Military Band Suites

  Telarc Dig. CD 80038 Cleveland Symphonic Winds, Fennell $$$

- Music for the Royal Fireworks; Water music (complete)
  Naxos Dig. 8.550109. Capella Istropolitana, Bohdan Warchal. $

The Baroque Mass

The music of the Reformation stemmed from the more rugged and sturdy temperament of Northern Europe. The titanic conflicts that attended the Protestant quest for spiritual values created a music of great inward strength with an intense concentration of purpose. Instead of the naiveté and childlike tenderness that had clothed the Renaissance Mass, the earthy Lutheran service was forged from the fresh memory of seasoned and storm-tossed men who had shed their blood on battle fields to uphold their religious convictions. The Baroque Lutheran service did not abandon the Catholic Mass, but shortened it to include only the first two parts, the *Kyrie* and the *Gloria*. These short Masses were appropriate for regular church services. An exception was the great *Mass in B minor* by Johann Sebastian Bach which is a Catholic and not a Lutheran Mass, and incorporates all the divisions of a complete Catholic Mass. Its three hours duration, and its elaborate orchestral accompaniment, make it unsuitable for routine liturgical purposes, and it has been performed, therefore, only as a concert Mass.

Exhibit 26 Bach: Mass in B minor[29]

This huge Mass represents the peak of the polyphonic tradition in church music. It is a vivid series of emotional tableaux presented by an organ and orchestra, with choruses ranging from four to eight parts to solos and duets, with each one expressing in music the emotional quality of the successive passages of the Mass' text. Some of the choruses are adaptations of music that had been written by Bach for other works, especially his cantatas.

The music of this Mass ranges in mood from ecstatic jubilation to touching simplicity.[30] It is strong and rugged, a song of strength attained through suffering and grief. The grandeur of the first *Kyrie* and the *Sanctus* has probably never been surpassed in choral music; in the *Sanctus* and *Osanna,* one part of the chorus is dramatically pitted against another. On the other hand, there are moments when the music is filled with the most intimate human expression. The solos and duets are typically introduced by an orchestral melody that weaves in and out of the musical texture in polyphonic combination with the solo voices.

Only random selections of this great work have been chosen for comment below in the *Listening Notes.*

No. 1 *Kyrie* (first part)

The first part of the *Kyrie* is a great five-part chorus set to the intensity and simple directness of the words *Kyrie eleison* (Lord have Mercy) that is the chief element of all prayer. The movement begins with an agonized repentant cry for mercy by the full chorus. This is followed by an instrumental introduction of the main theme which is first heard in two of the inner voices and then in the bass. The theme gets more clearly defined as the singers pick it up in their sequential entrances: tenor, alto, soprano and bass. For each voice, the word *Kyrie* is repeated as a single simple syllable, but the word *eleison* is drawn out and ornamented with characteristic delicate baroque artistry. The entire movement is, therefore, made up of a statement of the main theme by the various voices that is interspersed with brief instrumental interludes. Together, they give the movement an effect of inevitable and relentless forward motion that leads to a tremendous climax before the end.

The second part of the *Kyrie* is a tuneful duet between two solo soprano voices to the words *Christie eleison* (Christ have Mercy), and the third part is a four-part chorus, quieter in mood than the first, repeating the words *Kyrie eleison*. With these three parts, a musical interpretation of the Father, the Son, and the Holy Ghost of the Trinity are effectively represented.

No. 15-17 The *Credo* (fragments)

This fragment begins with a five-part chorus sung to the words "And was incarnate by the Holy Ghost of the Virgin Mary, And was made Man." The first words, *Et Incarnatus*, enter separately in the voices, accompanied by a repetitive melodic and very expressive motive on the violins with a constant bass rhythm. The fragment ends with the words *et homo factus est* that add a feeling of suspense to the air of mystery that already pervades the piece.

The *Crucifixus* that follows is a four-part chorus that is set to the text "was crucified also for us under Pontius Pilate, He suffered and was buried." It is the most dramatic and mournful part of the Mass in which the reiterated descent of the bass, and the motive of grief in the strings, gives a vivid tone painting of Christ's suffering on the cross. Here is music profoundly intense, that could only have come from the spirit of a man who was moved to the utmost of his being.[31] Over this moving accompaniment, the voices enter fragmentarily, in accents of deep grief with the word *crucifixus*. With the words *etiam pro nobis sub Pontio Pilato passus et sepultus est* the chorus gets richer, and there is an effect of climax. The voices enter separately again with the word *crucifixus*, and the conclusion upon the words *et sepultus est* leads the voices into a low register with a feeling of profound dejection.[32]

The tragic feeling of the *Crucifixus* is dispelled immediately with the jubilant opening chorus in the next piece. This fragment is in three parts: the Resurrection, the Ascension and the Second Advent.

No. 20 *Sanctus*

This is the most inspired music of the Mass. The angels themselves appear to swirl in numberless hoards as a six-voiced chorus sings, like radiant sunlight, the praises to God: "Holy, holy, holy, Lord God of Hosts! Heaven and Earth are full of Thy glory". Here is a jubilation of cosmic proportions with a festive orchestra that gives a sense of overpowering celebration, a breath-taking voice from nature, man, the planets, and the whole universe reaching out together to the heavens to fill the entire macrocosm with glorious music.[33]

No. 23. *Agnus Dei*—Aria

The concluding portions of the Mass are quiet. The first section "Lamb of God, have mercy on us" is a solo of great beauty for alto voice with a sobbing accompaniment by the violins in an imitative relationship with the solo voice. It is a grief-stricken personal utterance of some deeply suffering sinner, prostrate in prayer.[34] The melody contains an unusual motive that appears in the beginning on the violins, and lends a feeling of great poignancy to the music.

- Mass in B minor
  DG Double 439 696-2, Janowitz, Ludwig Schrier, Ridderbusch, BPO, Karajan $

- Mass in B minor
  EMI forte Dig CZS5 68640-2 (2). Donath, Fassbaender, Ahnsjo, Bav. R Ch. & O, Jochum $

1 Moore, Douglas, *From Madrigal to Modern Music* (WW Norton, NY, 1942)
2 Vienus, Abraham, *The Concerto* (Doubleday, Doran and Company, NY, 1944)
3 *Ibid*
4 Ewen, David, *Music for the Millions* (Arco Publishing Company, NY, 1944)
5 Kerman, Joseph, *Listen* (Worth Publishers Inc, NY, 1972)
6 Vienus, Abraham, *The Concerto*
7 Kerman, Joseph, *Listen*
8 *Ibid*
9 Downes, Edward, *Guide to Symphonic Music* (Walker and Company, NY, 1981); see also Hurwitz, David, *Beethoven or Bust* (Anchor Books, NY, 1992)
10 Vienus, Abraham, *The Concerto*
11 Hurwitz, David, *Beethoven or Bust*
12 *Ibid*
13 Downes, Edward, *Guide to Symphonic Music*
14 O'Connell, Charles, *The Victor Book of the Symphony* (Simon & Schuster, NY, 1945);
15 Rudel, Anthony, *Classical Music Top 40* (Simon & Schuster, Fireside Book, NY 1995)
16 Music of the Baroque Era, *A Listener's Guide to the Recordings* (Time-Life Records, Chicago, 1966)
17 *Ibid*
18 Downes, Edward, *Guide to Symphonic Music*
19 Kerman, Joseph, *Listen*
20 Downes, Edward, *Guide to Symphonic Music*
21 Kerman, Joseph, *Listen*
22 Moore, Douglas, *From Madrigal to Modern Music*
23 *Ibid*
24 *Ibid*
25 Downes, Edward, *Guide to Symphonic Music*

78

26 O'Connell, Charles, *The Victor Book of the Symphony*; see also Downes, Edward, *Guide to Symphonic Music*

27 O'Connell, Charles, *The Victor Book of the Symphony*

28 Kerman, Joseph, *Listen*

29 Moore, Douglas, *From Madrigal to Modern Music*

30 *Ibid*

31 *Ibid*

32 *Ibid*

33 Kerman, Joseph, *Listen*

34 *Ibid*

7   The Classical Style

To a musician, *classical* refers to a style expressing the spirit that seeks to recapture the qualities of universality, equilibrium and perfection of form, and the discipline of mind that has for long been associated with the arts of classical Greece. A Classical composer is concerned as much with what is being said, i.e. the melody, as with the perfection of the manner of saying it, i.e. the form.[1] Rather than seeking out new pastures, he is content to raise established traditions to their highest ideals. Such a system produces stability, and with it all the attributes of the static: Fixed grandeur, dignity, and authority. In the individual, it produces morality and peace by showing him or her the values that are rooted in the universe, rather than those that are dependent on one's fallible and changing judgment.[2]

Under classical rules, we are told, the artist is not a rebel at war with society and the public; he or she satisfies a settled taste, and is a willing supporter of the established regime.[3] Under classical morality, the good man is reasonably happy; he is not driven by the chaos of manners and codes into a morbid guilt or fanatical efforts at reform.[4] And, under classical religion, the human mind finds an unshakable embodiment of its own permanent values, making impossible any freakishness or irresponsibility of belief which can turn every person into a puzzle or a threat to every other person. In a word, the classical order acts as an infallible balance wheel to steady human emotions.[5]

Long before the emergence of the classical school of composers, Vienna, the seat of the Hapsburg Empire, had acquired a reputation for its music. It was a highly cosmopolitan city, susceptible to Italian, French and German influences, and these it transformed into something unique. Owing to the great number of Austrian composers who occupied leading positions in this era, and to the prominent role that Vienna played in musical life, the Classical period has also been called the Viennese Period or School, although the style was not restricted to Austria.

The Symphony

Few persons have, as yet, been able to uniformly agree as to what one means by a symphony (Greek: syn, "together", phone, "sound"). And yet it remains one of the most popular and prestigious of musical forms. It has been used to express subjects as divers as a heroic struggle or a religious or philosophic belief, or describe a Nordic landscape, or explore a nation's soul or a person's psyche. Some have defined it historically in terms of a series of cut and dried rules such as the sonata form, home keys, first and second subjects, and so on. Others have focused on its large-scale integration of contrasts, and its sequences of moods and events as expressed in the traditional four movements.

New orchestral techniques came to be first developed in the opera-house. Historically, the symphony grew out of humble beginnings in Italy where its primary purpose was either to announce a call to order at the beginning of an opera, or to declare that a performance had come definitely to its end. It was born from such varied sources as the Baroque suite, the operatic overture, and the serenade, and it carved out its mature identity from the changes in musical style that characterized the waning of the Baroque era and the advancing of the Classical period. The baroque *concerto grosso* contributed to the development of the style of the symphonic slow movement, and the baroque Italian *overture* standardized its form into three movements—fast, slow, and fast.

The symphony became the musical centerpiece of the Classical style. The structure of a symphony was composed from its four, thematically independent, movements, and its main foundation was centered on the sonata form. A first movement (*allegro*: quick and vigorous), occasionally with an introduction, invariably expressed in its music the serious themes of the human spirit, and was always cast in the sonata form. The second movement (*andante*: smooth and flowing, or *adagio*: slow), though of no less dignity, was made to contrast with the stress and strife and the stirring conflicts of the first. It did not display the deep discussions of the earlier music; simplicity of statement, expressed in the calm and poignant verses of a lyrical melody, were usually its natural utterance. In the third movement (*minuet*), a mood of relaxation overshadowed all else, and this was usually expressed, quite fittingly, in a dance. The complexion of the music hence passed from a tension and stress, through pathos, to humor.

In the early years of the symphony, this effect of relief, or restraint from tension, was carried over into the fourth and last movement (*finale*). This was generally cast in a *rondo* form which was particularly suited for the expression of carefree joy—the melody appeared and vanished with graceful interludes, which later developed into lesser tunes. There were no serious discussions in the *finale*, just a set of constant and playful alternations of the melody. As the symphony matured, the movements became proportionately enlarged. The *minuet* became frequently replaced by a *scherzo*, and the last movement changed its spirit from an entertainment piece to a more serious idiom of poetic feeling.

The *rondo*, therefore, yielded to the sonata form in the *finale* which often ended in a grand climax.

The modern symphony probably began as a *salon* amusement with the first symphony of Haydn. In its early years, this musical form exhibited a simplicity and a primitive clarity that was necessary to express the new secular feeling that was evolving in music, and to convey in absolute music what had before depended on words. Its attention was centered, therefore, more upon the structure of the musical sounds, and their conformity with established standards. The goal was to produce a tuneful well-built composition, rather than an eloquent expression of something abstract or even programmatic. But over the 36 years that spanned his 104 symphonies, things had begun to change and, in his last dozen or so such compositions, Haydn reached a height of poetic expression and exuberant joyousness that were expressed in magnificent lyrical passages. He was the first to put a mood into a symphony: He was the first great secular tone poet. There were no notes of defiance, or awful depth and sublimity in his music, but his works had a serene profundity of their own and a true lyric beauty.

With Mozart, the symphony deepened in intensity and broadened in scope. Losing the trappings of *bourgeois* humor and joy, it took a more cosmic view. Boyish exuberance yielded to matured serenity. Mozart crowned the secular musical outburst by deepening its pathos, idealizing its humor, and adding, in his final compositions, a serious heroic note that was afterwards expanded by Beethoven. His very completeness of form was typical and expressive of the breadth of his sympathy. Nonetheless, in both Haydn and Mozart, the music had a strongly entertaining attitude with its purpose being principally to give pleasure. Theirs was a sound where pure beauty, unalloyed with dim meaning or grim woe, was filling the courts and aristocratic households of Europe. There was no suggestion of prophecy or warning, no defiant proclamation of truth in general, or of any definite truth in particular. Music did not as yet "strike fire from the soul of man."

Depth of pathos was first explored by Beethoven. Whereas Haydn's was the song of the child, Mozart's was that of the youth, and Beethoven's of the man. Haydn and Mozart had tied the melodic sections together for their own sake, and they had accepted their fate, their surroundings, and their institutions murmuringly. They had been content to be happy out of doors in the woods and the meadows, and to go to an established church, and sing its services and obey its authorities. They had been glad to be allowed their wages and please their patrons. But Beethoven called no man master; nobody but Beethoven could govern Beethoven; and when, as happened when the fit was on him, he deliberately refused to govern himself, he was ungovernable.

In Beethoven, everything became subordinate to the expression of a great, continuous, homogenous thought or feeling. He was a giant wave in that storm of human spirit that produced the French Revolution. He was first a thinking man, and he took himself, his institutions, and his social and political ideals seriously. He reflected in his music the cosmic breadth and mystic depth of his great contemporary, Goethe. Meaning was more important than beauty; indeed, beauty was merely a means to the chief end of music which was to communicate emotional feelings. Feelings, for him, were at the root of all music and, for their expression, he often found it necessary to break the fetters of form, or ruthlessly violate the sacred canons to shock the ears of his audience with discord, and yet fill them with a sense of vital meaning. And this is not unworthy for, when traced thoroughly, feelings are the original fount of all heroic action, of all statesmanship, ethics, poetry and of humanity; indeed, feelings are but the cold expressions of that which is the living sentient fire. Over time, Beethoven's audiences were willing to be awed and identify with his sounds of personal and national aspirations, and his military conflicts and moral resolve, with the whole blended into a rhetoric of heroism.

The symphony of Haydn's early days may well be considered chamber music in a modern sense. When Haydn began his long service at *Esterhaza,* he had under his direction a very small band of players for whom he composed his symphonies: six first violins and other strings in proportion, one flute, two each of oboes, bassoons, horns and trumpets, and drums. Some believe that even today, the best performances of his music are generally obtained when this small size is borne in mind. The string family formed the core of his orchestral group, and the wood winds and brass were given the task of building up the sonority of the climaxes or sustaining the harmonic background. But there was also a lively exploration of the melodic possibilities and tone colors of the flute, oboe, clarinet, bassoon, horn and the other brass instruments. The horns served equally as members of the wood winds choir and the brass choir. The oboists doubled on the flutes so both could not be played simultaneously. This was not seen as a disadvantage, since musical color and contrast in his time varied from movement to movement rather than within each movement. Mozart and Beethoven added a trombone, the clarinets and extra horns and eventually the piccolo, double bassoon, triangle, bass drums and cymbals. The addition of a vocal choir in his last symphony (*Choral* Symphony) paved the way for the great orchestral advances of the nineteenth century.

After Beethoven, the Viennese symphonic tradition was continued by Schubert, Mendelssohn and Schumann. Berlioz considered himself the natural successor to Beethoven when he released the symphony from its Classical shackles, and introduced in it his revolutionary Romanticism. The legacy of Berlioz was considerable. The symphony, which had endlessly reconstructed and reflected literature, now began, in its own way, to absorb literature. His *Symphonie fantastique* opened the door to countless symphonic scores with literary inspirations. Composers now invariably began to give their symphonies a variety of particular programs. At first, the themes were either evocations of nature, or were drawn from areas such as Classical literature which were appropriate for,

84

and acceptable to, the aristocratic patrons. Poetic subject-matter was translated into music in the "program" symphony that bonded, in a subversive marriage, both the popular dramatic story-telling, and the high aims and philosophical seriousness of Romantic idealism. In addition to a relaxation of the symphonic form to allow an expression of romantic moods, Berlioz further opened the full range of orchestral sound through the use of new instruments, and through effects that required a larger number of players. With Berlioz, all the basic instruments were now at hand in a symphony orchestra that formed a palette, from which a composer could select virtually any combination of tone colors. The range of orchestral sound, and the sheer volume of sound that could be produced, were extended.

The Classical rules and ideals of craftsmanship, that had been loosened in the diversity of form and expression practiced by the Romanticists, were resurrected by Brahms, and German romanticism reached its twilight with the gigantic compositions of Mahler and Bruckner. But, as the politics and sociology of the time began to change, the symphony went on to voice the concerns of an increasingly urban and politically aware middle class that wanted to have its national identity asserted. In Dvorak and Tchaikovsky, the Viennese tradition became blended with a strain of nationalism and the Berlioz love of the ultra-dramatic and grand orchestration. The symphony orchestra reached its heights with Wagner who contributed to its modern standardization and fixed seating plans, since the scores of his monumental compositions required a minimum complement of instruments without which his music could not be performed. And, in the so-called *Symphony of a Thousand,* Mahler gave to the world one of its finest completely choral symphony.

Exhibit 27 Beethoven: Symphony No. 5

"Thus Fate knocks at the door." With these ominous words, Beethoven is reported to have given, casually, an interpretation of the opening theme of this symphony. And, starting with his words, it has become commonplace to build up in this music a complete picture of the strife between the spirit and Fate. The music addresses, even harangues, the whole of mankind; the last vestige of the courtly, deferential manner of the age of elegance has been scornfully discarded.

This symphony is not for the young and shallow; a listener must be capable of feeling the grimness, the terror, and the fight of life and living, so that he may exult with the composer in the triumphant joy of the undaunted. It is as tragic as the Book of Job and very like it in its content.[6] And, as in all great tragedies, it is burdened with the stern awfulness and merciless drive of the external destiny with which even the strongest can, at best, struggle. Fate, however, can have no power over man himself, the inner man; it cannot control the human character under which great deeds are done and genuine greatness achieved. Although there is an expression in this music of a monumental and overpowering external evil and of hopeless supplication, there is also a declaration of sacred faith and assured triumph which is typified in the triumphant *finale*.

Four harsh, purposeful chords—three quick notes followed by a longer one—are thrust forward by all the strings and clarinets, and the first movement plunges forward immediately like a merciless raging organism to establish the dynamic principal theme. Nothing so original, so forceful and concise, had hitherto opened any piece of music. No other great music had been built from an initial figure of just four notes, perhaps the most well-known chords in all music. The very life-blood of the fourth sustained note seemed to be squeezed out of it to the last drop: here, it has been said, was a force that was enough to arrest the waves of the sea and lay bare the ground of the ocean, that seemed to stop the clouds in their courses, dispel the mists, and reveal the pure blue sky and the burning face of the sun himself.[7]

These four powerful utterances, as persistent and almighty in this music as Fate itself, saturate the movement, recurring constantly and unrelenting in endless versions. And instead of building up from these musical fragments, the music breaks down into other fragments of even greater rarity and breadth. From these awesome beginnings, the music drives forward impetuously, and expands swiftly until, suddenly, its driving force becomes suspended by a violent and forceful climax put forth by the whole orchestra.

The main theme returns in an altered and gentler guise in the horns, and then a soothing song-like second tune enters in the violins. It is a sort of broadening of the first theme to form a second theme. No greater contrast can be imagined than that between these two themes: the first, a constant vital impulse devoid of joy, while the other a pleading and pious spirit, like the sweet protest of a woman against the fury of her oppressor. The new song is taken up by the strings and wood winds in a lovely and pensive dialog that beseeches peace and solace, and seeks, as it were, a refuge from the first theme which continues to be reflected softly in the basses. But there is no room for tenderness or grace in this music. Mustering the orchestra's mightiest forces, the awful four-note phrase returns with overwhelming strength to destroy the new melody. A solitary oboe, lone and forlorn, raises a piteous cry, but this only seems to provoke new torrents of rage in the strings. Once more the placid and comforting horn emerges to give pause, and once again the impetuous strings move the whole angry orchestra to crush this outrage with its omnipotent fateful utterances.

Now follows a development of the struggle, the bitterness, and the vehemence that underlies the whole movement. Here, it has been said, are revealed all the secrets of being—the private grief, the lonely meditations, the bursts of enthusiasm, and the anxious searches for love that tore at the composer's heart. The merciless drive of destiny, expressed in fitful hammerings of the principal theme, sweeps forward in a wild rush of rude and clamorous sounds to end in an earsplitting climax. There is little sign of the second tune, now appearing more helpless and pitiful than ever before; just the utterances of a supreme and ruthless ego, momentarily frustrated but unconquered, brooking no interference. There is no mercy as yet in the terrifying tread of ruthless Fate. The tension rises to an unbearable hush. Then the whole orchestra bursts out in a cosmic apotheosis of the mighty principal theme. The music is borne upwards in a responsive succession of the four deadly chords, tapering of, at times, with monotonous repetitions into a timid expectancy, only to be renewed in terrible clusters of tone to ring their incessant fateful blows.

The entire exposition is now repeated, but with an extremely affecting moment expressed in a slow solo by a lonely oboe. It is a perverted version of the gentle theme, and is mocked with brutal imitation by the entire string section with a sense of demonic humor. Presently, the whole orchestra storms in again, playing the main theme over and over with an infernal fury, showing a degree of vehemence and defiance that is, until now, unknown. The movement ends abruptly with two loud chords.

The second movement is built upon two lovely themes, each of which is of a quiet pastoral nature. The first possesses an irresistible grace and a beauty seldom equaled; the second is scarcely less beautiful. The music opens with a gentle sentimental song sung by the cellos with an exaggerated accent, that is somewhat reminiscent of the first movement's main theme. The violas join in, accompanied by the plucked basses, and are answered by a touching phrase in the flutes and oboes that is echoed in the violins. It is a simple tune, exquisite to hear, that forms the centerpiece of this movement, and it appears several times throughout the music in simple variations. The persistency of the simple phrase makes a profound impression. There is a distinct feeling of prayer, perhaps Faith, in this whole music; the assaults, struggles, conquests, and the abandoned passion of the preceding movement seem to have all melted away into an uneasy serenity.

Presently, a new and mournful tune emerges in the clarinets and bassoons with the four accented notes, that dreadful knocking of Fate, appearing once again in the background. An obvious impatience pervades the orchestra as this annoying knocking persists to mar the peaceful mood. The instruments voice their objections, and soon the protest rises to a violent crescendo culminating in a powerful note thrown out by the deep-throated basses.[8] The variations return, veiled by new figures of rhythm and setting, with changes made in color and treatment to perpetuate the prevailing emotional state of stability and calm. Somewhere, a succession of chords in the strings lead in a touching little duet between a clarinet and a bassoon, with all the air of a farewell, and this is prolonged by the wood winds in a humorous passage.[9] The remainder of the movement is extraordinarily noble, pathetic and beautiful, and the violins, full of unspeakable emotion, seem almost to go up into heaven.[10] The end comes in the form of a distinctly joyful prayer that seems to herald a vision of coming victory, a spirit of reassurance. The wood winds and strings unite in a loud acclaim of the melody, the horns sound the harmony, the drums beat the rhythm, and the lower strings strum a rapid accompaniment.[11] But beneath this joyousness lies an uneasy suggestion that violence and ruthlessness are not dead yet, but merely sleeping.[12]

From the shadowy and haunted recesses of the lowest strings of the cellos and basses arises a mysterious tone, an ominous breath of premonition, that opens the third movement. The air hangs heavy with anticipation: the lights seem to be lowered, and something terrible is going to happen. The gentle and tentative responses of the upper strings and the wood winds go unheeded and are of no import. There is a lull. Then a lingering note emerges on the wood winds, and suddenly, in the arrogant voice of a horn, comes a mighty and defiant warning. And forthright, the whole orchestra takes up this bold assertion loudly, with intonations of rebellion and power. But hark! Note the rhythm: it is that terrifying and wicked four-note summons of Fate that has returned![13] Perhaps, the best response to this grotesque and bitter twist of life, the music seems to say, may well be to humor it.

And so the music embarks on a tripping theme, a kind of heavy waltz sounded by the horns and strummed by the strings with periodic halts. It is played with the utmost vehemence, and is immediately answered and extended by the whole orchestra with martial vigor.[14] It is a grotesque and cumbersome gambol, choreographed for the great contrabasses, and to which the orchestra unwillingly joins in. None can, however, fail to miss its relation to that awful four-note motto; instead of the dull thuds with the ominous pauses, it now has the guise of a newer rhythm. There is almost a touch of sardonic profanity in this music, almost of blasphemy and an unholy jesting about unspeakable things.[15]

A lighter rhythm now emerges in a trio of strings. It is a rumbling movement in the spirit of a rough boisterous humor, almost like the dance of elephants. The profound and ponderous humor rises in a great bacchanal, only to dwindle away into a sinister and cavernous gloom brought about by that grim and awful rhythm that never seems to cease. Again, the puzzling beat rises, only to descend, once more, into still lower depths of the profoundest gloom with a demoniac perversion of the melody. Then, without the slightest change in color or power or tone, with nothing but an alteration of rhythm, this overcharged atmosphere marvelously clears. Suddenly, there is a clear ray of hope as the musical phrases become more piquant. The music is transferred from the horns to the oboes, clarinets and the first violins that together play a cheery and quiet new delicate arrangement.[16] There is a fiercely brilliant crescendo, a golden blaze of color and tone from the whole orchestra.

To the blare of three trombones, with depth added by the contrabassoons, and brilliance flashed by a piccolo, the fourth movement bursts into a triumphal opening march that sings out an exuberant joy. The clarinets, joined by the violas and cellos, join in the celebration. Here, it seems, is a heroic lift from the abode of devils to that of angels, from hell to heaven, from sinister and overwhelming evil to a moral triumph and an emancipation of the spirit.[17] Awaiting no pause, throwing off its shackles, the music steps forward in exultant marching chords to embody, as it were, the living and beautiful spirit that denotes a freedom from all outward conditions. The unrestrained jubilation continues confidently, varying in profundity and in sparkling humor, ending in renewed bursts of exultant triumph where articulate tone seems lost in vague intensity. Strange and disorderly, almost appalling like some divine power working under the rushing surface of this mass of sound, the creative force of law and order seems to be at work here.[18] At last, out of the suspense and repetition and the mystery which has, for so long, enveloped the music, there bursts out a new world, radiant with an eternal sunshine, and welcomed by the jubilant sounds of ionian strains as if all the heavens were shouting with joy.[19]

Suddenly, without warning, in the midst of this frantic rejoicing, comes a replay of the dreaded summons of Fate: the four terrible chords! Why? Why is there this return of the early terror? Perhaps it may be that an unpleasant remembrance makes more sure the reality of the victory, and the certainty of disarming that dreadful visitor and robbing him of his terrors. Perhaps it is a reminder of the bitter laughter that once seemed the only answer to that dreadful knocking; perhaps it is a realization that in all our deliberate acts, we ourselves are both Heaven and Hell.[20] Again, the triumphant song continues, first vague, then more defined. The music grows faster and fiercer, not feverish, but with a festal assurance of the highest joy. Still faster it races on, into a final reaffirmation of the assured victory over the original theme—but the music cannot stop here. It rushes on until, after endless vague reiterations, the end at last comes because it must, in a concluding climax of overwhelming excitement, power and brilliance.[21]

- Symphony No. 5; 7 in A
  DG Dig. 447 400-2, Vienna Philh, Carlos Kleiber $$
  A most electrifying recorded performance.

- Symphonies 1-2;4-5.
  DGG Double 439 681-2 (2). VPO, Karl Boehm $

Exhibit 28 Beethoven: Symphony No. 6 (Pastoral)

Though his ancestry was from Belgium, Beethoven was, nonetheless, a German, with a German's passionate love of nature and the outdoors with its birds and brooks and every creeping thing. Many of his music ideas took form when he rested in the shade of a favorite tree, or during his long, lonely walks which he took in all weathers in the woods and countryside outside Vienna.[22] Nature was to him not only a consoler for his sorrows and disenchantment; she was also a friend with whom he took pleasure in familiar talk since she was the only intercourse to which his growing deafness posed no obstacle.[23] In the *Pastoral* symphony, he presented a poetic picture of country life, complete with the scenes of nature that he loved so well: the broad meadows, the rocky clefts, the elm-girt woodland paths, and the murmuring rushing brooks.[24] More significant, he also expressed in this music the spirit of nature, and the feelings aroused by the sights and the sounds of a natural world. He was not charting landscape or seasons or country happenings, but the interrelationship between landscape and the conscious mind. Nature's beauty and symmetry always remained for him a reassuring testimony that God was truly in his Heaven and all was well with the world.

Historically, the *Pastoral* marked an important stage in the development of program music. Although descriptive titles and realistic evocations

90

of bird song and thunderstorm had been long familiar in instrumental music, never before had naturalistic details and intensity of feeling been more palpable, or more powerfully or more vividly expressed. The choice of five movements for this symphony, instead of the traditional four, was also unusual, with the last three running together in a continuous sequence. The "extra" movement was the thunderstorm, which constituted a dramatic transition to the *finale*.

The first movement opens with the music played by small combinations of instruments. Certain of the tiny melodic fragments are repeated over and over again, sometimes as many as twenty times in succession, in a sort of naive joy to express the constant and repetitive sounds of nature. The real meaning of these bird-song repetitions, however, is not that they represent birds in particular, but that birds themselves repeat their songs continually when they are happy and have nothing else to do.[25] So also does a brook go on for ever, and the murmur of the music often becomes continuous because it evokes the course of its untiring flowing waters. It has been said that this symphony has the tremendous strength of someone who knows how to relax; whereas most symphonic developments build up in tension, this one enlarges upon tranquillity.[26] As the music unfolds, the overall effect is that of a steady gaze, gradually revealing ever more distant horizons.[27]

The first movement recalls the *Awakening of Joyous Feelings on Arrival in the Country*. Indeed, *feelings* is the key word that pervades the entire work. The cool fluttering air of incense-bearing morn envelopes the opening. Without any introduction, the first melody is given out by the first violins, as sweet and soft as the air of May itself, with buds and blossoms and the new-mown grass. The song is answered by a four-voiced string choir.[28] It is an old Croatian folk-song, and it seems to contain in its heart the whole of the wonderful movement that it starts. The entire first movement is constructed from its fragments, germinating off phrases that are closely related to the parent stem in rhythm and interval.[29] It teams with life and vigor, conveying the verdant freshness and burgeoning loveliness of spring-time in the open country.

The melody passes from the strings to the wood winds and is then picked up by the full orchestra. A happy mood clothes the air; the sound of babbling brooks and singing birds are suggested or imitated by the tremulousness of the cellos and tiny arabesques from the flutes. Clarinets and the other wood winds strike a fast rhythm, and the strings glide freely on a strain of the tune. Presently, the full orchestra strikes in to reach a climax, and the violins slip easily into the second theme.

This is a more thoughtful and dignified melody than the first, and is repeated, in turn, by each component of the string section: First violins, second violins, violas, cellos and bass. It causes a monotony which, however, is never monotonous, akin to the constant sounds of Nature: The monotony of rustling leaves and swaying trees, of running brooks and blowing wind, and the call of birds and the hum of insects.[30] The wood winds pick it up, embellished by dainty flourishes from the flutes. A third tune arises high in the flutes, and soon all the birds in the woods seem to be singing bits of this song which dies down with a cheery call in the strings and a caroling note in the wood winds.

Both themes, especially the first, are now developed. It is carried first in a low duet by the strings, then in a single song by the violins, again in duet, and then in a full hymnal chorus.[31] There is much repetition of the first theme by the instruments and the full orchestra, but despite all this repetition, there is no weariness: When the sameness of the fields, woods and streams can become distasteful, then will this music weary its listeners![32] A rollicking dance tune is added, delicate and jubilant, and full of the spring feeling that animates this music, at the end of which the first theme returns softly, initially in the strings, then all alone in the high flutes, answered mockingly by a playful burst from the whole orchestra to bring the movement to a long close.

A limpid stream descending from a neighboring height, and shaded by leafy elms on both sides, describes the exact spot at Heiligenstadt that is the *Scene at the Brook*.[33] Often called the most serene slow movement ever written, its slow tempo makes the second movement the longest part of this symphony. The movement opens to the murmuring of tremulous strings suggesting the rippling of running water—the more the water, the deeper the tone. The murmur of the brook becomes more continuous throughout the rest of the movement, and its incessant gurgling in the background cannot fail to be recognized, however slightly it is touched in: the peaceful waters form a rippling accompaniment throughout. Above and through the ceaseless waters are heard the various motives, none of them directly imitative, but all suggesting the delights of the natural world, the glories of summer, and the busy noises of the country life swarming upon the senses.[34] The horns drone as the first violins slowly sing an articulate song. The lower strings soon emerge from the background and grow louder in their waving and swaying as the lower wood winds now sing the melody.[35] Here is the kind of mood, drawn into a state of timeless contemplation, where one would say to oneself on a sleepy summer's day by the brook, "How beautiful!"[36]

The final trill dies away into a dreamland, but it is so beautiful, and the sunlight appears to have so shifted through the trees to such new purpose, that the music must look again at the scene. The coloring is now slightly grotesque but it is still all too beautiful.[37] The song soon breaks into a verse of more human clearness, first in the high strings, then in the low cellos. The melody is taken over by a clarinet, a high trill on the strings, sweetly discordant, seems to be added to the branches above, the first violins give a series of trills, and the horns add on a charming vagueness. The song ends to the high notes of a flute and the music returns, once again, to the tremulous murmuring of the strings.

A new scene now emerges with the wood winds starting afresh into a melody, brought in first by the rich tone of a bassoon that is played to the murmuring of the high strings. The violas and cellos join in to add a summer feeling to the song, and the singers trip into a jolly measure. The clarinets enter, and the other instruments join the dance which soon ends in an united chorus. The verse is now repeated; the mood emulates the sweet conflict of the forest sounds of insects, birds and waters. Everything is in perfect keeping, and to comment upon such beauty is to gild refined gold.[38] A new verse, echoed higher in the flutes, digresses from the original tune, but this melody soon returns with more readiness and variety.

Suddenly, for a moment, all is silent, even the rippling brook. And through the silence comes the famous passage imitating the singing of the birds that has been called a master-stroke of pure musical form: The flute's trill imitates a nightingale; the call of the oboe, a quail; of the clarinet, a cuckoo. Here is a reminder that birds are nature's own musicians. But not even a bird-call can disturb the sweet complacence in which the movement ends.[39]

The atmosphere of the third movement depicting the *Joyful Gathering of Peasants* is jolly and carefree. So far the music has had to do with nature; now it turns to the human beings who people this delicate landscape.[40] The sentiment at once changes completely, and one is carried from graceful and quiet contemplation to rude and boisterous merriment. Here is music of the rural bands that played at the taverns in the countryside outside Vienna that Beethoven so often frequented. The movement begins with a soft and lightly tripping downward-moving tune, the first theme of which is played by the stringed instruments. Flutes, bassoons and oboes, the wind instruments most appropriate for the rural artists, then take up the melody to a most expressive jolly jingle in the quickstep of a tuneful Irish jig. Many instruments join in loudly, and the rustic music ends in a climax.

The real dance now begins, its rhythmic tones being played by groups of instruments. An old-fashioned waltz rhythm on the first and second violins ushers in a second theme, a true gay waltz tune, but more a song than a dance, played by the solo oboes with a continuous accompaniment by the violins. It is a quaint little German folk-tune that every schoolboy probably knew, and it gains more body and color when picked up by a horn.[41] Now occurs the well-known humorous incident of the bassoonist in the village band who has only three notes left on his battered instrument which he plays at full force whenever he should, and sometimes when he should not![42] Trumpets now appear for the first time in the symphony, and their dying tones lead to another simple rough dance tune played by a trio of strings. The full orchestra joins in loudly and leads, without a pause, to a repetition of the first theme, then directly on to the next movement.

The Storm breaks suddenly, as the village dance is in full swing, and throws a mystical cast over the rustic gaiety, much as a dark cloud might do on the actual field. Hitherto, only the idyllic aspects of Nature have been celebrated; now, the formidable hidden power behind these, the divine might of the Creator, are unleashed. Thunder, hail, lightning and blustery wind are all suggested in this superb musical evocation of nature as a splendid war of the elements rages. The strings start the fourth movement, followed by a clarinet call that is echoed promptly by a horn. The horn repeats, and the melody now enters on the strings, three times in succession. Basses and kettledrums sound the distant thunder as the storm breaks loose and the dancers run for shelter. The second violins elicit the light patter of sprinkling rain, with the larger drops echoed by the first violins. Winds tumble in the descending violins, and the trumpets, trombones and piccolos sound the tempest peals and the more furious rattle of rain and lightning flashes.

Presently, as suddenly as it began, the storm begins to blow itself out. Low thuds of pelting rain strike more gently, and here and there a loud bolt recurs. A distant thunder rumbles in the timpani, and a calm oboe melody transforms the image of raindrops into a glistening of leaves. As the last growls recede, the higher strings and clarinet sound the first notes of a hymn of thanksgiving. The first timid bird lifts up its tiny song, a shepherd plays upon his pipe, and the sun shines once more.[43] For this was not a raging storm at sea, but a thunderstorm that had interrupted

94

something like a dance around a may-pole, and which, far from being a danger, has given rise to happy and thankful feelings afterwards.[44]

To keep sheep was the occupation of those who lived in the age of innocence. Apollo, the God of song, tended the flocks of Admetus, and it was the shepherds who received the news of the Nativity.[45] A shepherd's song of thanksgiving merges imperceptibly into the final movement to express the *Gladsome and Grateful Feelings After the Storm*. It is a song of gratitude to the Creator for the useful shower, a countryman's thanksgiving of unaffected devoutness. The first violins start the tune, it is repeated by the second violins, and then the music expands broadly as the melody is taken up the violas, cellos, clarinets and bassoons in unison. The violins keep the tune as the flutes play a suggestion of it, or it is plucked by the strings as the other instruments play arabesques. After a majestically joyful climax, the movement ends slowly with a gradual subsidence of the music. Against the softly sounding violins, violas, cellos and basses, there arises a hymn-like, faintly blown, reminiscence of the opening theme, feeling now like a slight autumnal chill, perhaps the chill of dying, sounded distantly on a muted horn that dies away into the distance, breathing a majestic splendor, glorious as the fields refreshed by the rain.

- Symphony No. 6 (Pastoral); Overture: The Creatures of Prometheus; (i) Egmont: Overture; Overture: Trummel geruhet; Freudwall und leidvoll; Klarchens Tod, Op. 84.
    EMI CDM7 63358-2, Philh. O, Klemperer; (i) with Birgit Nilsson $$
- Symphony No. 6 (Pastoral); Symphony No. 4
    Sony SMK 64462, Columbia SO, Walter $$

Exhibit 29 Brahms: Symphony No. 1

A first symphony, it has been said, carries the charm of novelty like a maiden speech. It bears the stamp of the man's spirit, his personal tone, like the philosophy of a new teacher.[46] And it comes as no surprise that Johannes Brahms (1833-1897) is one of the very few composers who delivered an important message in his very first symphonic work. Though the germ of this first essay existed in his mind quite early, the work was left, like strong wine, to lie upon the lees for almost twenty years before it was offered to the world as a product of his full maturity. To some extent, these years reflected the awe with which he regarded both the symphony form and its greatest artist Beethoven. On the other hand, it may well have taken such a long time for a great man's experience to work out the grand transition from the immense tragedy of the first movement to the triumph of the *finale*.[47] Certainly, no other first symphonic work is such a completely realized masterpiece: Its grand style, its earnest spirit and monumental pathos, its virile, concentrated and defiant energy spared nothing to stir the innermost depths of one's soul. It maintained, even in its moments of exaltation and joy, a certain restrained and remote quality.[48]

The first movement opens with an expectant but majestic introduction that gathers mass forcefully and slowly to set a *Pathetique* mood for the entire work. The violins soar ecstatically in circuitous paths against a determined background of measured throbbing timpani. Fragments of melody, the poignant portents of the main theme, arise in the flute, oboe and violin. Hollow plucking strings and strangely piping wood winds answer with what seems to be the first fervent strain of human appeal in this music.[49] The sublimity dissipates in a big concluding sweep of dissipating tones, and the plaintive wailing of an oboe, rising and falling, and losing itself among the other instruments, introduces a simple first theme characterized by an especially striking phrase of four notes. This is picked up passionately by the violins.

A severe second melody enters, borne by the oboes, clarinets, bassoons and horns, and bearing a close resemblance to the passage in the wood winds that had introduced the first subject. Indeed, the second tune, though gaining eminence, is soon accompanied in the lower strings by a steady phrase from the leading theme itself. There are no strong emotional contrasts between the two themes, no opposing effects of sunshine and shade, or tragedy and comedy. It is as if joy has been completely shut out—only a monumental primeval sorrow prevails, joined in an intimate musical relationship to a striving and restless feeling of aspiration.[50]

A lovely fragment by the clarinet rises above the gloom to hold the ear and lift up the spirits, and it is imitated with tender reflection by the other wood winds that flit, like pairs of butterflies, in flickering shades of changing tone. Here is a bewildering wealth of lesser melodies! But the urgent predominating rhythm allows no dwelling upon gentleness, and the energetic strings break into this calm to carry the first section to a virile and agitated end.

The entire section is now repeated. The simple first theme, so amenable to varied and forceful development, undergoes vital and throbbing manipulations—full-blooded and muscular, defiant but encouraging—though always dwelling in the contained realm of a sober, almost fearful, joy. Somewhere, a long conversation between the violins, basses and contrabassoons begins peacefully but then runs amuck, loud and strong like unruly horses. The strings victoriously seize the fragmentary theme, and though the thematic piece has been torn away from the other wood winds, the bassoon still joins them. Then the violins abandon it, and pour out instead a lovely melody, sad and reflective, which presages the end of the movement.[51] The movement comes to a close softly, in a warm and enveloping wave of waxing and waning tone, recalling the song of sorrow that had been played by the wood winds in the introduction.[52] With a mighty sigh, the melody sweeps into silence. A single note is plucked by the strings: The tragedy, it appears, has ended!

The second movement is one of the most melodic music pieces ever written. It is dreamy and melancholic, and is wrought out of two beautiful melodies. The first is played conspicuously at the opening by the first violins, and the second equally lovely tune follows, pensive and longing, voiced by a singularly poignant oboe. It is a gentle, contemplative melancholy, like an acceptance of things as they stand, born out of the inevitable disappointments, grief and futilities of life.[53] The music rises, lone and trembling, urged on by a pulsing rhythm by the strings and wood winds to a point of emotional delirium, and then subsides to an introspective calm. Solo violin and solo horn accompany the orchestra in a clever and delightful duet, with the violin eloquently hovering above the orchestra, star-like and bright, guiding the music to its delicate end.

The third movement, as expressed by this childless companion of children, is lively and graceful, but with the gentle and artless whimsical humor reminiscent of youngsters.[54] A clarinet begins a children's folksong, mellow and with a fluid melodic flow, that moves gracefully above a plucking accompaniment by the cellos. The tune is reinforced, first by the violins and violas and then, gently and softly, by the strings and the wood winds. A new theme, emotionally touching both in rhythm and melody, briefly surfaces in the wood winds but the first melody returns by degrees, clothed in decorative figures of great delicacy and beauty. The main second melody now enters, lively and graceful, announced gravely by the wood winds but transferred quickly to the caressing utterances of the strings. The second tune dominates the movement and brings it to a gentle close.

Had he written nothing else, the magic evocation of power and beauty, and the outpouring of passion and exhilaration in the fourth movement would have ranked the composer among the immortals of music. Here is leonine majesty and epic grandeur at its best![55] Words fail to express the incomparable grandioseness and sublimity of this music, the likes of which the world has rarely heard. The movement undergoes a strange and wonderful metamorphosis from the depths of an agonizing tragedy to a brief delirious madness, which gives way to a philosophical complacence, and then to a final exaltation.[56] It has been said that this sequence of music is virtually inevitable, for in the first movement the tragedy is completed and done with, and the rest of the work is concerned with the issues that make tragedies so beautiful.[57]

A poignant, awful cry emanates from four descending notes in the bass, followed by a fragment by the violins. An enigmatic strangeness sweeps through the orchestra and then, from the depths of the basses, arises the plucking of strings, seemingly like the heavy throbbing of a torn heart, mounting more swiftly and boldly until, with a final leap, it reaches out and touches the whole string section. Above the heaving sobs of the violas and cellos, the other orchestral voices lament sadly. Again that fearsome throbbing breaks in, pulsating through the plucked strings, progressing like the somber footsteps of some menacing beast, or a strong gusty wind, before which the deliriously whirling figures of the strings and the wood winds seem tossed about like helpless leaves. A terrifying roll of the timpani ends this harrowing scene.

Amid hushes and the tremulous harmonies of the strings, a calm and lovely song now unfolds like a breath of spring air blown softly and sweetly, first by the horn and then by the flute. Here, it seems, are the chiming clocks of the world, a soothing and heartening chorale of festal bells sounding, accompanied by the warm complacency of the strings. As the horn gradually dies away, and the cloud-like harmonies in the strings sink lower and lower like a mist veiling the landscape, there is a pause. Then the most exuberant and jubilant music bursts forth in the strings, and the whole orchestra plunges into a high-spirited, almost ecclesiastical, tune ranging from a passionate pleading to a wild elation, trying to forget that awesome terror of the earlier music. This is a heaven-storming proclamation of joy rarely paralleled in music, a mighty unconstrained and electrifying paean of exultation to the Highest. And when one believes that the uttermost limits of power have been explored by the orchestra, the chorale bursts forth once more into an even more glorious splendor, with the brazen voices exerting their most Olympian powers in a grand triumphal procession. The bold brass descends mightily, and the end comes in a single long-drawn conclusive tonal cluster of noble simplicity.

- Symphony No. 1 in C minor; SCHUMANN: Overture, Scherzo and Finale
  DG 431 161-2 , BPO, Karajan $

Exhibit 30 Brahms: Symphony No. 4

It has been said that before he started work on his last symphony, Johannes Brahms (1833-1897) drank deep from the cup of grief and terror offered by Sophocles' tragedy *Oedipus*. There is something of the gloom and melancholy of that awesome work in certain parts of the fourth symphony which, unlike virtually all other symphonies, also ends tragically. A tragedy usually tells a story that is eventually weakened, or even falsified, by a happy ending. In this work, on the other hand, a tragic tale is told from beginning to end, with only fleeting uplifting interruptions.[58] It has been described as a great autumnal landscape, a composition built upon a theme that fills the soul.[59] It is not a hysterical grief that is expressed here, but a restrained, self-contained and disciplined emotion of a heroic character producing, in effect, the same catharsis that Greek tragedy purportedly produced on its ancient audience.[60]

In an exaggeration of the traditional Viennese style, Brahms composed not just the first, but all the first three movements in the sonata form, and for the last movement he resurrected the baroque *passacaglia*. Perhaps this was a manifesto to proclaim his traditional orientation to the new generation of modernists who had surrounded him in a Vienna dominated by Johann Strauss. This may well have been a reason why the city was the slowest to warm up to this work. Yet gradually she took hold and, at the last performance before the composer's death, a devoted Viennese audience lauded enthusiastically after each movement. At its end, with tears streaming down his cheeks, a dying Brahms, shrunken in form with his white hair lying lank, stood weakly before an applauding and sobbing public, for each knew that he was saying his last farewell.[61]

The first movement opens with a moving dialogue between the strings and wood winds that seems to have come out of nowhere, but of which one suddenly becomes conscious.[62] Blaring fanfares by the horns, and cries of pain, interrupt the narration which passes into an earnest and ardent long melody with little swells, up and down, suggesting the general fluctuating current of life, with life's constant questionings and half-answers.[63] Although the rhythm of the melody is not of the flowing type, its notes, when sung in even rhythms and without rests, suggest the melody of an old German song that was probably known to the composer from his childhood. Commencing in a somewhat melancholy and halting fashion, it soon gains in brightness and impetus. The main melody is met with a response from the violins.

A second theme of quite a different character now appears. It is made up of a group of well defined melodies beginning with one played by the violins, followed by a contrasting phrase that is proclaimed loud and clear by the horns and wood winds, with upward directions and irregular rhythms suggesting a gay bravado. This is succeeded by a tender and deeply felt tune for cello and horn played against a very moving tone in the bass. Lyrical melody prevails with vigorous rhythm in this music. There are three motives here: the first is an expressive melody with a constant rhythm, while the second and third are differing rhythms arranged in a melodic pattern.[64]

Presently, the long theme starts to repeat itself, with a variation in the wood winds and the plucked strings. The movement proceeds with a rare variety of expression and power of climax—at times powerful and prayerful, at times caressing, tender, mocking, homely, at times far away, at times near, now hurried, now quietly expanding, ever surprising, ever welcome—all unified into a perfect whole, more by their emotional bondage than by any structural integrity.[65] A variant is presently introduced by the flute, clarinet and horn to a continuing plucking of the strings. Later, the theme is heard softly on the trumpets, growing more distinct and assertive when transferred to the wood winds. A sense of uncertainty that has been called the questioning phrase of the music persists with a slight variance, and still without a definite answer. The wild fragments of the horn return with more emphasis to gain a momentary dominance, but then the solemn vein takes over again. The climax of this movement is as great as ten minutes of crowded drama can allow: a climax greater than any of the preceding ones unfolds, and the music soars in spirit until its final insistent questions are put down unanswered by mighty tonal clusters and the loud beatings of the drums.

The second slow movement, pastoral though in style, also has an eventful tale to tell that lifts one from the world of tragedy to some ancestral land of legend. It begins with four herald-calls by a horn that are echoed by the bassoons, oboes and flutes. These introduce a music of great simplicity and appealing tenderness to set the bucolic character of a song that seems to be woven of dreams under a summer sun. The melody is sung softly by a clarinet, and it flows over an almost imperceptible accompaniment by the plucked violin strings. Gone are the feverish questionings, the inadequate answers, the strife and the overbearing gloom of the first movement.[66] A modification of this song is expressed by a violin above a wood winds and horn accompaniment, and this is followed by yet another motive by the strings, echoing the wood winds with emphasis. Then the second theme, more serene than the first, sails grandly in, ushered by the cellos. It is repeated in soaring triumph when, suddenly, it melts into tenderness; a shadow comes over the music, and wistful questions from a clarinet and oboe bring back the close of the first theme with an added sweetness.[67] The entire music is recapitulated. A plaintive summons arises from the clarinet, and the movement dies away with allusions to the opening call of the horns.

The third movement, suggestive of folk-spirit, is a rondo-like interlude filled with a joyous outpouring of verve and vigor, a furious attempt to attain happiness.[68] The first gay tune is announced loudly by the whole orchestra; a subsidiary tune is given out by the strings and continues the energetic mood. More grace and calm prevail with a second tune. It is a folk-song kind of melody that starts in the strings and is then carried by the wood winds. The jolly atmosphere persists, with little swirls of runs played softly by a piccolo, clarinet and oboe to close the movement in bright spirits. But beneath this facade of gaiety and light-heartedness, an undercurrent of foreboding and agitation can be palpated, even a pious supplication as if in atonement for this forbidden exuberance.[69]

Far from explaining the tragedy or resolving it, the fourth movement presents a reality from which there is no escape—here, the entire range of tragic emotion from rage to solemnity, pathos and resignation are penetratingly explored.[70] The main theme of the fourth movement opens mightily in the brass and wood winds which express an eight-note melody, and its first variation appears immediately when the theme is repeated, ornamented by the plucked strings. The whole movement, in fact, consists of an extraordinary and ingenious procession of variations, about thirty two in all, with combinations of strings and violins, flutes and oboes, and double basses and bassoons among others, carrying the theme.[71] But it is not essential to abstract one's attention to follow the structural elements of the variations in order to appreciate the magnificence of this music as a whole; indeed, it is impossible to consider these oft disguised variations individually, though they have been frequently dissected out.[72]

The theme stated by the trombones descends angrily with rolling drums and plucked chords into the depths of the orchestra, while plaintive melodies crowd above in the wood winds.[73] Then the violins take up a striding declamatory tune which becomes more flowing, and is agitated by a lovely cross-rhythm in the wood winds. The storm subsides into a sympathetic dialogue between the violas and the wood winds.

Now follows one of the most touching flute passages in all music, followed by a little variation involving a conversation between the flute, oboe and clarinet.[74] Then the trombones come forward with perhaps the

101

most wistful passage in the whole symphony, and when this has died inconclusively away, the theme returns in the wood winds only to be fiercely cut across by the indignant strings.[75] Somewhere, there is a volcanic outburst, a powerful and unexpected climax of blazing loudness followed by the next variation, in awesome softness, to relieve the tension. Yet, with each recurring statement of the theme, one feels a reserve, a something left unsaid.[76]

So far this symphony has shown us life and action. This is what heroism fights for, but the hero is not fighting for his own happiness. He is to die fighting.[77] And so the music continues, executing a grand series of modulations until, with a despairing new derivation, a something *is* finally said in a gorgeous and intoxicating rhythm as one of the greatest orchestral works of all time storms to its tragic close.[78]

• Symphonies Nos. 3 in F; 4 in E minor
  DG 437 645-2, BPO, Karajan $$

✳ ✳ ✳ ✳ ✳ ✳

Exhibit 31   Mozart: Piano Concerto No. 21

Wolfgang Amadeus Mozart (1756-1791) lavished his most exquisite care and unstinted inventiveness on his twenty five concertos for piano and orchestra. In his poetic hands, both piano and orchestra knew their place, based upon a mutual respect arising from a well-defined comprehension of one another's functions. The piano could listen patiently through long orchestral passages with unfailing good temper, its good breeding enabling it to withstand even the temptation of clearing its throat.[79] The orchestra, for its part, allowed the preeminence of the piano as a general proposition, and kept its own more unruly members in restraint. Etiquette did not always prevent a bassoon from sly humor, nor a horn from becoming, on occasion, slightly sentimental.[80] But all subscribed to a certain standard of decorous behavior that breathed the very essence of the Viennese spirit and the age of elegance.

If Mozart had written a musical autobiography, one would hardly have failed to hear echoes of this assertive and sunny masterpiece. He composed this imperial Concerto, his twenty first, at the peak of his most prosperous season in Vienna. The technically demanding solos were undoubtedly written for Mozart to show off his own brilliance at the keyboard. However, as Mozart himself put it, while a soloist playing this piece may well be sweating at the end of the *finale* of the music, it will be with the gentle perspiration of a drawing-room, not with the dripping exudation of a concert hall!

In true traditional form, the music opens with an orchestral introduction. In a restrained whisper, the strings announce the main theme in unison, to which the wood winds reply with a delicate march-like phrase. This is repeated, with the wood winds alternating with the strings, until the whole orchestra, complete with trumpets, horns and drums, bursts out with the main theme in full golden resonance, setting the mood for the festive brilliance that marks the first movement. Short successive phrases by an oboe, bassoon and flute coax a shy piano to join in the music. The piano does enter, with a fitful and fluttering hesitancy, that soon becomes more confident to end in a brilliant cadenza. The violins return with a statement of the main theme, but the piano now takes over the melody boldly, playing it alone with an intermittent accompaniment by the strings.

Graceful piano runs and arabesques lead to a second theme carried by the piano alone, without accompaniment. It is a startling and sharply emotional figure—startling, because the first three notes of this theme are destined to form the basis of the whole second movement, and the next three notes are reminiscent, in more than one way, with the opening of the composer's last and most famous symphony, the *Jupiter*! Presently, the music flows into one of its simplest and most beguiling moments when the solo wood winds interweave their voices with the lonely piano: first the flute, oboe and bassoon, then the flute soars over the piano and is replaced by a sustained oboe, and all the while the strings set a pulse that wreathes the music in a romantic glow.[81]

A passage of vigorous virtuosity, with trills and a demanding series of runs up and down the keyboard, leads to a highly imaginative development of the main themes. Despite a heightening of tension and lines filled with sorrow and longing, the music never forfeits its melodious character. Virtuoso figures in the piano are balanced against broadly spun phrases in the wood winds and strings, and lead into a reemergence of the sunny main theme played by the whole orchestra.

The piano returns strongly to pick up the main theme which is now played with a flute. The oboes join in, then the strings, then the piano stops while the whole orchestra takes over for a brief symphonic interlude.[82] All the basic themes are recapitulated, and the material grows and expands with an endlessly fertile imagination. The music rises in power and grandeur, and just when one might have expected a brilliant close to this bright movement, the end comes quietly, on tiptoes, in a last whispered recall of the opening theme.[83]

The sunny festivity of the first movement becomes a thing of the past in the unforgettable second movement. For all its quiet, this is perhaps one of Mozart's most stirring utterances, where the music builds up into an overwhelmingly powerful tension. Over a murmuring accompaniment by the second violins and strings, to a steady pulse by the plucked cellos and basses, the first violins sing a long and languorous melody. The wood winds join in with bittersweet sustained notes, their voices blowing like a gentle breeze against the strings.[84] Soon the piano enters, and all the strings play a plucked accompaniment as it unfolds the main melody with a gentle poignancy. Piano and orchestra blend naturally; there is nothing ostentatious in the succession of ideas opened by the orchestra, on which the piano then discourses in several sequences of thought. It is an extraordinary dialogue: up above, there is a melody that proceeds with developing tensions and involvements, while down below are the plucked bass-notes, with occasional intensifying comments by the wood winds.[85] The music slips into a delicate duet between the piano and oboe, to which a flute and bassoon add their rich voices. The movement ends naturally, in total calm, as peacefully as it began.

The gay third movement is a lively *rondo* which, with its vivacity and good humor, typifies the Classical *rondo* finale that gives an impression of effortless motion. A simple tune, brisk and lively, played by the violins makes up its first theme which is soon taken over by the piano. After an orchestral interlude, the solo piano returns in a running passage with the three-note musical phrase that had figured so prominently in the earlier movement. The passage is repeated by the horns. A second melody is now introduced by the wood winds, the piano repeats the opening theme in a showy passage, and then the second subject is given out by the piano in a dialogue with the oboes and bassoons. The first theme is restated to begin each new section of the *rondo:* the musical figure appears again, this time answered by the horns, and later on, in a dialogue between strings and bassoons, with the piano playing independent filigree-like runs. The movement ends with a repetition of the first theme of the *rondo*.

- Piano Concertos Nos 19, 20, 21, 23, 24; Concert rondos Nos 1-2
  Ph Duo 442 269-2, Alfred Brendel, ASMF, Marriner $

- Piano Concertos Nos. 20, 21, 23, 27; Piano sonata No. 17; Rondo in A minor
  Double Decca Analog/ Dig. 436 383-2 (2). Vladimir Ashkenazy, Philh O. $

Chamber Music

Chamber music, as understood today, is a form of instrumental music suitable for performance by a few instruments in a small or private room. Its origin may be traced back to the royal patronage of the Middle Ages when it encompassed the vocal and instrumental music that was customarily played by the finest musicians in the private music rooms of the medieval princes and nobles, as opposed to the music of the Church. A viol was the instrument that was most commonly substituted for the voice, and a "chest of viols" became a common possession in any well-ordered home of that time. Among simpler folk, this music formed the "dinner music" that was sung seated about a table, where the familiar and popular airs of the day were accompanied by quaint domestic instruments.

The new division of instruments into groups or choirs in the Classical era led to the formation of standard large instrumental ensembles, such as the symphony orchestra, for which composers could write a symphony or a virtuoso solo concerto. The same organization also brought with it a standardization that had hitherto been lacking in the instrumental music for small ensembles. Before this time, the line of development between chamber and orchestral music had not been clearly marked. All music, including the *concerto grosso,* had been performed only by small instrumental groups, thus evoking the same effect as chamber music. For most Baroque composers, the distinction between orchestral and chamber music was one of little significance: the number of instruments mattered less than the type of music being played.[86]

The organization of a distinct chamber music in the Classical style resulted in the development of new musical forms, of which the standard became the string quartet with two violins, viola and cello. This evolved as an extension of the more established string trio but with one more violin added. Careful part writing for individual instruments established a musical genre for solo instruments of which the most important was the sonata for piano or violin. The meaning of *sonata* is literally "a piece sounded" as opposed to *cantata,* "a piece sung." In the Classical period, the sonata (not to be confused with the sonata form) had a more specialized meaning attached to it: namely, a piece of chamber music, usually in three or four movements, for one or two instruments, with the piano usually being one of the instruments.

It has become customary to classify chamber music according to the number of instrumental parts: duets, trios, quartets, quintets, and so forth. Such music has been composed for families of instruments: trios have been composed for wood winds or strings, and quartets have been written for four instruments of the same kind, such as for four bassoons or four saxophones.

Exhibit 32 Schubert: Piano Quintet in A major[87] ("Trout")

"The country around Steyr is inconceivably lovely," the twenty two year old Franz Schubert (1797-1828) wrote to his brother from an extended holiday in Upper Austria. "At the house where I lodge there are eight girls, nearly all pretty. Plenty to do, you see." And there was lots to do, for he was a guest at the home of a wealthy music patron where the happy days were spent outdoors walking in the open rural air, and the evenings were filled with exuberant and romantic music-making in the house.

At his host's request, he composed an adventurous work calling for the unusual combination of violin, viola, cello, doublebass and piano, the fourth movement of which contained a set of variations on his host's favorite Schubert *lied, Die Forelle* ("The Trout"). Schubert, himself, played the piano part from memory at its first evening performance because he did not have time to write everything out. Suffused with the warmth and intimacy of *haus musick*, the now famous *Trout* quintet, as it is popularly called, breathes the carefree spirit of irrepressible gaiety and the cheery joy that marked this memorable vacation. The music is unpremeditated and utterly relaxed, and the instrumental parts are sufficiently easy to allow even amateurs to play the many ingratiating tunes in its five movements.

A dramatic chord in the strings leads to an upward sequence of rising notes in the piano, and then the strings unfold some mysterious and delicate musical fragments on the viola and piano. The cello and violin interject occasionally, as the doublebass rumbles lowly in the background.[88] The violin now emerges with the main melody, a tune as natural as breathing, with its inhale-exhale rhythm repeatedly underscored by the piano. The lyrical melody meanders through a variety of tuneful excursions to end in a definitive statement of the second theme. This is an insistent, highly rhythmic tune, first announced by the piano, and then taken up by the violin and the rest of the strings. A series of exchanges take place between the strings and the piano, and then all the instruments race forward in unison to end, quite out of breath, in a brief pause.

Now arises an exquisitely tuneful development of the main theme. Over a throbbing figure in the viola, cello and bass, the violin slowly intones the melody. The piano enters, and then the tune is picked up sleepily by the doublebass to which the piano adds a delicate filigree accompaniment to energize the tempo. The music springs alive, the strings and piano flit delicately amidst a wealth of harmony and melody as the doublebass sets a steady pulse, until suddenly, out of nowhere, this parade of tunes is interrupted abruptly by a forceful chord.

The music returns to an almost literal repeat of the mysterious opening, the melodies sing again and rush forward with great bravado, and the first movement ends suddenly—by simply coming to a stop.

The atmosphere of cheerfulness that pervades the entire work is not dissipated even in the slow second movement which is quieter and more tender than the opening one. It would be difficult to find any trace of pain or sadness in this music. The piano announces a first melody, a romantic lyric ornamented by sweetly delicate trills. It is taken up by the violin with similar graceful adornments, the piano shifts to a series of notes in a rising sequence, and then a second melody appears, a rather morose tune for the cello and viola, supported discreetly by the rest of the instruments. A third tune follows forthright, a vigorous skipping song played rhythmically by the piano over a vigorous bass. The music tiptoes forward in a run, as if it were tripping down a long flight of stairs, and then the run is repeated—six times in succession on the piano, and three times on the violin, to fade away slowly into the distance.

Presently, the three melodies are repeated again, but clothed in different sets of keys that transform the music, much like the palette of changing colors that gently bathes a landscape as the light changes in the wake of a setting sun.

The third movement is a brilliant morsel of heady spirits. Gay and frolicsome, the violin and viola project forward at an exceptionally fast tempo into a four-note tune. An energized piano soon joins in the fray, and then the cello and doublebass reiterate the heavy notes. The music is bouncy and high-spirited as the piano and strings engage in a vivacious dialogue, almost as if they were debating as to who would have the last word.

Suddenly the momentum lapses, and a new lyrical melody unfolds in the violin and viola, and is picked up tenderly by the piano. This is the gentle Trio section of this movement with its own romantic tunes. The tune is played by the cello and bass, and then the whole sequence is repeated: the piano starts out with the amorous melody, joined soon by the violin and viola, and then by the cello and doublebass.[89] The serenity of the mood is briefly interrupted by a harsh chord as if the instruments were arguing vehemently on some vexed point, and then, as though embarrassed by this outburst, the music continues calmly with the piano and violin alone to end this section.[90] But the music springs once again to a boisterous pace, the spirited four-note melody returns briskly with bristling electricity to shatter the calm, and all the instruments race once more, fast and fierce, to end this movement.

The fourth movement was an additional one intentionally created before the finale to introduce the *Trout* theme and its variations. The original *lied* had sung a bucolic morality fable about man's ruthless destruction of all creatures great and small. The song had narrated a story about the treacherous hooking of a moody trout that used to wiggle, "alive as a straight arrow," in the clear waters of a brook that was its home. In the present movement, the *Trout* theme is announced simply by the violin, against a background of the other string instruments, with the doublebass playing heavily in the background. It appears just as it did in the original song, with only a few changes—the piano is silent in this exposition.

The first variation assigns the melody to the piano that decorates it with a series of brilliant trills, played against a series of sequentially rising notes and some plucking in the strings. When the viola and cello elaborate the tune in the second variation, the piano and other strings confine themselves to a quiet accompaniment. The violin, however, breaks loose to play a series of very fast distracting notes around the melody. Then the piano breaks away in a kind of perpetual motion in the third variation, dashing in loud bursts and runs from the middle of the keyboard to the top and back, as the doublebass tries to play the tune. The heavy music becomes transiently sunny as the violin sings a gentle song, but the storm returns as the cello picks up the tune and carries it into the fourth variation where the melody soon disappears behind clusters of tone and a changing rhythm and key. The fifth variation presents a whole new figure that starts out in the strings, with the cello being particularly tender.[91] The pace is slow and deliberate as the piano joins in and passes the music to the violin. The movement ends with a restating of the simple and unadorned *Trout* melody that is played again for the last time, underscored by the same rippling figure in the piano that occurs in the original song to simulate the trout's lively gliding in the stream.

The finale opens in a loud and long chord given out by the strings as a harbinger of the excitement to follow, much like a herald's signal to announce a tournament. It is an amazingly vigorous and imaginative piece of music, full of Hungarian dash and abandon with sudden stops and starts, and astonishing rhythmic and harmonic changes. A lively tune is played by the violin and viola, and this is vigorously and ingeniously developed before a second fresh and invigorating melody enters. Now

108

the first tune is played again, both themes are developed further, and the whole sequence is repeated. The tunes never seem to lose their delight no matter how often they recur. The music rises in intensity, the strings contrast in unison against the piano, and then all the instruments join together for a last joyous romp to the final chords.[92]

- Piano quintet in A (Trout)
  Decca Dig. 411 975-2, Andras Schiff, Hagen Qt. $$$

- (i) Piano quintet in A (Trout); (ii) String quartet No. 14 (Death and the Maiden)
  Decca 417 459-2 (i) Curzon, Vienna Octet (members); (ii) VPO Qt. $$

Exhibit 33 Beethoven: Piano Trio in B Flat Major[93] ("Archduke")

The Archduke Rudolf was only a small twig on the imperial Hapsburg family tree that boasted several dozen Archdukes of greater and lesser import. However, Rudolf played a very material part in the history of music, for it was he who, for over twenty years, had paid most of the yearly pension that guaranteed Ludwig van Beethoven (1770-1827) a livelihood in Vienna. The most devoted and loyal of his aristocratic patrons, he was the one friend that Beethoven never quarreled with, and he was the only one of two persons that Beethoven acknowledged formally as his full-fledged pupils. In return, Rudolf received the lion's share of Beethoven's dedications, including this most famous of trios for piano, violin and cello, commonly called the *Archduke Trio*. Some have suggested that the trio was really intended for the great secret passion of his life, the beautiful Countess Erdody, whose apartment Beethoven had shared for many months. The trio contains some of the finest and most moving music written by the composer; it shows an air of elegance and an aristocratic grandeur quite foreign to the emotionalism of the heroic age of Napoleon.

The music opens with a noble and majestic melody introduced quietly by the piano in an elegant and flowing phrase. The tune, marked by an initial five-note musical phrase, immediately sets the relaxed mood that is characteristic of the entire piece. The violin interrupts to restate the theme, accompanied by the cello and piano. The piano returns tenderly, but the violin and cello respond forcefully with powerful clusters of tone.

A second melody, graceful and delicate, opens in the piano alone. It is made up of pairs of musical fragments that seem to descend in a step-

109

wise and irregular fashion. Softly, the cello and violin join in, gradually building up volume to take over the tune, accompanied by steady beats from the piano. Now a related series of quick runs appear on the piano, down, up, down, up, and then down-up, up-down in a contrary fashion. Soon, the violin and cello pick up this idea, the one descending, the other ascending, until they, too, are dashing off in different directions at the same time as the piano.

For the rest of the movement, the main theme is expanded and magnified with vast creativity. Starting as a mere wisp of sound, the melody is made to grow each time with renewed energy to lead to an exuberant and joyous outburst. The music repeats itself, and then the piano lapses into an irregular background rhythm while the violin and cello soar over it with tender reminiscences of the main theme.[94] As the piano continues to meander quietly, the cello unfolds the main tune again, but leaves it midway to be completed by the violin. Somewhere, the melody is plucked out on the strings in a hushed and still moment, as the piano softly intervenes with quiet trills derived from the main theme. Soon the piano asserts itself, returning the tune with support from the strings. Now the piano and cello sing a duet, then the violin sings with the cello as the piano plays in the background. When each instrument has had its final say, the trio combine together, like a miniature orchestra, for one last restatement of the main theme to end the movement.

It has been said of the second movement that here, for the first time, the lion of wit has been successfully made to lie down with the lamb of melody.[95] The movement opens with the cello playing a bouncy rhythmic figure that is promptly usurped by the violin. It is a deceptively simple tune, almost like a huntsman's theme, that is picked up on its second repetition by the piano which then puts out a contrasting melody. The strings undertake to vary this melody by repeating some of the main notes, almost in a comical and absentminded fashion. It seems that all three instruments have agreed that this is a splendid and delightful thing to do, but close attention reveals subtle rhythmic disagreements between the piano and the strings, with the piano insisting on stressing the wrong notes![96]

Before long, a second melody is unfolded by the trio, a gay dancing theme cast somewhere between a sturdy peasant tune and a delicate and formal ballet.[97] It is a marvelously flexible and undulating melody that is repeatedly interrupted by a waltz-like musical fragment. The piano takes over the merry tune to the plucking of strings; the subdued exultation is captured by the violin, and then by all three instruments with great tenderness as the cup of joy seems to run over.[98] However, for all its force-fulness, the waltz theme is tinged with melancholy. The gentle flow of melody is stopped abruptly by two loud chords, a musical commotion sets in briefly, and then, as if from nowhere, the cello emerges boldly to announce, once again, the main theme. The violin continues the song, which is taken over by the piano, and then all three join cheerily to end the movement.[99]

It has been said of the third movement that it is, perhaps, one of the greatest slow movements in the annals of music. More than any other music, it seems to cast the dust more completely aside, and nakedly ride the air of a more astral world.[100] A pensive, hymn-like choral unfolds majestically on the piano, its dignity heightened by the joining of the violin and cello. This is the main theme, elegant and sad, that is subject to four variations of pure unearthly ecstasy that make up this movement. Here is music of ineffable beauty, serene and otherworldly, with the pi-ano serving as a carrier of the theme and an accompanist, partaking in sweetly ravishing and intensely moving duets with the violin and cello.

Variation 1 has the piano tracing the melody's outline in smooth trip-lets, while the violin and cello quietly interject.[101] With the second variation, the two stringed instruments introduce a delicate staccato phrase. The pace seems to quicken in Variation 3 played by the piano with united comments from the two strings. In the next variation, all three instru-ments combine to explore, for the first time, the richly melodic potential of the theme. The piano's left-hand figuration is so intricate that the tempo relaxes to allow a wonderfully serene melody to unfold from the key-board.[102] As this variation comes to a close, the chorale-like theme returns in all its unadorned simplicity. The music draws towards a serene end with a quiet figure introduced by the violin that anticipates the theme of the next movement into which it merges without a break.

And when all have been reduced to tears with this song, the last movement begins with jarring chords from the violin and cello that launch the piano on a raucous romp, as if to chide the listeners for being so foolish and sentimental during the preceding movement. It is in a rol-licking *rondo* form, with gaily alternating themes and frivolous trills, and down-to-earth jumps and scales. The third appearance of the dance in the *rondo* sequence exploits the higher notes of the cello against a tremulous piano with spectacular effects. A trilling piano giggles inces-santly and the ebullient strings bubble out dancing, giddy melodies. There is a transient lull, and then the three instruments romp merrily together to bring the music to an exuberant and flamboyant close.[103]

- Piano trios Nos 7 (Archduke); 9 in B flat
    EMI Dig. CDC7 47010-2, Ashkenazy, Perlman, Harrell $$$
- Piano Trios Nos 5 (Ghost); 7 (Archduke)
    Sony SBK 53514, Eugene Istomin, Isaac Stern, Leonard Rose $

Exhibit 34 Haydn: String Quartet Op. 76 No. 3 (Kaiser: "Emperor")

It was at the encouragement of a devoted amateur musician that Franz Josef Haydn (1732-1809) composed his first string quartet. The form so captivated him that over the next few months he brought out one such piece after another. The earliest of his eighty three quartets were but small suites for four string instruments; it was not until he had composed almost forty that he achieved a perfection of form, both graceful and charming, that brought to life each of the four stringed voices, individualized yet unified under a common will.[104] Transparency, neatness and clarity dominated this music which became his happiest and most popular medium. Each instrument had its role, according to the capacity of the instrument and the balance of the part, so that each individual part was neither a solo nor a mere accompaniment to the others.

When Count Erdody asked Haydn for a set of quartets, the sixty four year old composer had not only established this form, but had also imbued it with its more spiritual qualities: A tenderness, playfulness, pathos, and a curiously impersonal and remote melancholy. The third of the Erdody quartets was the *Kaiser* ("Emperor"), so-called because the theme of its slow second movement was a hymn that Haydn had written to honor the birthday of Emperor Franz II—a melody that was destined to become the national anthems of both Austria and Germany.

The music opens lightly, with a bright sunny theme that dominates the first movement. The tune is unfolded simply, without frills or repeats, and then undergoes several transformations. Eventually it develops a striking dance-like tempo reminiscent of a genuine peasant festival. All the instruments have important parts, especially the first violin, and the music itself is substantial and virtuosic.

The theme of the notable second movement stems from a Croatian folk melody that was revised to form a highly emotional and dignified hymn-like melody, somewhat more flowing than a chorale. It is constructed of two repeated phrases, with contrasting phrases inserted between the two.[105] In the variations of the theme that make up this movement, one of the instruments always continues to play the melody as the variation is being introduced. Each instrument has a chance to play the tune, and the variations never obscure its nobility or its deeply religious color.[106]

Variation I is in reality a duet in which the melody is in the second violin while the first violin plays a contrasting line that embellishes the tune. The other two instruments are silent. In Variation II the melody is sung by the cello, and is supported by the second violin. As this is happening, the first violin and the viola play a rhythmic counter melody. It is the viola that picks up the melody in Variation III while the other instruments play the contrasting parts. In Variation IV, the first violin again plays the tune, while the other three instruments play an intricate chordal accompaniment. The cello, in particular, holds a long anticipatory note that adds unity to the music, allowing it to resolve in a satisfying manner. The movement ends with the entire quartet giving out the tune in a hauntingly beautiful piece.

The next movement is a minuet that begins and ends with a loud and simple, heavy-footed peasant dance, with a softer and melodious trio interspersed between.

The finale is a fast and exceptionally long piece of music that is throughout quite stern and foreboding. Three powerful chords that are answered by a rhythmic phrase pervade the movement and set up an anxious mood.[107] The music ends more cheerfully on a happier key.

• String Quartets No. 75 in G; 76 in D (Fifths); 77 in C (Emperor); No. 78 in Flat (Sunrise); 79 in D; 80 in E flat
    Naxos Dig. 8.6550129; 4550129. Kodaly Qt. $

---

[1] Stringham, Edwin, *Listening to Music Creatively* (Prentice Hall, NY, 1946)

[2] Barzun, Jacques, *Classic, Romantic and Modern* (Doubleday Anchor Books, NY, 1961)

[3] *Ibid*

[4] *Ibid*

[5] *Ibid*

[6] Goepp, Philip, *Great Works of Music* (Garden City Publishing, NY, 1913)

[7] Grove, George, *Beethoven and his Nine Symphonies* (Dover Publications, NY, reprinted 1962)

[8] O'Connell, Charles, *The Victor Book of the Symphony* (Simon & Schuster, NY, 1935)

[9] Grove, George, *Beethoven and his Nine Symphonies*

[10] *Ibid*

[11] Goepp, Philip, *Great Works of Music*

[12] O'Connell, Charles, *The Victor Book of the Symphony*

[13] *Ibid*

[14] Goepp, Philip, *Great Works of Music*

[15] *Ibid*

[16] Grove, George, *Beethoven and his Nine Symphonies*

[17] Goepp, Philip, *Great Works of Music*

[18] Grove, George, *Beethoven and his Nine Symphonies*

19 *Ibid*
20 O'Connell, Charles, *The Victor Book of the Symphony*
21 Goepp, Philip, *Great Works of Music*
22 O'Connell, Charles, *The Victor Book of the Symphony*
23 Ewen, David, *Music for the Millions* (Arco Publishing Company, NY, 1944)
24 Osborne, Richard, *Beethoven,* in Layton, Robert, Editor, *A Companion to the Symphony* (Simon & Schuster, NY, 1993)
25 Tovey, Donald Francis, *Symphonies and other Orchestral Works* (Oxford University Press, NY, reprinted 1990).
26 *Ibid*
27 MacDonald, Calum, in *The Symphony, Past, Present, Future.* BBC Music Magazine, Summer Special, 1995
28 Grove, George, *Beethoven and his Nine Symphonies*
29 *Ibid*
30 *Ibid*
31 Goepp, Philip, *Great Works of Music*
32 Grove, George, *Beethoven and his Nine Symphonies*
33 Ewen, David, *Music for the Millions*
34 Grove, George, *Beethoven and his Nine Symphonies*
35 *Ibid*
36 Tovey, Donald Francis, *Symphonies and other Orchestral Works*
37 *Ibid*
38 Grove, George, *Beethoven and his Nine Symphonies*
39 O'Connell, Charles, *The Victor Book of the Symphony*
40 Grove, George, *Beethoven and his Nine Symphonies*
41 O'Connell, Charles, *The Victor Book of the Symphony*
42 Kinscella, Hazel Gertrude, *Music and Romance* (RCA Manufacturing Co. Inc, NJ, 1941)
43 O'Connell, Charles, *The Victor Book of the Symphony*
44 Tovey, Donald Francis, *Symphonies and other Orchestral Works*
45 Lam, Basil, *Ludwig van Beethoven,* in Simpson, Robert, *The Symphony* (Penguin Books, NY, 1966)
46 Goepp, Philip, *Great Works of Music*
47 Tovey, Donald Francis, *Symphonies and other Orchestral Works*
48 Ewen, David, *Music for the Millions*
49 Goepp, Philip, *Great Works of Music*
50 Newmarch, Rosa, *The Concert-Goer's Library of Descriptive Notes, Vol. 4* (Oxford University Press, London, 1931)
51 O'Connell, Charles, *The Victor Book of the Symphony*
52 *Ibid*
53 *Ibid*
54 *Ibid*
55 *Ibid*
56 *Ibid*
57 Tovey, Donald Francis, *Symphonies and other Orchestral Works*
58 *Ibid*
59 Newmarch, Rosa, *The Concert-Goer's Library of Descriptive Notes, Vol. 4*
60 Hurwitz, David, *Beethoven or Bust* (Anchor Books, NY, 1992)
61 Downes, Edward, *Guide to Symphonic Music*
62 O'Connell, Charles, *The Victor Book of the Symphony*
63 *Ibid*
64 Moore, Douglas, *From Madrigal to Melody* (W W Norton, NY, 1942)
65 *Ibid*
66 O'Connell, Charles, *The Victor Book of the Symphony*
67 Tovey, Donald Francis, *Symphonies and other Orchestral Works*

114

[68] Hurwitz, David, *Beethoven or Bust*

[69] O'Connell, Charles, *The Victor Book of the Symphony*

[70] Hurwitz, David, *Beethoven or Bust*

[71] Kinscella, Hazel Gertrude, *Music and Romance*

[72] Tovey, Donald Francis, *Symphonies and other Orchestral Works*

[73] *Ibid*

[74] *Ibid*

[75] *Ibid*

[76] O'Connell, Charles, *The Victor Book of the Symphony*

[77] Tovey, Donald Francis, *Symphonies and other Orchestral Works*

[78] *Ibid*

[79] Ewen, David, *Music for the Millions*

[80] *Ibid*

[81] Rudel, Anthony, *Classical Music Top 40* (Fireside Books, Simon & Schuster, NY, 1995)

[82] *Ibid*

[83] Downes, Edward, *Guide to Symphonic Music*

[84] Rudel, Anthony, *Classical Music Top 40*

[85] Haggin, BH, *The New Listener's Companion and Record Guide* (Horizon Press, NY, 1978)

[86] Hurwitz, David, *Beethoven or Bust*

[87] Rudel, Anthony, *Classical Music Top 40*. The *Trout* quintet is described in detail, line by line, in Rudel's book from which portions of the present *Exhibit* have been adapted

[88] *Ibid*

[89] *Ibid*

[90] Berger, Melvin, *Guide to Chamber Music* (Anchor Books, Doubleday, NY, 1990)

[91] Rudel, Anthony, *Classical Music Top 40*

[92] *Ibid*

[93] *Ibid*. The Archduke Trio is described in detail, line by line, in Rudel's book from which portions of the present Exhibit have been adapted

[94] *Ibid*

[95] Ewen, David, *Music for the Millions*

[96] Rudel, Anthony, *Classical Music Top 40*

[97] Berger, Melvin, *Guide to Chamber Music*

[98] Rudel, Anthony, *Classical Music Top 40*

[99] *Ibid*

[100] Ewen, David, *Music for the Millions*

[101] Donat, Misha, *BBC Music Magazine*, January 1996. This paragraph is adapted from the listening guide in the magazine.

[102] *Ibid*

[103] Rudel, Anthony, *Classical Music Top 40*

[104] Ewen, David, *Music for the Millions*

[105] Hoffer, Charles, *The Understanding of Music* (Wadsworth Publishing Co, Belmont, CA, 1967)

[106] Hurwitz, David, *Beethoven or Bust*

[107] Berger, Melvin, *Guide to Chamber Music*

"If music be the food of love, play on;"
— William Shakespeare

8   The Romantic Period

If there is anything indeterminate in music, it is the definition of the *Romantic*. Indeed, it has been pointed out that every musical era is *romantic* towards the past and *classic* for the future.[1] And is not every great master's youth his romantic age, when he reacts against the formal dominance of his predecessor? Classic and Romantic have, from the beginning of time, corresponded to the two basic instincts of human nature: on the one hand, the need to control and moderate the emotions and, on the other, to express an uninhibited emotional longing for the forbidden, the unknown and the unattainable.[2] Whereas the Classical aroused sentiments of repose and serenity, the connotations of Romantic suggested restlessness and disorder. Eternal longing, regret for the lost happiness of childhood, or an indefinable discontent that gnawed at the soul formed the ingredients of the Romantic spirit.[3] And so it came to pass that whereas the Classical had found inspiration in the gods and heroes of ancient Greece, the Romantics discovered the Dark Ages: King Arthur and Siegfried, the quest for the Holy Grail, fairy tales and medieval sagas, folk dances and nationalism.[4] Here were the great themes of the triumph of good over evil, of God and nature, of life and death and man's destiny, and of the struggle for freedom. In its music it found expression in the great heaven-storming climaxes, the violent contrasts between deafening loudness and a whispering softness, and in deeply affecting melodies of enduring lyricism.

The Classical period had emphasized those qualities that bound mankind together; hence the symmetry, balance and universality of its music.[5] The Romantic period, on the other hand, laid stress on the qualities that marked off one from the other; hence the diversity of form and expression of its music. Here was a new spirit of individualism, a sense of uniqueness: If the Romantic was not any better than his fellow man, at least he considered himself different.

One of the salient characteristics of this period was the overshadowing of external beauty of form by an urgent intensity of mere emotional content, an emphasis on inner expression as against outer symmetry.

Music found expression in the Romantic period in the art-songs (*Lieder*) and the piano pieces, the overture and the program symphony and, above all, in the symphonic poem.

Exhibit 35 Smetana: The Moldau (Vltava)

The country now called Czechoslovakia, embracing former Bohemia, Slovakia and Moravia, was the most deserving in Europe of its unique musical genius. Many a visitor had marveled at the teaching of music in all Bohemian village schools, and at the making and playing of violins even in the poorest of homes. For as long as they could remember, the musically talented people of the Bohemian nation had been under Austrian rule, taxed to maintain foreign armies, suppressed by the police and its censorship, and offended by the use of German as the official language. Over the centuries, a long line of Bohemian fiddlers, flautists and minstrels had wandered away from the Fatherland to enrich the artistic life of other free lands. It came, therefore, as no surprise that when the great wave of revolutionary nationalism swept through Europe in the nineteenth century, the Bohemians made a strong movement for cultural and political autonomy. The undoubted leader of their nationalistic movement in the arts was Bedrich Smetana (1824-1884), whose intensely patriotic songs had been sung on the military barricades of Prague.

Much of the history of Bohemia, its Teutonic origins and its legends, its history and its landscape, may be traced by following the Moldau river as it winds through the fertile Moldau valley in the heart of Bohemia. Smetana put together all his love for the scenic beauty and charm of his native land in a cycle of six symphonic poems, *Ma Vlast* (My Fatherland), of which the second was a tone picture of the *Moldau*. The music touches Mother Earth herself and her charming and serene songs, for the minstrel in this music seems to be a peasant in his own village dress, resplendent in color and proud of his rank.[6] And the mighty river is his great song.

Deep in the shades of a Bohemian forest, two springs arise: one is warm and sparkling, the other cool and tranquil. Here is the *Source of the Moldau River*. Their clear waters that run so gaily over stone and pebble unite and sparkle in the morning sun. The music opens with a gentle undulating musical fragment—one tiny air, played softly in unison by the sweet-voiced instruments.[7] Another rippling fragment arises in the waving, tremulous strings and the strands of a harp, and the fragments grow louder as one tiny brooklet joins another and the waters gather together. A solo flute plays a single weaving figure as a single brook emerges, cool and tranquil like a sylvan stream. Soon the warm tones of a clarinet merge with the music with a melodic figure as a second brook, warm and sparkling, blends with the stream. Then arise the violas, yet another stream, all accompanied by a gliding harp and plucked strings as the confluent waters spray on the pebbles.[8] The weaving figure grows louder as the bassoons and strings join in the music.

Presently, the main theme is heard, unfolded by the oboes and first violins. It is a beautiful native melody, taken from a Swedish folk-song that praises the beauty of a country province.[9] The tune is repeated four times. The music grows deeper as the flutes and bassoons join in, and repeats itself over and over as the flowing waters chatter along, transparent and ceaseless, gradually building up in volume and body and in chordal accompaniment.[10]

In time the brook broadens out to become a river, the Vlatva, breathing the spirit of the Bohemian countryside. It flows through dark and mighty forests, and its banks echo to the horn of a hunter high on the hill, confirming *The Hunt in the Forest*. Oboes, horns and bassoons sound the bugle call which is echoed by all the choirs of the orchestra as the ceaseless flowing waters, still sounded by the tremulous strings, fade very softly in the distance. The hunt comes to a close with a prolonged note on the horn.

As the echoes of the hunt and the rushing movement of the river die down, a new rhythm takes over: a lively folk dance of a *Peasant Wedding*. All the instruments of the orchestra, except the horns, join in the rustic wedding procession that moves slowly along. Fragments of a melody, a simple folk air, are repeated. Presently, a triangle gives out the tinkling of church bells while a kettledrum softly accents the rhythm. The music becomes softer, and to the strains of the strings, clarinets and the kettledrum, the festive rhythm, too, fades away into the distance.

Night falls, a mysterious quiet surrounds the river, and the high muted strings sound a diaphanous tone as the shimmering moonlight floods its banks.[11] Delicate patterns sung by a flute, perhaps the very strains of Pan himself, set the stage for the *Moonlight and Dance of the Nymphs*. Weaving strains of flutes and clarinets, and arabesques from a harp, are tossed in the ensemble as the waters splash, and the *rusalkas* or water nymphs dance to celebrate *al fresco* nuptials in a gay and vigorous rhythm.[12] The main theme enters, introduced by the muted violins as a sweet and sustained song-like melody which is repeated softly by the whole orchestra while the flutes, piccolos and clarinets frolic above.

Presently, a trumpet asserts its martial rhythm, softly at first, then louder and more livelier as the trombones and tuba join in the strain.[13] Now the Moldau broadens as its melody is carried forward with rising volume by the full orchestra. Suddenly, the flutes, piccolos, oboes, bassoons and violins give out fragments of the main theme as the music surges ahead, gathering momentum.[14]

The strong river rushes over the rocks and through the gorges in foaming waves, as it approaches the *St. John's Rapids (St Johann)*. The orchestra churns up a jagged rhythm, the strings sound the rush of eddies and, to the surge and stride of currents with leaps of dashing spray, fragments of the main theme are tossed around the orchestra in confusion as the music builds up to a mighty tempest. An overpowering climax explodes, the brass repetitively blare out phrases of the main theme as the broad and turbulent river is forced down the narrow rocky precipice and crashes down mightily on the rocks below.

Suddenly, the music sinks into a quiet hush as do the waters, and a delicate figure on the violins and violas leads to the *Grandeur, Widest Part* of the Moldau. The river now flows in triumphant grandeur over a smooth bed through broad open meadows. In its quiet waters are reflected many a fortress and castle, witnesses of a bygone splendid age of chivalry, solitary guardians of a vanished martial fame that is no more. A swelling chorus of the main theme rises in the wood winds like an exalted melody, accompanied by full and majestic chords from the double basses, drums, triangle, harps and strings.[15]

As the pilgrim goes to his Mecca, so, too, are the native waters wafted to the welcoming banks of their own great historic city. The water rises, and the full orchestra, except the strings, also rises in the broad and majestic rhythm of a hymn-like strain as the stately river passes under the old bridges of Prague, "the city of a hundred spires." The tune is a long-forgotten chant melody that used to be sung in a cathedral that stood, in former times, within the walls of the great castle *Vysehrad*, so rich in heroic legends. They are now in ruins, but it was around these fortress walls that a splendid city had once flourished. The main theme soars out jubilantly in the strings, the peace and majesty of the river prevails, and then, as in a dream, the shining waters fade away from sight. Two chords strike out, and then a silence.

- Ma Vlast (complete)

Telarc CD 80265, Milwaukee SO, Macal $$$

- Ma Vlast (complete)
  Naxos Dig. 8.550931. Polish Nat RSO. Antoni Wit $

Exhibit 36 Berlioz: Symphonie Fantastique

"Immediately after the composition of the Faust pieces, and still under the influence of Goethe's poem, I wrote my *Symphonie fantastique*; very slowly and laboriously in parts, with extraordinary ease in others. The *Adagio* (the Scene in the Country), which always affects the public and myself so keenly, cost me nearly a month's arduous toil; two or three times I gave up. On the other hand, the *March to the Scaffold* was written in a night." Thus wrote Hector Berlioz (1803-1869) in his *Memoires* about the premiere performance of this volcanic musical revolution, played by an unprecedented large orchestra, that burst upon an astonished Parisian audience just six short years after the death of Beethoven.

Few works in the history of the symphony have exerted such an influence. Subtitled "Episodes in the Life of an Artist", this was the first major symphony to include an explicit story, or program, for each of its five movements.[16] Berlioz was a twenty six year old student at the Paris Conservatory when he wrote it, and the program strongly paralleled his own life. At the age of twenty three, he had become madly infatuated with an Irish actress Harriet (Henriette) Smithson whom he had seen on the stage in the roles of Shakespeare's Orphelia and Juliet, and who eventually became his wife. But his love was at first unrequited, and the symphony tells the tale of an artist driven to distraction by love.

The Beloved in this music is represented by a particular melody (the *Idee fixe*) and is heard throughout the work. It ties the five movements into a unified whole. To illustrate the shifting nature of the artist's dream, it is transformed into numerous guises at different stages of the music. This was not a new idea for Berlioz, because the germ of an *Idee fixe* had dated back to his first love in his twelfth year, and he had already used the actual melody of the current *Idee fixe* earlier in his *Herminie*. In the present symphony, it is heard in every movement, and is changed symbolically as demanded by the mood and atmosphere of the movements.

The first movement expresses the *Reveries, Passions* of our lovesick artist. The music begins in a romantic mood with a dreamy melody that seems to grow imperceptibly out of silence. After some feverish strains, the music bursts out fervently into the first tune, not the *Idee fixe*, but a halting and passionate melody. It expresses the remembrances of the uneasiness of mind, the aimless passions, and the baseless depressions and elation that were felt by the frustrated lover. The song closes softly, and a bright cluster of tones heralds in the theme of the Beloved, the *Idee fixe*. This is a love lyric of sweeping beauty, with its essence most centered in the first phrase. The middle verse stresses its passion with many striking slowdowns and arresting up-and-down sweeps in the music. Somewhere, a fiery dialogue of profound beauty ensues between the wood winds and the low strings; then the sovereign beauty of the song reigns alone. A second climax is reached as the *Idee fixe* returns noisily at a faster tempo to end in a crowning verse of pure melody. The movement comes to an end in soft solemn chords, animated by fragments of the *Idee fixe*.

Sounds of glad expectancy usher in the second movement where the artist meets his Beloved at *A Ball* amidst the tumult of a brilliant festival. The *Idee fixe* appears as a lilting rhythm in the clear notes of an expressive waltz that flows gaily through the middle section of this opium dream. Two harps feature prominently in the music which comes to a bright end, and the love-lyric is played again, but this time alone, in the softest confidence, as a lingering farewell.

Bucolic reeds expose the long *Scene in the Fields* on a summer evening in the country with two young shepherds. An English horn, probably a boy herder, and an oboe, his female companion, echo a pastoral tune in a lovely duet *(Ranz des Vaches)*. The quaint simplicity of this idyllic scene, and the impromptu song of the shepherds, brings a new calm to the artist's heart and a brighter color to his thoughts. The movement continues with another long tune, a rustic theme, first played by the violins and a flute, then by the violas, cellos, and four bassoons. But it is not all a placid pastoral. The *Idee fixe* reappears, the artist's heart misses a beat, and grievous forebodings of deception and infidelity pass through his narcotized mind. A tremulous pulse emerges in the strings and is answered by the love-lyric that swells up to a surprisingly forceful climax. Peace comes with a return of the initial idyllic theme, the male shepherd's song, played to the accompaniment of distant thunder sounds evoked by sponged-tipped sticks beating on four differently tuned timpani.

The final two movements of this symphony, the *March to the Scaffold* and the *Dream of a Witches' Sabbath*, are described elsewhere in this book (See *Exhibits* 52 and 65, respectively)

- Symphonie fantastique; Overtures: Le Carnaval romaine; Le Corsaire; Harold en Italie; Symphonie funebre et triomphale
    Ph Duo. 442 290-2 (2) Nobuko Imai; John Aldis Ch. LSO, Sir Colin Davis $

Exhibit 37 Strauss: A Hero's Life (Ein Heldenleben)

Heroes exist, have existed, and will forever exist, universally in the great music of mankind. For some, the standard of grand and manly heroism is a life of valor, with its material and exterior rewards. To others, it is a general and free ideal that describes the inward battle of life, the aspiration to achieve through effort and renouncement the elevation of the soul. Such is the ideal man that Richard Strauss (1864-1949) depicts in this symphonic poem, a human being who lives and loves, knows victories and defeats, understands tears and laughter, and faces his physical and spiritual powers, and the autumnal peace of his closing years, with all the nobility and vitality of his manhood.[17] Rendered here is not only the struggle and immediate triumph over adversity, but the gentleness and complacence that comes with years of fulfillment.[18] Whether or not Strauss made himself the depicted hero remains conjectural; it *did* amuse him considerably when he learned that his critics, whom he abhorred, thought that they recognized musical portraits of themselves in the grotesque chattering noises and the ponderous pedantry of the low brass![19]

The mighty theme of the Hero is announced forthright as the music opens, put out boldly by the horns and the low strings, joined later by the violins. It is a compelling phrase, more a rhapsody than a melody, gallant and incisive, yet with a certain beautiful wildness that is full of youthful fire.[20] The music rises to a climax, and a second phrase emerges in the soft rich murmurs of the harps and strings. Quickly, even this tune changes to a different hue as a third brighter melody arises, as if in answer to its forerunner. And so the development of the music continues, interrupted by a blast of the Hero theme, to carve out the character of the Hero in its many aspects and varying qualities. The subsidiary themes grow out of the bare structure of the Hero theme, as if they were outgrowths of his essential nature, to suggest his pride, his depth of feeling, his ambition, and his sensitivity.

Somewhere, there arises in the music a struggle between languorous beauty and heroic resolve, Apollo versus Mars so it seems, but just as it appears that the heroic drive has been lulled and conquered than the Hero's theme breaks out again as a lusty and fierce tune.[21] The virility of the Hero's song continues to grow in successive bursts of expanding triumph, unfolding a full portrait of the pride and glowing power of youthful manhood, while the lesser themes play about in exquisitely delightful verses. The music becomes deafeningly loud until, in a mighty projection of sound, the main theme brings the section to a close in a defiant and heaven-storming climax.

A musical confrontation would seem inevitable if the purity and power of young manhood were to be pitted against envy and malice. The second section of this music, therefore, depicts the Hero's adversaries who are made to look petty and small beside his noble spirituality. Flutes, oboes, piccolo, clarinets and an English horn utter a shrill and snarling phrase, the theme of the Hero's enemies. It is a rough and scraping amalgam of noises borrowed from the most hostile sounds of nature, a wild and spiteful cacophony that seems to override order and reason. Tenor and bass tubas blow out a ponderous phrase. Sad and meditative fragments of the main theme protest gently in the cellos and double basses. Slowly, the music strengthens and grows in passion as the Hero resolves to take up arms against this sea of troubles, and by opposing, end them.[22] Brasses blare out a martial fanfare of the Hero's theme, the music grows forceful and more assertive and, just as the mocking hordes are put to flight, the music stops suddenly.

A sweet and lovely melody, sung by a solo violin, opens the third section. This is the theme of the Beloved, to which the Hero responds in deep and manly tones uttered by the briskly plucked strings of the cellos and the basses. Again the sweet voice of the beloved breaks in with dreamy and ethereal tones as the sprightly lass cajoles her lover. Now follows a marvelous duet between a seductive solo violin and the orchestra, the latter softly playing the passionate melody of the Hero himself. The sultry violin begins a long flight of fantastic monody, with short melodic outbursts of swiftly changing humors alternating with phrases of sentimental quietude.[23] One of her impish musical outbursts is flippant, then comes an insolent turn, then a full gamut of rich moods on a virtuoso violin: playful, amiable, jolly again, faster and more raging, suddenly quieter and full of feeling, insistent and soothing, angry, scolding, tenderly expressive as the coquettish Beloved feigns indifference to arouse the Hero to more and more vehement protestations of his love.[24] A lively joy turns quickly into a yearning, then breaks into a jolly fling. And now and again, between these fleeting whims, there sounds a motive of peace and solace from the orchestra.

Hitherto, the quieter orchestral motive has hovered throughout in the background, but now the orchestra grows louder and takes charge to end this strange chase of elfish moods, and breaks out into a love song of heroic sweep and passion. The strings sweep rapturously, gorgeously

124

adorned with gliding harps. Somewhere, an oboe sings an ardent and tender song. The section ends subtly, to close in an almost hypnotic calm.[25]

Yet hardly has the first fierce flame of love calmed into a lambent glow than from the distance arise the echoes of ancestral voices, prophesying war. Once more the Hero feels the old pain of remembrances of things past; once more the odious sneers of his adversaries intrude upon his consciousness.[26] A fragment of the main melody on the strings expresses his distress, and wafts softly away into silence.

A martial fanfare by a single trumpet; then by two trumpets, followed by three, and the call to arms is sounded. So all day the noise of battle rolls, as the blood and sweat of countless warriors mingles with the clash of waving spears and crashing swords. Violins sweep up and down with incredible agility, the strangest cries arise from the brass and wood winds, drums rattle and boom, and ever and anon a trumpet cries loud its piercing alarum.[27] Here, in a quick chase of chords in the wood winds, a pursuer seems to bring down his lingering foe; there, arises a horrid clash, deemed to destroy all beauty and reason. And above the stirring chaos, for one brief moment, the Hero's theme arises in the deep voices of the bass strings. On goes the furious din of fierce war as the whole orchestra reaches climax after Gargantuan climax in a massive edifice of deafening sound. The theme of the Hero emerges again, projected triumphantly in the massed strings, followed by the theme of his Beloved, and then the main theme returns in all its fullness and majesty as the Hero rejoices his military victory, alone, as the orchestra chants a victory paen.[28]

The fifth section begins a celebration of peace, and it is the spiritual evolution and achievements of the Hero that now sweep by in the music. The mood is serene and contemplative, and a maze of divers musical fragments and melodies flash by and keep rising, each new strain growing out of another in quick succession or in ingenuous polyphony, as if eager for a hearing before the music were to end. At times, a broad and serene theme is put forth by the tuba, viola and bass clarinet; at times, another motive unfolds in the voices of the horns and cello. The melodies, however, are not new; they are all a series of themes from Strauss' earlier works, like the reminiscences of a Hero's whole musical life (could it be Strauss' own?) skillfully blended to yield the most sublimely beautiful music that seeks to embody the Man's "works of peace."

Sinister mutterings by a tuba open the final section: all the glorious achievements of the Hero seem to have won only more envy and derision from his uncomprehending critics. Presently, a serene melody is unfolded by an English horn, accompanied softly by the strings, flute and brass to the gentle and persistent percussions of the timpani. Tranquillity reigns over the orchestra as the Hero gradually comes to understand that spiritual triumph is not a matter of recognition by the world, but rather one of being at peace with one's own conscience.[29] A solo violin affirms the sympathetic presence of the Beloved at his side.

Final peace comes in a purified version of the main theme guised in a soft pastoral hue. The strings bring forth a final theme: the fulfillment of the Hero's life. It is blended subtly from fragments of the easily recognized phrases that had represented the Hero's spiritual works of peace, which are mingled with fragments of the tune of the Beloved. Here, it seems, is a final peace and calm brought about by love and spiritual triumph![30] It is a golden tranquillity, blessed with a solid and everlasting form. A solo violin returns once more to sing an unbelievably moving and lovely melody of profound pathos. The trumpets blast out the Hero's theme, the orchestra builds it up, broad and solemn and majestic, to a gigantic mass of tone, as if the heavens themselves were blaring out the song of heroes, and the music ends in a climax of incredible splendor.

- Ein Heldenleben; Also sprach Zarathushtra Op. 30
  BMG/RCA 09026 61494-2 Chicago SO, Fritz Reiner $$

- (i) An Alpine Symphony; (ii) Also Sprach Zarathushtra; (iii) Ein Heldenleben; (ii) Till Eulenspeigal
  Double Decca 440 618-2 (2). Bav. RSO; (ii) Chicago SO (iii) VPO, Solti $

Exhibit 38 Berlioz: The Corsair, Overture

Much has been written about the sources of Hector Berlioz's overture *Le Corsaire*. Berlioz, himself, talked of "drinking in that burning poetry" of Byron's *Corsair* and, during a dangerously stormy boat voyage when he was nearly wrecked in a gale, he had made the acquaintance of a real Venetian corsair-type adventurer.[31] Some have even drawn attention to a probable association with James Fennimore Cooper's *The Red Rover*. In the final analysis, Berlioz's *Corsair*, of course, is Berlioz himself, masquerading as Byron's hero. It was written while the composer was recovering in Nice after a romantic and ineffectual suicide attempt. The whole piece is an extraordinary work of brilliant romantic tone painting.

This Overture is as salt a sea-piece as has ever been written.[32] Two sharp opening chords, and the violins are off, fast and fierce, as the winds howl and the sea foams to an accompaniment by the wood winds. A

126

transient soft lull—perhaps the contrasting nature of Byron's *Corsair,* pitiless yet generous, with a love for women and hatred for his kind— and the orchestra rushes out again to a fiery tempo. Presently, a lovely lyrical theme, full of feminine chastity and tenderness, is unfolded by the violins, but the tempestuous music returns and propels relentlessly forward, with the beautiful lyric woven into a complex orchestral fabric.[33]

- Overtures: Le Corsaire; Le Carnaval romaine; Beatrice en Benedict; Benevuto Cellini; Romeo et Juliette: Queen Mab scherzo; Les Troyens: Royal hunt and storm; SAINT-SAENS: Le rouet d'Omphale
  BMG/RCA 9026 61400-2. Boston SO, Munch $$

Exhibit 39 Liszt: Hungarian Rhapsody No. 2

It was Franz Liszt (1811-1886) who established the rhapsody form in romantic music, and who popularized the term *rhapsody*. Rhapsodies have one uniform characteristic: They offer a breath-taking contrast between *lassan*, slow and languorous music, and *friskan*, gay, abandoned, passionate music, which are the two conventional movements of the Hungarian national dance, the *Czerdas*. After years of research into Hungarian folk music, Liszt composed sixteen Hungarian Rhapsodies in which he incorporated the melodies, rhythms, sentiments, yearnings and passions of Hungarian gypsy music. Combining his own flair for theatrical effects with the fiery and seductive, often jovial, native character of this music, he produced an effect that was at once electrifying and extraordinarily stimulative.[34] Originally scored for solo piano, an orchestral version of the Second Rhapsody was also put together by the composer.

The music opens with the *Lassan* played earnestly by the clarinets, violins and violas in unison, accompanied by clusters of tone in the horns, trombones and basses. The first theme, slow and mournful, unfolds in the clarinets and the high strings accompanied, once more, by the horns, trombones and basses. After a flourish by the clarinets, the melody is picked up by the flutes and oboes.[35] A new, more colorful dance theme now appears, one that is suggestive of the fast *Friska* movement. It is proposed by the harp, flute and violas to the ringing of a triangle and bells and the plucking of strings, and is then picked up in a more spirited way by the violins and wood winds.[36] There is another flourish by the clarinets, and then fragments of the melody are repeated with some variations to bring the movement to a quiet close.

Now the *Friska* opens, fast and fierce, in a brilliant dance theme played by an oboe to the accompaniment of the violins, piccolo and clarinet. The music grows faster and louder, the pulse quickens, there is a wild fierce rush, and the whole orchestra pitches in to carry this dashing song to a most energetic and exhilarating climax. A transient lull follows, a clarinet and bassoon air a quiet little melody, another pause, and then the music takes off again to end in a deafening climax.

- Hungarian Rhapsodies 1-16; ENESCU: Roumanian Rhapsody No. 1
  Mercury 432 015 -2, LSO, Dorati $$

Exhibit 40 Mendelssohn: Symphony No. 4 (Italian)

More than one hundred and fifty years ago, Felix Mendelssohn-Bartholdy (1809-1847) arrived in Rome for a stay of several months. The grandeur of the city, the serene beauty of the Alban Hills, the grand coronation of a Pope at which he was a spectator, the popular colorful festivals, the ever-near spectacle of the sea, and the sights and sounds of the sunny land all left their mark upon the music that he composed during his Roman visit.[37] "This is Italy," he gushed in a letter, "The whole country has such a festive air that I feel as if I were a young Prince making his entry."[38]

Blessed with an innate gift of melody, and easily prone to find emotional content in historic sentiment or in scenic description, Mendelssohn did not sing in this music of the blue Italian skies as he saw them. It was, rather, an inner picture of enchantment that he painted, one that every German Romantic had envisioned for this classic heroic land of beauty and art that had held Germans captive from the earliest invasions of the Goths to the poetry of Goethe.[39] There is little trace of Italian nationalism, or the graphic or picturesque, in this music. It is German, with a pure German expression of delight, and a highly poetic utterance of a German idea of Italy.[40] Mendelssohn himself never heard this symphony; it was found nine years after he had written it, among the great mass of manuscripts that he left behind after his death.

The well known opening musical phrase expresses at once the simple joyousness and contagious exhilaration of the whole first movement. The melody flows spontaneously—rarely a deep flow, but always clear and shining, right from its beginning.[41] The principle theme, gay and spirited, is entrusted to the violins, with the wood winds and a horn providing a richly colored accompaniment. Here, it seems, is the young Prince

128

making his entry! There is an air of lightness, a wonderful freshness bubbling in every move. By deft turns and by trick of sequence, the tune evolves into ever newer guises whose subtle similarities are virtually impossible to trace outwardly except in their merry pace. A second melody, which continues the happy spirit of the first, is played by the wood winds with the strings dancing about playfully.[42] The tune extends into a pure song, at times almost resembling a dance. Suddenly, a solo clarinet calls faintly, as if from some distant Roman ruins, and a merry orchestral chorus of the first theme comes bustling in again, drowning, with its festive jostling, the more delicate strains of the second tune.[43]

Now arises a sparkling dialogue between two themes that plunges one suddenly from a world of prosaic merriment into a dim and mysterious land of strange legends. From which realm it arises one cannot tell, but a restless fragment of a tune winds its way off from the melody. However, it is too volatile, too incessant in its chatter, to take the lead, and it soon subsides to a subordinate position as a new theme of greater distinction and dignity enters.[44] Again, one feels its kinship to the others and its fitness in the whole scheme, but the tune defies all attempts at following through. The two tunes are so different in their natures: the one full of dark romance, the other like a frivolous holiday warmth and gladness.[45] Not to be outdone, the first theme now bursts in strongly, initially in the wood winds, then alternating with the brass, and the duel is on again as each gains successive assertion over the other, often with equal insistence of both at the same time.

The official second theme has been strangely quiet during this exchange. Soon, after a lull, this second tuneful and rhythmic melody reappears, sung as a duet of cellos above the violas. Even here, that other mysterious darker-hued melody intrudes, first lightly, and then more vehemently.[46] After a brief struggle, the sweeter song triumphs, and holds its cheery sway to the end of the movement.

Like the cry of a muezzin from his minaret, the wailing wood winds (flute, oboe and bassoon) and the upper strings intone the second movement. It is a mysterious and lyrical melody, almost a litany, that reappears frequently throughout this section. The combination of violins and flutes in the repetitions of this tune has been described as one of the most delightful *tours de forces* in all orchestration.[47] This introduction is followed by the main theme of this movement, heard in the mellifluous combination of an oboe, bassoon and viola to an accompaniment by the low strings and the wood winds. Often labeled as the *Pilgrim's March,* its music has been alleged, perhaps erroneously, to describe a religious procession passing through the streets of Naples. It adds a note of human wistfulness to the austerity of the litany.[48] Others have likened it to a Bohemian folk-song. Here is pure Italian poetry as it appeared to the German mind: indefinable, and burdened by a wealth of legendary feelings like a strange folk-ballad from a foreign land.[49]

Much of the charm of this lyrical and moving song, telling its sad tale without reflection or overflowing emotion, lies in the melodious strain of the strings as the tune flows above in the wood winds.[50] Later, the violins take over the theme, and the flutes pick out a shadowy counter-melody. The next verse is mysteriously narrated by the violins to a fateful, ever present accompaniment of the lower strings.[51] A new melody by the clarinet, rudely interrupted by fragments of the main theme, ends the movement in an atmosphere of mystery.

The third movement is bucolic and playful; there is, to German ears, an unmistaken essence of their own folk-songs in the opening melody of this minuet.[52] But the real gem of this music is the intensely romantic melody played by a trio of horns and bassoons, quite reminiscent of a midsummer-night's dream. A combination of strings played against a combination of bassoons, brass and timpani ends the movement with color and rhythm.

The fourth movement sports a *saltero*, a rowdy Italian peasant dance performed by men and women in pairs, with hops, skips and rapid steps that draw the dancers in a circle, now advancing, now retreating, with great vigor and abandonment. The peculiar rhythm of this "carnival of the Campagna" is introduced by the wood winds and strings. The melody is played by the flutes, followed by a new musical idea that is discussed between the two sections of the violins. A new eel-like rhythm now enters, the *tarantella,* a wildly exciting and exhausting dance that was supposed to drive out from the body the poison of the deadly tarantella spider. The violins evoke a mad and frenetic rhythm and, in an outburst of the *saltero*, the music comes to a frenzied halt.

- Symphony No. 4;—SCHUBERT: Symphony No. 8 in B minor (unfinished)
  DG Dig. 445 514-2. Philh. O, Sinopoli $$
- Symphonies Nos. 4 in A (Italian); 5 in D minor (Reformation); (ii) A Midsummer Night's Dream Overture
  Erato/ Warner 2292 45932-2, (i) ECO, (ii) LPO, Leppard $

Exhibit 41 Chopin: Polonaise in A flat

Both the march and the dance came together happily in the sixteenth century in the *polonaise,* a courtly dance designed to allow the dashing

130

Polish nobles to file ceremoniously past the throne in all their regal splendor. Slavic in color and spirit, filled with an abandoned fervor, and abounding with unusual progressions and harmonic schemes, its texture was essentially of native growth and native substance.[53] In his sixteen *Polonaises*, Frederic Chopin (1810-1849) expressed the soul of his native country. They became idealized in his imagination as a symbol of that unappeasable longing which every Romantic artist carried in his heart: the longing for the lost native land of happiness that may never be found again.[54] These short piano pieces were consistently tempestuous and stormy in temper, cogent and demoniac. Here was a far different Chopin from the familiar introspective dreamer of the Paris *salons*.

The *Polonaise* in A flat (*Polonaise Militaire*) offers this march-dance in its proudest and most ceremonial mood. It begins with a long introduction. The majestic opening theme that follows is proud and chivalric, and full of embellishments. Notice the peculiar and moving rhythm of the accompaniment. Suddenly, the rhythm stops as the piano takes off on a sweeping run. The theme is repeated, then follows a short contrasting melody, and the section closes with a reiteration of the main tune.

The following section is the epitome of the grand style in piano music and brings out the heroic side of this genre. The virtuosic left hand takes on an unsurpassed brilliance, approaching the limits of what the piano can do. The emotional fervor drops perceptibly, and then the tension returns in a roaring and torrential emotional outburst. Now the music takes on a rhapsodic character, with part of the melodic phrases being derived from the contrasting section. The music ends with a statement of the original theme.

- Polonaises 1-16
    Decca Double 452 167-2 (2) Ashkenazy $

1   McKinney, Robert , & Anderson, WR, *Discovering Music* (The American Book Co, NY, 1934)

2   Machlis, Joseph, *The Enjoyment of Music* (WW Norton , NY, 1984)

3   *Ibid*

4   *Ibid*

5   Layton, Robert, *The Common Pursuit*, in The Symphony, Past, Present and Future. The BBC Music Magazine, Summer Special, 1995

6   Goepp, Philip, *Great works of Music* (Garden City Publishing Co, NY, 1913)

7   Kinscella, Hazel Gertrude, *Music and Romance* (RCA Manufacturing Co, Camden, NJ, 1941)

8   *Ibid*

9   Downes, Edward, *Guide to Symphonic Music* (Walker & Co, NY, 1981)

10   *Ibid*

11   *Ibid*

12   O'Connell, Charles, *The Victor Book of the Symphony* (Simon & Schuster, NY, 1935)

131

13   Kinscella, Hazel Gertrude, *Music and Romance*

14   *Ibid*

15   *Ibid*

16   This paragraph is adapted from *The Symphony, Past, Present, Future* (BBC Music Magazine, Summer Special, 1995)

17   O'Connell, Charles, *The Victor Book of Symphony* (Simon & Schuster, NY, 1935)

18   *Ibid*

19   Downes, Edward, *Guide to Symphonic Music* (Walker & Co, NY, 1981)

20   O'Connell, Charles, *The Victor Book of Symphony*

21   Goepp, Phillip, *Great Works of Music*

22   O'Connell, Charles, *The Victor Book of Symphony*

23   Goepp, Phillip, *Great Works of Music*

24   *Ibid*

25   O'Connell, Charles, *The Victor Book of Symphony*

26   *Ibid*

27   *Ibid*

28   *Ibid*

29   *Ibid*

30   *Ibid*

31   Downes, Edward, *Guide to Symphonic Music*

32   Tovey, Donald Francis, *Symphonies and other Orchestral Works* (Oxford University Press, NY, reprinted 1990)

33   Downes, Edward, *Guide to Symphonic Music*

34   Ewen, David, *Music for the Millions* (Arco Publishing Co, NY, 1944)

35   Upton, GP & Borowski, Felix, *The Standard Concert Guide* (Blue Ribbon Books, NY, 1940)

36   *Ibid*

37   Newmarch, Rosa, *The Concert-Goer's Library of Descriptive Notes, Vol. 4* (Oxford University Press, London, 1931)

38   Downes, Edward, *Guide to Symphonic Music*

39   Goepp, Philip, *Great Works of Music*

40   *Ibid*

41   O'Connell, Charles, *The Victor Book of the Symphony*

42   Goepp, Philip, *Great Works of Music*

43   *Ibid*

44   *Ibid*

45   *Ibid*

46   *Ibid*

47   Tovey, Donald Francis, *Symphonies and other Orchestral Works*

48   *Ibid*

49   Goepp, Philip, *Great Works of Music*

50   *Ibid*

51   *Ibid*

52   *Ibid*

53   Ewen, David, *Music for the Millions*

54   Machlis, Joseph, *The Enjoyment of Music*

"Was it a vision, or a waking dream?
Fled is that music:—Do I wake or sleep?"
                                    — John Keats

9   Impressionism

Impressionism developed in the arts as a revolt against the sentimental extravagances, the richness of feelings, and the deeply intellectual emotional attitudes of the great Romantics. It evolved to become a purely surface art, committed to capture for posterity an impression of the fleeting loveliness of a moment, the evanescent colors and elusive contours of a shifting external world. Here was a form of musical painting that conveyed, for example, the emotional suggestions of a landscape rather than its physical description. The momentary interplay of light and shadow, and the sheer delight of contrasting sounds and colors resulted in a purely superficial pictorial canvas. Sensibility, nuance, suggestiveness, and subtlety were the marks of this new music. Clear outlines gave way to misty impressions dissolved in a natural light. The Impressionists touched no high spirits of exaltation or despair; it was not for them to explore the vast issues of the human spirit or probe the innermost passions of the human soul. Their music was made not according to fixed formulae, but simply and logically in accordance with the poetry it sought to express. And, within their style, they wrought patterns of loveliness and charm that recalled a worry-free age of innocence and beauty.

Impressionistic music, therefore, is for the moment and for the senses, not for the intellect. It is not difficult to understand; indeed, it is not meant to be understood but merely to be heard and felt. It does not require guiding directions or formal analyses. It is evocative; the effects are those of passing colors and forms, ephemeral melodies and contrasting contours that require an imaginative attitude to listening. Here, more than anywhere, the listener is on one's own.

Exhibit 42 Debussy: Prelude a L'Apres-Midi d'un Faune

In this sophisticated inspiration of musical impressionism, Claude Debussy (1862-1918) was the first to point out that this piece was intended to evoke the subtle and suggestive amorous scenes described in a poem by Mallarme bearing the same title: *The Afternoon of the Faun.* The faun was a simple and sensuous primitive child of nature from classical antiquity, born in the shape of a man with the horns and feet of a goat. In this music, it is transported, perhaps from the slopes of pagan Greece, to the aesthetic subtleties of a hot afternoon in a Parisian wood.[1]

The slumbering faun awakens and attempts to recall his experiences of the previous afternoon. He wonders whether it was a dream, or a reality, that he had been visited by nymphs, those white and golden, divinely tender, goddesses? He cannot tell, for they were no more substantial than the sweetly melodic notes from his own flute. Suddenly, he glimpses a vision of naked whiteness amidst the brown reeds at the side of the clear lake. The impression fades, and he snuggles back in the warm luxuriant grass to recall that delicious perfumed dream once more.

A mingling of low-pitched arid flutes, sensuous oboes, distantly calling horns and antique cymbals, accompanied delicately by the orchestra, evokes that mysterious and heathen enchanted world that lies between waking and sleep.[2] Presently, a melody is announced by a flute, perhaps the flute of the faun himself, and is picked up sweetly and expressively by a piano before it fades away to the limpid silvery tones of a harp. It is a song full of desire, with a strange tenderness and melancholy. The theme is repeated by the flute, but this time against a background of tremulous strings. Slowly, a strange and evanescent, almost magical, tapestry unfolds, exposing transiently a glimpse of warm sunlight, a glitter of shimmering water, or the scent of a lightly passing breeze, all tossed fleetingly among the oboes, clarinets and French horns. The music becomes steadily more urgent, a lively dialogue ensues to reach a momentary crescendo, but it dies away at once, and the lazy flute melody returns, now decorated with fanciful arabesques.[3]

The heat and voluptuousness of the afternoon's golden hours grows. An oboe weaves out a new erotic melody, plaintive and rapturous, perhaps about remembrances of things past. It gets steadily more urgent and louder, almost orgasmic, to strain into a third melody put out by the wood winds, expressive and very sustained, suggestive of a desire satisfied. The music once again grows more rapturous, faster, and very loud to capture a momentary climax—a fleeting glimpse of pursuits and embraces and escapes—and then, once again, it dies away forthright amidst disappointment.

The sensuous flute melody returns languorously in a mist; muted horns skip daintily with light-footed oboes and flutes, answered by the whole orchestra in the lightest chords imaginable, to create a soft haze as impressions of raptures and laughter emerge and vanish. A tremulous harp suggests the fleetness of the passing vision. The impression fades, the faun settles down again as a solo cello lingers with the flute to recall the same thought with which the music had opened. With dreamlike softness, in an unforgettable passage for muted horns and strings, the sounds slowly dissolve as the enchantment melts away into thin and silent air.

- Prelude a l'apres-midi d'un faune; Jeux; La Mer
  EMI Dig. CD-EMX 9502; TC-EMX 2090 [Ang. CDM 62012]. LPO, Baudo $$

- (i) Prelude a l'apres-midi d'un faune; Images; Nocturnes; Le Martye de Saint Sebastion; 2 fanfares and symphonic fragments; Printemps; (ii) 3 ballades de Francois Villon; (iii) La Demoiselle elue
  DG Double Dig/Analogue 437 934-2 (2), O de Paris, Barenboim with (i) Ch. de l'O de Paris; (ii) Dietrich Fischer-Dieskau; (iii) Barbara Hendricks $

Exhibit 43 Falla: Nights in the Gardens of Spain

Spain! The land of Don Juan and Don Quixote, the home of Carmen, of multicolored cruel bullfights, of proud arrogance and fiery love.[4] In this music, composed initially as three nocturnes for the piano, Manuel de Falla (1876-1946) captured the soft and undulating, poetic suggestiveness and the popular soul of his native land. Based on musical fragments, and on rhythms and scraps of melody peculiar to the folk songs of Andalusia, he evoked the memory of certain places, sensations, and sentiments. Here are visions of the Alhambra outlined against the warm nights of a radiant Andalusian sky, testament to a glory passed forever, or an Andalusian trio of two mandolins and guitar, playing from the heart in one of the old gardens, flooded with moonlight. The music has no pretensions of being descriptive; it is merely expressive, a tone painting in the most delicate colors, giving an impression in sound of something joyful and exuberant, yet melancholy and mysterious.

The palace *at the Generalife* (Moorish: *Jennat al Arif*, Garden of Arif), a thirteenth century villa overlooking the romantic gardens on a hillside, lies outside the Alhambra, the residence of the Moorish monarchs of Granada. The music begins without introduction, as if it has already been playing for some time. It is cast in the form of variations on a single musical idea that is stated at the outset by the violas, then eerily reproduced by the second violins. This is a very spare theme, hardly more than an ornament.[5] When the piano makes its first appearance, it takes up this theme in an altered version, with the rhythm punctuated by the strings and brass.

A second melody grows out of the first, and this, too, is varied by the piano. The sounds, with their tinkling mandolin accompaniments, create an impression of rich gardens with gushing fountains and flowering pomegranates, of mysterious cypress thickets and dreamy patios that still harbor the unrevealed secrets of the ghosts of yester-years.[6] The melody grows, expands, and luxuriates in a dazzling feat of virtuosity.

Suddenly, the music comes to a halt, and one is transported, it seems, to another garden, scented with orange trees and myrtle and palms. There is a vague music of a *Dance in the Distance,* with whirring trills and runs and the rhythmic strumming of a Spanish guitar. The music opens with trills and sinuous runs on a viola, against a background of plucked cellos and basses. The piano also adopts this pattern. Soon, a new and more important tune is unfolded in the flute and strings, and is taken over by an English horn, clarinet and the violins.[7] The persistent rhythm of this dance tune dominates the entire piece, and never loses the feeling of being heard at a distance, through a veil of shimmering sound.[8] One whirling dance follows another, the piano plays brilliantly and then, without a break in the music, the scene changes to one *In the Gardens of the Mountains of Cordoba.*

Here is a gay and lively party under the trees, a nocturnal revelry with long tables spread out sumptuously, with wine and laughter flowing freely as a *zambra* of gypsy musicians play, sing and dance. This time the dance is close at hand, and the piano responds with an artful statement that sounds like embellishments on a guitar, full of shifting accents and irregular ornaments.[9] Somewhere, a dancer steps out with flaming eyes and stamping feet to the wild rhythms and the rude songs, her seductive gestures flashing in the moonlight. It is a dream like *The Arabian Nights,* and yet the music, rich and lustrous, seems to transcend the barriers of time and place to have one see things, and hear things, with senses other than one's own. The spell persists in a long and surging summing-up as the dance rhythms fade into the night.

- (i) Nights in the Gardens of Spain; (ii) El amor brujo (ballet, complete); RODRIGO: Concerto

136

Decca Dig 430 703-2; 430 703-4. (i) De Larrocha, LPO, Fruhbeck de Burgos (ii) Tourangeau, Montreal SO, Dutoit $$

- Nights in the Gardens of Spain;—GRANADOS: Danzas espanolas
  Ph. 442 751-2 (2) Eduardo del Pueyo, LAP, Jean Martinon $$

Exhibit 44 Respighi: The Fountains of Rome

Here is picture-painting and story-telling at its best, with an intense dramatic feeling and a vividly convincing realism teamed with an orchestral *tour-de-force* of the highest order. In this suite of Italian pictures, Ottorino Respighi (1879-1936) presents a set of musical impressions to evoke the sensations, emotions and images inspired by four famous fountains in Rome at various times of the day. These are the hours when their character is most in harmony with the surrounding landscape, or during which their beauty appears most impressive to an observer. This personal form of symphonic poem, where the descriptive and colorful elements blend with the lyrical and sentimental elements, is in four sections.

Dawn breaks slowly at the *Fountains of Villa Giulia*. The murmuring of muted second violins, combined with the first violins playing a weird harmony, evokes a delicate atmosphere of mystery. A tender melody is sung by an oboe and is accompanied by the flutes and an English horn. Here is an image of the eternal Roman countryside, beautiful and serene in the soft fresh light of the morning, with its ancient landscapes and grazing animals. A lowing herd winds slowly o'er the lea, and the ploughman leaves home in the damp gray mists of a breaking day. In the distance, the unforgotten marble columns rise high and unmolested in their solitary splendor. Presently, the music becomes very slightly more firm through the soft addition of clarinets, bassoons and the lower strings. A triangle taps gently eight times. Muted instruments, tremulous strings, and delicate running passages from a sweet-voiced cclesta blend to create an atmosphere as mysterious and vague as the quiet hours of dawn.[10] Suddenly, a loud insistent blast of horns rises above the delicate and dainty trills of the whole orchestra as a myriad birds awaken to the first rays of the sun.

A sudden loud summons by the horns, and brilliant orchestral flourishes, depict the precipitate gushing and splashing waterfall of the *Triton Fountain* in the bright sunshine of the late morning. It is the joyous call to the Naiads and Tritons who come prancing forth, pursuing each other amidst embraces and laughter between the jets of water, dancing ever faster to a frenzied climax. A light and playful rhythm in the flutes, clarinets and harps follows and leads in the first theme, with the harps adding airy embellishments to suggest a play of the waters. The melody is taken up by the first violins and then passed to and fro among all the instruments. Many trills are heard, as well as the plucking of strings and the sliding of tones from a celesta, harp and piano. The varied combinations suggest the singing and twittering of birds, and the dance of the Naiads and Tritons as the morning advances. The music ends poetically with a progressive softening and muting of first one, then the other sections of the orchestra.

A solemn undulating theme announces the great baroque *Trevi Fountain* at noon. The theme is taken over by the wood winds, and then passed on by the brass as a triumphant peal in an effort to recall the pomp, wealth, and majesty of the glorious baroque era. A piano adds a tripping accompaniment, harps glide to augment the atmosphere, and the music grows faster and louder. Trumpets blare as great Neptune's chariot, drawn by prancing sea-horses, sweeps over the radiant waters, followed by a parade of Sirens and Tritons. The procession then vanishes, the music becomes slower and more calm, and finally diminishes to a softness as the trumpets fade into the distance and, imperceptibly, one is transported to the gardens of the Villa Medici.

It is the nostalgic hour of sunset at the *Villa Medici Fountain*. A sad theme suggesting the end of the day, a subdued hymn-like melody, is played, divided between the first and second violins. The song is taken up by a flute and an English horn to a constant accompaniment of delicate arabesques by a celesta and harp. The dripping water, drop by drop, sparkles like brilliant jewels in the dying rays of the sun. A curfew tolls the knell of parting day as, from all directions, a final ringing of bells, large and small, merges with the twitter of birds and the rustling of the leaves. As the daylight fades away, the orchestral strings blend peacefully into the twinkling silence of a star-cool night.

- The Fountains of Rome; The Pines of Rome;—MUSSORGSKY: Pictures at an Exhibition
    RCA 09026 61401-2 Chicago SO, Fritz Reiner $$

- Feste Romane; The Fountains of Rome; The Pines of Rome
    Naxos Dig. 8.550539 . RPO, Batiz. $

1   O'Connell, Charles, *The Victor Book of the Symphony* (Simon & Schuster, NY, 1935)
2   Stringham, Edwin, *Listening to Music Creatively* (Prentice Hall Inc, NY, 1946)
3   *Ibid*

[4] McKinney, HD & Anderson, Wr, *Discovering Music* (American Book Company, NY, 1934)

[5] Time-Life Records: The Story of Great Music. *A Listener's Guide to the Recordings: Music in the Spanish Style.* NY, 1967

[6] McKinney, HD & Anderson, Wr, *Discovering Music*

[7] Time-Life Records: The Story of Great Music. *A Listener's Guide to the Recordings: Music in the Spanish Style.*

[8] *Ibid*

[9] *Ibid*

[10] Kinscella, Hazel Gertrude, *Music and Romance* (RCA Victor Company, NJ, 1930)

Part 3

The Varieties
of
Musical Experience

Life is short and the art is long. And very old is the art through which man has sung of the things of enduring beauty that have sprung out of mankind's own consciousness and experiences. Ever since the original Sin, his first great Fall, man has had the same emotional, moral and physical experiences over the centuries, the same agonies and ecstasies, triumphs and frustrations, shames and glories. He has had the same yearnings, and the same struggles to satisfy those yearnings. He has faced the same problems, and asked the same questions, and has found himself entangled in the same conflicts in his relations with himself and others. A few have preserved in music the matchless stories of man, a monument of blood, imagination and intellect running together. For we are the music makers, the dreamers of dreams, the world movers and world forsakers. Without our will we are born, and against our will we die. We suffer and make suffer, and to what end this comes to pass is the story of our mighty theme.

All music is a response to human experience, a report on one's inner life. Every composer creates his own world. Behind the symphonies, behind the songs, behind the piano pieces, behind the gush of chamber music and chorales, behind the operas, behind the entire cross-section of a composing career, there is a human mind, a human frame, with human characteristics and foibles and interests, human opinions, all the concentrated disparities that make up a man, the man behind the music.[1] There are feelings that can be evoked by all objects in proportion to one's intelligent susceptibility, and a great master of any language can invoke the deepest part of these feelings in his own terms.

The music *Exhibits* that follow in this section represent some of the workings of this process. Such is the bloom of perpetual newness, as it were, upon these works, that it makes them look always untouched by time, as though the unfaltering breath of an ageless spirit has been infused into them. Here, therefore, are a series of images and lines of thought derived through the senses and the imagination, more the expression of feelings than the illustration of things, which set for the listener a point of departure for his or her own flights.

---

[1]   Abraham, Gerald, *The Music of Sibelius* (W W Norton & Co., Inc., NY, 1947)

"...the rude sea grew civil at her song,
And certain stars shot madly from their spheres,
To hear the sea-maid's music."
—William Shakespeare

10 The Sea

God almighty created the first waters under the Heaven and bid them be gathered together, and the waters He called Seas. Since the first great river that flowed out of Eden, the life of man has converged about the sea and its rivers. The sea brought life and wealth, and along its undulating waters, men have dreamed their never-ending dreams, spun their legends and poetry, and have made their music. Perhaps, even the first ideas of movement, of the dance, came from the rhythm of the waves.

Tradition has it that Venus sprang forth from the waters. It was across Homer's wine-dark sea that the Acheans sailed in a thousand ships to burn the topless towers of Ileum, and the same waves tossed Odysseus haplessly from shore to shore. The demonic Ahab met his fate in the tempestuous ocean, lashed to the crooked jaw of an infernal snow-white humpback. Although death is at all times solemn, it is never so much as at sea. The slow and mellow voice of the waters moans ceaselessly over the unbroken slumbers of those that it holds in its vasty depths, without a grave, "unknell'd, uncoffin'd, and unknown."

There can be nothing so desperately monotonous as the sea, and one no longer wonders at the cruelty of the men before the masts: at the plundering Vikings in their dreaded longboats, or at the pirates who made the innocent walk the plank to Davy Jones' locker along the Spanish Main. The sea is a mystery. Here is a society that none can intrude. To some, its mysterious untiring waves, never resting, embody a great natural power that renews its strength and, without reference to joy or sorrow, follows the eternal laws imposed by a higher power. Go to the sea, they have said, to him that will learn to pray. Yet, no matter what its smiles may be, one doubts its friendship.

The music composed about the sea is incessantly and everywhere alive. Energy runs through it like coursing blood, heating it to the high color that shows in wine-dark seas and in black ships with vermilion prows.[1] But the

145

sounds are neither monotonous nor meaningless. If they are packed with fury, they are not noisy. If the music is restless without end, it is not sick of a fever.[2] Its abundant life is brilliant with form. In steady unceasing rhythms, or in an orchestral roar, the waters seem to oscillate between bustle and quiet, between masses of tone colors and one lonely harp making music alone, between the din of furious battle and the domestic peace of a star-cool shore.

Exhibit 45 Debussy: La Mer

Claude Debussy (1862-1918) had an almost religious adoration of the sea. "Here I am with my old friend the sea," he wrote to a friend, "always beautiful."[3] In this musical excursion to the sea, it was not his intention to paint a programmatic picture of the movements and tides of the sea, or allow one to hear, see or feel its waters. Rather, this music was about the reveries and emotions which the sea inspires in one who is sensitive to its varied beauties. Here is an unpeopled world; only the observer and the sea exist. Nonetheless, nowhere in music has there been presented so magical a suggestion of the open sea with its incredible shades of blue and green, its sparkle, motion and depth, and its mysterious and everlasting magic and power. This symphonic poem is in three fragments.

The first sketch opens with an impression of the awesome soothing power of the resting ocean at dawn.[4] Muted strings and murmuring drums, and slowly loudening notes on a harp merge to create an image of a shadowy mist that seems to arise slowly over the orchestra. The landscape of the night has faded and all the air holds a solemn stillness. There is a mysterious, eerie quality in the undulations of this music which seems to be at once an incantation and an awakening. A strange note, as of a distant trumpet, blows a gentle wailing phrase. Suddenly, as the shady hues of darkness are dissipated, the sense of desolation yields to a soothing song played softly by the horns against softening strings, as the limitless line of the horizon unfolds through the mist. The soothing cheer is interrupted by pleasant and strange sounds, and the sweet song of the horns returns in a quieter rhythm. The song continues amidst a chorus of splashing waves and swirling breezes by the strings, its tune picked up by a muted trumpet and the ringing notes of a clarinet. Slowly, it fades away.

A stirring orchestral shock announces a single flash of awakening light. The first rays of the sun spreads its welcome warmth over the waters, and the light grows. The sea is now awakened. The music rises as life picks up to the soft and busy sounds of another new day. The sounds shift in color and transparency like the sea itself, and it is not possible to separate from its curiously amorphous structure the myriad beauties of which it is compounded.[5] As the light seems to grow clearer and the air more boisterous, the waves of this chimerical sea ride higher, throwing their spume into the new sunshine, exultant and tumultuous.[6] Ever-changing fragments of rhythm and tones, echoed in golden notes by a horn and a hushed trumpet, seem to cast shifting reflections of gliding seabirds, gilded clouds, and bright sunlight on the shimmering waters of the orchestral sea.[7] The sketch ends at high noon in a short but impressive chorale by the wood winds as the tossing waves, like a last shake of the mane of sea horses, flash under a bright clear sky to the triumphant blare of the brass.

The second fragment starts romantically with the most delicate of beginnings. There is a touch of romance in the tone of the clarinets, and an unavoidable feeling of fable and legend in the unconscious concert of natural sea sounds: The deeper pulse of the ocean in the horns, and the sharp dash of the lighter surf in the *glockenspiel* set against the constant and unstable flowing ripples in the trembling strings.[8] Here the sea—that placid, deceiving monster—is revealed in a different mood: the now thoroughly awakened sea is at play.[9]

A resonant clash by the spray of colliding waters announces the play of the waves. A thousand voices seem to entangle and crash, frothy waters spume upwards, and long rollers rush towards the shore to dissolve in a snowy foam.[10] There are waves of every color and mood in this capricious sport of wind and waves. Here is a wild ocean, alive with manly fury. Vagrant winds lash the waves loudly across the shore in tossing billows, dashing them upon the rocks. The elements dance, they romp and race through immemorial games the secrets of which will never be known to man; against this the wood winds sing a simple song of lightly lapping and cradling waters, and the strings converse in a higher, quicker play resembling the unpredictable tantrums of a mermaid.

A myriad colors now appear and vanish in the fountains of spray; like a fairy tale, the scenes change quickly. A shower of gliding harps breaks the tune, the song reappears and is taken up by the golden notes of a horn, and the waters seem to shimmer and sparkle to a harp and the trilling wood winds and strings.[11] Against this background, the horns come in to tell another chilling tale in an ominous melody. The scene vanishes. Later, two mermaids seem to sing in a twining duet.[12] In a warm hue of light, the horns sound a new weird song taken up by a chorus of lighter voices that ends, with a rising volume, in a clear, almost martial, call by the brass.[13]

A new scene appears, and the slower air of trembling strings and the quicker play of the wood winds, harp and bells wanders through new and ever-changing phrases. Strings and shaking brass now bring back the horn's ominous melody, but the music soon emerges out of its gloom with a burst of profound cheer by the trumpets accompanied by the dying peals of bells. There is a brief moment of uncertainty between joy and doubt, but the lighter mood prevails and the music, stirred up by its own sportiness, soars into higher flights until a mighty chorus of all the instruments rises to a triumphant climax of joy.

But it is all a sport of the waves. The music wearily subsides into calm, and one is left once again with the impersonal scene that prevailed at the beginning of this piece, and an unavoidable feeling of legend still hovers over the dying music. On the sea's vast stage, a trance-like phantasmagoria, so evanescent and fugitive, leaves behind only the vagueness of a dream.[14]

The third fragment is almost the obverse of the first; the themes seem the same but the hue and mood has changed from the youth of dawn to the sadness of dusk. An ominous voice, as if auguring an approaching upheaval, opens a stormy dialogue between the wind and the sea. From the great deep to the great deep it goes, gathering its forces, prophesying war. There is a shiver of anticipation in the music as a tempestuous storm seems about to unleash its dreadful fury. Instead, there is a lull . . . and from afar arise ancestral voices, a nostalgic siren song set against a continuous rippling of harps, intermittently repeated or answered by Triton's horns. The music grows louder and faster, strings and wood winds pit against each other in bewildering and wonderful acrobatics. An ever-growing chorus of acclaiming voices takes up the unrestrained song, the brass peals forth in shining splendor, the wind heaves madly against the blast, and the waves rise higher and crash resoundingly in a fervor of great festivity as if all the creatures of the water, like steeds galloping at an eager spirited pace, were holding high carnival. The dialogue of wind and wave is of cosmic things, whatever be the puny destiny of man.[15]

The immemorial fascination lures and enthralls and terrifies, so that one is almost tempted to fancy that the wet winds and tossing spray and the inexorable depths and reaches are but the magic casements of the dreaming mind.[16] Yet beneath these elusive and mysterious overtones, the reality of the living sea persists. The chorale returns to a jubilant climax till at last, wavering as the waters themselves, an uncommitted curious melody ends the perennial tale of the sea.

- La Mer; Jeux; Prelude a l'apres-midi d'un faune
  EMI Dig. CD-EMX 9502; TC-EMX 2090 [Ang.CDM 62012]. LPO, Baudo $$

- (i) Berceuse heroique; (ii;iii) Danses sacre et profane; (ii) Images; Marche ecossaise; La Mer; (ii;iv) Nocturnes; (ii) Prelude a l'apres midi d'un faune; (11;v) Premiere rhapsodie
  Ph Duo 438 742 (2) Concg O (i) Eduard van Beinum; (ii) Haitink with (iii) Vera Badings; (iv) womens Ch of Coll Mus.; (v) George Pieterson $

Exhibit 46   Debussy: Sirenes from Nocturnes

Three numbers make up Debussy's exquisite set of orchestral nocturnes: *Nuages* (Clouds); *Fetes* (Festivals) and *Sirenes* (Sirens). The title *Nocturnes* was intended to have a more general meaning, a diversified impression. The *Sirenes* movement has the collaboration of a female chorus.

"When one has just heard *Sirenes*, one is tempted to sigh."[17] It is the third Nocturne, *Sirenes,* that describes the sea and its endless rhythms on a rich star-cool night. There, amidst the billows silvered by the moonlight, a mysterious song of the sirens beckons. It is their voices that do much of the silvering.[18] About their melodic line the orchestra billows and casts up arabesques of spray. All is undulant, spacious, airy. The music arises largely from two notes that rise or fall with something of the fixity of waves, yet seem as changing as the incessantly moving sea.[19] Rhythmically altered, the motive of rising or falling moves against backgrounds of varying lights and shadows.[20]

There are no words to this strain, no meaning to the voices, no witchcraft or exorcism here, just a pure sound that laughs and passes. To each listener the sirens sing languidly of whatever might lure and seduce him. Happy or disillusioned, wild with desire or weeping, the sirens are ever calling, ever calling . . . thcy disappear little by little in the distance, but they carry away with them their precious torment, an infinite melancholy, an eternal ardor, a ravishing tenderness in which the most sensual caress seems to be only the shadow of the intoxication of the soul.[21]

- (i) Berceuse heroique; (ii;iii) Danses sacre et profane; (ii) Images; Marche ecossaise; La Mer; (ii;iv) Nocturnes; (ii) Prelude a l'apres midi d'un faune; (11;v) Premiere rhapsodie
  Ph Duo 438 742 (2) Concg O (i) Eduard van Beinum; (ii) Haitink with (iii) Vera Badings; (iv) womens Ch of Coll Mus.; (v) George Pieterson $

Exhibit 47 Mendelssohn: Fingal's Cave, Op 26

Off the western coast of Scotland, in the Hebrides, lies a small, wind-swept island called Staffa, scarcely a mile in length, and half that at its greatest breadth. The island rests like a table upon a wall of colored and strangely formed stone columns and, on its southeastern corner, opens one of the most marvelous of nature's exploits: Fingal's Cave. Some say that, in ancient times, the Highlanders called it the Cave of Finlin after the Celtic giant who allegedly built the Giant's Causeway many miles away so that he might step over from Ireland to Scotland without wetting his great feet.[22] Still others have heard of it as the Cave of Music because of the monotonous murmurs of the waters as the tide flows in and out in calm weather. When the seas are heavy, the huge waves pound through its caverns with enough force to shake the earth and fill the air with its thunder.

There is a story that the twenty year old Felix Mendelssohn Bartholdy (1809-1847) returned to the house of a Scottish family after an unforgettable visit to Staffa. In a tossing skiff with the hissing sea close beside, he and a friend had seen this largest and most wondrous of caverns. Scenery had always impressed his romantic imagination and, as he sat in the skiff, a melody was already beginning to evolve in his restless mind. What a vivid and splendid impression this had been: The red, maroon and brown basalt pillars lining the sides of the caverns, smothered with green and gold lichen, the surging sea and waves resounding in the rocky caves, the harsh cries of the sea gulls, the sharp smell of the damp salt air mingled with the aroma of seaweed, and the melancholy soul of the whole barren northern scene.[23] The story goes that there was a piano in the room, and he dashed off the melody. Thus was born this delicate and polished masterpiece, more commonly known as the *Hebrides Overture*.

The overture opens with the main theme played, in turns, by the bassoons, violas and cellos, describing the roll of the ocean waves on the shore at the mouth of the cave. A greater roar of waves surely never rushed into a stranger cavern! The theme expands as it is taken up by the first and second violins, then by the flutes and the clarinets with punctuations from the kettledrums, and so on until nearly every instrument of the orchestra has sung it.

Presently, a second longer and quieter melody unfolds in the cellos and bassoons accompanied by a waving figure from the strings. The two melodies develop and expand, endlessly advancing and retreating like the waters, evoking the radiant clearness of the air as if an unknown, majestic and wild spirit were pervading the caves when the mist is completely dissolved.[24] Somewhere, an oboe rises above the other instruments with a plaintive wail, like sea winds over the seas. But throughout the music, there is no forgetting the constant agitated rhythm of the sea, repeated over and over in the accompaniment. The music reaches a powerful climax as though a storm has brewed up, and then the melodies blend again in ceaseless action and rise to a second climax. The trumpets return softly at the height of this crescendo to announce a return to calm. The opening theme reappears, less somberly now, and the second theme joins in—for its part, less lyrically. The music dies away slowly and quietly to the mysterious strains of the trumpets and flute.

- Overtures: The Hebrides (Fingal's Cave),Op 26; Athalia, Op 74; Calm Sea and Prosperous Voyage, Op 27; The Marriage of Camascho, Op 10; A Midsummer Nights Dream, Op 21; Ruy Blas, Op 95.
  BMG/RCA Dig. 7905-2-RC. Bamberg SO, Flor $$$

- Overtures: The Hebrides (Fingal's Cave),Op 26; Calm Sea and Prosperous Voyage, Op 27; Ruy Blas, Op 95.; Symphony No. 3 (Scottish)
  Naxos Dig 8. 550222; Slovak PO, Oliver Dohnanyi $

Exhibit 48   Rimski-Korsakov: The Sea and the Ship of Sinbad from "Scheherazade"

Nicholai Rimski-Korsakov (1844-1908) had known the sea as a young officer in the Russian Navy. He had been impressed by the brilliant hues of the tropical seas and the tropic skies that his naval ship had traversed as it cruised around the world. From this experience, and an imagination fired by the fantasy of the Arabian Nights, he created a splendid picture in music of a sunlit sea, brilliant as a jewel, on which the Sultana Scheherazade could send forth her fabled boats as she spun a nocturnal web of magic and a thousand and one adventures. *The Sea and the Ship of Sinbad* is the first movement of his tone poem *Scheherazade- After a Thousand and One Nights - Symphonic Suite for Orchestra.*

The story of Scheherazade is well known. The Sultan Shahryar had put to death each of his wives after the first nuptial night. The cunning Scheherazade, however, postponed her execution by entertaining her curious lord each night with one wondrous unfinished tale after another, of magic lamps and genies, harems and eunuchs. Adventure upon adventure continued for a thousand and one nights until the Sultan finally repudiated his deadly practice. The music is descriptive but hardly narrative; there is no connected story expressed in this piece.

151

The introduction opens broad and majestic with a low-pitched musical theme, announced loudly by the orchestra, projecting a sense of the gently rolling spaciousness of an open sea. This bold musical motive, sounded in unison by trombone, tuba, horns, and the wood winds with the strings in their lower pitch, probably represents the gruff Sultan and is, therefore, commonly described as the theme of the severe monarch.[25] There is a brief interlude, and then Scheherazade begins her exotic tale to the rich strains of a tripping harp, her voice, trembling and diffident, rising slowly and expressively in the high florid notes of a solo violin (Scheherazade's theme) as she launches Sinbad's ship on its virgin maritime voyage. The Sultan and Sultana are strikingly contrasted: the former embodied in the conventional brusque rhythm of the whole orchestra, while the latter, a free spirit, is played by the solo violin in highly ornamented free flowing arabesques.

Now we feel the long swell of the heaving restless sea.[26] The movement following the introduction develops from two melodies of which the first, call it the Ship theme, is really the Sultan's theme shifted in rhythm and provided with a rolling accompaniment—it is as though the Sultan were, in fancy, projecting himself on to Sinbad's ship as the story unfolds.[27] The theme is repeated over and over to hold the picture together, but each time with ever-changing tone colors that allow our wily storyteller to paint a magnificent picture of the sea: A brazen sun hanging in a brazen sky, a painted ship upon a painted ocean.

The music almost seems to articulate those wondrous wide-eyed words: "Once upon a time there was. . ." A fabulous canvas in music appears to unfold: strange birds seem to glide overhead, awful shapes materialize from nowhere to move dimly in the green deeps, a shapeless shadow darts swiftly across the sunlit decks, and a short fierce storm rages invisibly in the infinite blue depths of the tropic sky.[28] The string melody is taken up initially by a reedy oboe mingled with the warmer hues of a viola; then it is played on the horns as if a dreamy voice were emerging from a distant fog, decorated by a flute with polished tones that appear as glittering as a dash of sea-spray in the sunlight. The flute sings along with the clarinets and violin. Here is the stuff that dreams are made of; never before was such a ship drawn across such a sea! Finally, the whole orchestra rises up in a surge of storm and thunder like a weary heaving giant as the ship rolls continuously to the gentle accompaniment.

The Ship theme, as it works itself up to become gradually louder, soon alternates with a second melody representing the sea, call it the Sea theme: A happy inspiration of clustered tones played first by the clarinets and bassoon, then by the flutes and clarinet, to evoke the serene calm of shimmering undulating waters. The two themes form a desirable contrast: the low-pitched irregular rhythm of the ship set against the high-pitched perfectly regular calm of the sea. Variety is displayed by a wonderful blending of different tonal instruments. An oboe solo plays the countermelody to the Ship theme echoed by the clarinet, then a solo violin interposes with Scheherazade's song. The violins now take over the Sea theme while the clarinet and flute provide the countermelody. The four themes and countermelodies, the steady underlying beat, and the brilliant interplay of instrumental timbres fuse imperceptibly into a composite and unified whole.

Suddenly, the exotic picture dissolves and the story reappears; the stern voice of the Sultan is heard again and the tremulous accents of Scheherazade go bravely on.[29] The dynamic scheme is very simple; loud (Sultan) and soft (Sultana) as in the introduction, thereafter a softness that repeatedly builds up to a loud and peaking wave only to crash low again, and then die away in gentle eddies. In the quiet calm that closes the movement, one feels reassured that for one additional day, at least, our wily narrator has successfully postponed her terrible fate.[30]

- Scheherazade; Capriccio Espanol, Op.34
  Telarc Dig. CD 80208. LSO, Sir Charles Mackerras $$$

- Scheherazade, OP 35; BORODIN: Polovtsian dances
  EMI CDC7 47717-2 . RPO, Sir Thomas Beecham $$$

- Scheherazade; Tsar Sultan: orchestral suite
  Naxos Dig. 8.550726 Phil O. Batiz $.

Exhibit 49 Wagner: Der Fliegende Hollander, Overture (The Flying Dutchman)

There is an old legend of the sea about an ancient mariner, a Dutch sea captain, who is damned to sail the infernal oceans to the end of time in a spectral galleon with blood-red sails, *The Flying Dutchman*. Every seven years he is allowed a brief landing, in the hope that he would find a woman who can love him to the death and thus lift the curse. When Richard Wagner (1813-1883) composed this overture to his second successful opera, he, too, had been a wanderer. Like the doomed sea captain he, too, sought two things: The rest that comes by settling in one's own homeland, and the peace that can arrive when one has found a faithful wife.[31] The bygone sea tale became for him a very personal experience when he found himself with his young wife in a hazardous and stormy sea trip, tossed about as the only passengers on a small boat driven by superstitious sailors who blamed him as the evil omen that had evoked the inclement weather. Here, amidst the lashing waters, he recalled the legend, and outlined in his head this score.

The music breathes the out-doors; the sweep of the winds, the scurrying of water and foam in an angry sea, and the maritime chorus of a phantom sailor's song brings together one of the grandest of all musical pictures of the sea.[32] This now famous overture is based on two themes of rare pathos and romantic beauty: That of the awful Curse, and Senta's ballad, the song of the faithful girl who gives up her own life to prove her love and free the wretched seaman.

The overture opens with a long-held, tremulous cluster of tones announced by the wood winds and violins, colorless yet strong and fierce as a stormy wind, creating an aura of mystery. Almost immediately, the call of the *Dutchman* (the Curse theme) is unfolded by the horns and bassoons, after which it is echoed by a trombone and tuba as though from far out at sea. Now begins one of the most brilliant storm pictures in music. Fragments of the melody are sounded loudly in tearing discord by all instruments, followed by a rushing ascending and descending passage, the ebb and flow of the wild and tempestuous waters, echoed softly by a viola and cello. The storm spent, the orchestra grows fainter and fainter, till finally nothing is heard but the calm of the kettledrums.

Then, after a pause, arises a new fragment filled with tenderness and quiet sentiment to contrast against the wild and tempestuous music of the storm. This is Senta's song, or the Redemption theme, singing of she who has gone to join him in his entranced unreality, adrift in space and impervious to time.[33] This melody is played in the beginning by an English horn; then an oboe takes the tune, and soon the melody reverts back to the horn. This is followed instantly by an uncertain motive whose melody is played only upon two notes before the Curse returns in the horn to sound a weary song, a wilted tune of endless wandering combined with a fervent prayer for death.

The mood changes, and the wood winds sing a new melody, a jolly sailor's song echoed from the cliffs of the fjord as a stately ship sweeps happily home past the phantom vessel. Haunted by the depths of his own misery, the enraged mariner rides madly into the storm, crashing through the tempest to seek the one who can bring his release, with the sailor's song now plainly heard as a theme signifying unrest.

Suddenly, a ray of light pierces the gloom like a lightning flash. The light comes and goes, and the beautiful fragments from Senta's ballad are heard again, full of sublime sorrow and sympathy, as the mariner steadfastly drives towards it, reaching out for the love that will finally bring salvation and peace.[34] The Redemption theme is delivered several times, a joyous rhapsody sounds as the spell is lifted, and the Curse theme thunders out its freedom in the heavy metallic brass and the full orchestra.

. And just when one believes that the music is about to end, the orchestra tones down for a moment, and lets the wood winds, accompanied by a harp, fade out the Redemption theme softly and gently. The movement, instead of ending loudly, closes softly and slowly in a sort of spiritualized transformation as the unhappy seaman rises from the waves, hallowed and whole, led by his redeemer's rescuing hand to the dawn of an exalted love.[35]

- (iii, iv) Overture: Der fliegende Hollander. (i; ii) Siegfried Idyll, (i, v) Gotterdammerung: Siegfried's Rhine journey; Lohengrin: 9i;ii) Prelude to Act 1; (vi; iv) Prelude to Act 3. Die Meistersinger: (vi; iv)Overture; (vii; viii) Prelude to Act 3 (ix; viii) Parsifal: Prelude and Good Friday Music. Overture (vi; iv) Rienzi; (vii; x) Tannhauser. Tristan: (iii; iv) Preludes to Acts 1 and 3; (vi; iv) Death of Isolde. (i; v) Die Walkure: Ride of the Valkyries.
  DG Double 439 687-2 (2) (i) BPO; (ii) Kubelik; (iii) Bayreuth Festival O; (iv) Karl Boehm; (v) Karajan; (vi) VPO; (vii) Deutsche Oper, Berlin O; (viii) Jochum; (ix) Bav. RSO; (x) Otto Gerdes. $

1   Van Doren, Mark, *The Noble Voice* (Henry Holt and Company, NY, 1946)
2   *Ibid*
3   Downes, Edward, *Adventures in Symphonic Music* (Farrar & Rhinehart, NY, 1944)
4   *Ibid*
5   O'Connell, Charles, *The Victor Book of the Symphony* (Simon & Schuster, NY, 1935)
6   Thomson, Oscar, *Debussy, Man and Artist* (1937, reprinted Dover Publications, NY, 1967)
7   O'Connell, Charles, *The Victor Book of the Symphony*
8   Goepp, Philip, *Great Works of Music* (Garden City Publishing Co. Inc., NY, 1913)
9   O'Connell, Charles, *The Victor Book of the Symphony*
10   *Ibid*
11   *Ibid*
12   Goepp, Philip, *Great Works of Music*
13   *Ibid*
14   Thomson, Oscar, *Debussy, Man and Artist*
15   *Ibid*
16   Gilman, Lawrence, *The Music of Claude Debussy, Musician*, Boston, 1907 (Quoted by Thomson, Oscar, *Debussy, Man and Artist*)
17   Thomson, Oscar, *Debussy, Man and Artist*
18   *Ibid*
19   *Ibid*
20   *Ibid*
21   Suares, A, *Debussy*, La Revue musicale, Paris, 1920 (Quoted in Thomson, Oscar, *Debussy, Man and Artist*)

155

22   Goepp, Philip, *Great Works of Music*

23   Ewen, David, *Music for the Millions* (Arco Publishing Co., NY, 1944)

24   O'Connell, Charles, *The Victor Book of the Symphony*

25   *Ibid*

26   *Ibid*

27   Stringham, Edwin, *Listening to Music Creatively* (Prentice Hall, NY, 1946)

28   O'Connell, Charles, *The Victor Book of the Symphony*

29   *Ibid*

30   *Ibid*

31   *Ibid*

32   Kinscella, Hazel Gertrude, *Music and Romance* (RCA Manufacturing Co. Inc., NY, 1941)

33   Peter, Conrad, *A Song of Love and Death* (Poseidon Press, NY, 1987)

34   Newmann, Ernest, *Stories of the Great Operas* (Garden City Publishing Co., NJ, 1930)

35   *Ibid*

"He is dead, the sweet musician!
He the sweetest of all singers!
He has gone from us for ever...
To the Master of all music,"
                        — Henry Wadsworth Longfellow

11   Death the Leveler

Legend has it that upon having their glorious life cut short by death, the heroes of ancient Greece received as consolation the promise of immortality. At banquet feasts in the pleasant company of other youths, they lived a perennial afterlife of pleasure. But even heroes had to die first before the immortality that was promised to them came true. For the valiant, death was no dread, but a mere passing from one adventure into another. Yet, over the ages, its finality as the end of life and the physical being, of the known and the recognizable, has invested it with an overwhelming significance. Death remains for ever unchangeable: if it is not now, yet it will come! It may be made magnificent as when Cleopatra puts the asp to her breast. Or it may fill the mind with images of horror of an ugly, violent and viciously cruel thing that, like a fierce impersonal beast, kills without passion or feeling, without pleasure or reluctance, simply because its nature is to kill. To some, after the struggles and frustrations of life, it reaches out as a serene and glorious experience, a magnificent apotheosis of man's last and futile gesture. For those left behind, the pain of personal loss, however agonizing or haunting in memory, quiets imperceptibly into an acceptance, a quiet consummation, as the currents of active living and of fresh emotions drown it into the subconscious.

Where, and to what, does the spirit depart? One cannot answer, but listening to the music in the *Exhibits* in this chapter, one must believe that it is to something glorious and serene and comforting. Death may ultimately be beautiful; in his stern and implacable face may lie a promise of deliverance, a facade that appears to be cruel only to be kind.

157

Exhibit 50 Beethoven: Funeral March from Symphony No. 3

The slow second movement of Beethoven's Third Symphony, the *Eroica,* is more than just an outpouring of grief for an individual hero; rather, the movement is an epic lamentation for all mankind. Impersonal as the tomb of the Unknown soldier, it remains a monument to the deathless spirit of man.[1] The poetic concept of sorrow has rarely found such musical characterization as in this Funeral March with its high and proud grief, its infinite shades of pathos that appear as the movement progresses, and its ending that yields to a tragedy of Greek proportions, causing the very voice of the orchestra to break. Here, for the first time in the annals of music, was a real, heart-rending human experience.

This movement, where the greatness lies in its exalted tone and its symbolic depth and unity, is a fine illustration of a situation where the melody itself becomes subordinate. In fact, we are told, the listener is advised not to tie one's interests only in seeking out the melody.[2] The simple march-like theme of mourning, broken-backed and dragging, is announced by the violins with a quality of intense feeling and purity of expression that sweeps on in lonely grandeur as it is taken up by the whole orchestra. The marching steps seem to falter as the shuddering rhythm begins, but the tread soon becomes firmer.[3] There is no possibility of misconstruing the message of the music. That agonizing slow beat can only be the terrible rhythm of a march towards the grave. The theme that begins the dreadful march, although first presented softly and sadly, is sometimes uttered with vehemence, as if to push aside the weeping musical creatures that seem to move along with every passing interval of time.[4] One feels an impatience, a resentment towards death, the one obstacle that stands in the way of the noble impulses and heroic designs that life encourages us to feel and undertake, the one enemy that cannot be overcome.[5]

Until we reach the second theme. This new melody is rich in courage and humanity. Here, it seems, is the Hero's own attitude towards death. A serene oboe, succeeded by a flute, and then the violas and cellos, sing a subjective exaltation of the dead Hero, recalling happier times, with the violins humming a simple and placid pastoral with no funereal strain save the beating of the drums. Each musical instrument tries to surpass the other in eulogizing the Hero.[6] This works up to an extremely tense climax that is shattered by a menacing blare of the trumpets accompanied by tramping strings. For a moment it seems that we are lifted away from the objective grief of mourning, the unreasonable and inexorable taking-off of one beloved. But not for long.

Back to the thud of drums the funeral march returns, with the tearful wood winds and violin striking out the dimly familiar theme, sad and lovely and resigned, played in polyphony. All the instruments join in the fateful chant in succession. The broken disjointed fragments march softly, with pauses of silence in between, as these last words of leave-taking and homage get choked by the sobs.[7] The music becomes overwhelming when the basses enter: Here, surely, is the meaning of life and death, the Resurrection Day and the life thereafter.[8] There is a lull for a moment with the wailing of violins, then the brass and strings crash in thunderously, the sullen bass reenters to mutter its compelling message ceaselessly until, quite suddenly, one hears in its climax the original funeral melody, marching in the wood winds almost like an afterthought!

Where the end might be there is again a sudden lull. A new song arises with a new tune suggesting a transfiguration of the Hero. The ending itself is solemn and subdued save for a single triumphant burst at the last.

- Symphony No. 3 (Eroica); Symphony No. 5
  Archive Dig. D 106963, Orchestre revolutionnaire et romantique, Gardiner $$$

- Symphony No. 3 (Eroica); Overtures; Leonora Nos. 2 & 3
  EMI mono CDM7 638552-2. Phil. O, Klemperer $$

Exhibit 51 Strauss: Death and Transfiguration (Tod und Verklarung)

It was the discovery of Wagner's *Tristan und Isolde* that inspired the twenty six year old Richard Strauss (1864-1949) to compose this symphonic poem describing the last hours of a man who had striven all his life for the highest ideals. After the music had been written, a vague explanatory poem was appended to it as a program. In a bare and dimly lit little room, it said, a very ill man wrestles despairingly with Death, trying to overcome its power by his will to live. Exhausted, he sinks back into his bed, his wan face damp with the dew of death, distorted by the memory of past agonies. In a frenzied fever, he sees his life pass before his mind's eye: The dawn of childhood and the ripeness and passion of youth, the relentless but unfulfilled fight to shape all his ideas and ideals to embody an almost sacred perfection, despite the seemingly endless barriers that a cold world had knowingly piled before him. And now on his deathbed, the one ideal that he had sought with his heart's deep desire—that one high purpose of shaping all he saw transfigured into a still more transfigured form—he still seeks in his death sweat. "Then clangs the last stroke of Death's iron hammer breaking the earthly body in twain, covering the eye with the shadow of death." The soul leaves the body, but only to discover, finally, in the eternal cosmos, the magnificent realization of the ideal that he had so yearningly sought here below: deliverance from the world, and transfiguration of the word.

There is a grisly suggestion of failing heart beats in the strange rhythm that begins the prologue, very softly, in the strings.[9] Here is an indescribable suffering, expressed by gloomily descending pairs of chords, with a hopeless cry above in the flutes. A brief but lovely musical fragment sung wistfully by an oboe introduces the motive of childhood, and of the remembrances of things past.

But this respite proves to be deceptive. Death pounces in and pommels powerfully upon the exhausted frame of the dying victim who, in turn, strikes back with a sudden renewed energy. A whirling frame of musical phrases ensues, paroxysms of warring themes rise to a climax, intermittently broken by a wistful melody, or dominated by a harsh intruding chord. Suddenly, there arises in the murmuring strings, to one's great relief, the serene intimations of the great theme of transfiguration. A blissful melody sings a full song that is often disguised as a dance. After a short intervening tune, the hymn-like melody returns, only to be rudely arrested by a fearful discordant chord. But the melody returns with a greater energy to carry the music through to a joyous mood.

The birds of evil omen seem to withdraw for the moment, and in this brief and joyful respite, the poor victim dreams once more of a boy's happiness, sung by a harp and the wood winds. But the deathly struggle resumes; past furies are like nothing compared to the dreadful turmoil that now rages through the orchestra.[10] Harsh trombones and booming drums announce the dark powers, the music rises swiftly and, as eerie as the chilled night wind, the man's spirit departs to the loud and solemn metallic clang of the gong.

Now, hardly dimmed in mood, the music turns suddenly into a phase of languorous passion set in the rich and sweetly vibrant sounds of the strings and a pulsing harp. The music rises and falls, and then soars again in the path of an endless melody, returning to its own line of flight, playing as it were with its shadow, catching its own echo in the ecstasy of the chase. A clarinet and the strings call in the theme. The glorious music of liberation and transfiguration now takes full form in the majesty and power of the brass to reach eloquent heights of splendor, and attain a spiritual exaltation that lies beyond the description of words. Victory is here! A triumphant shout dispels all doubt and fear. All the former themes sing anew, merging the tale of their strife into a recurring verse of united bliss. The movement ends in the gentlest whisper of slow vanishing echoes, with all the gladness of an enchanting dream.

- Death and transfiguration; Metamorphosen for 23 solo strings
  DG Dig. 410 892-2. BPO, Karajan $$$

- Death and transfiguration; Sinfonia domestica Op. 53; (ii) Salome's dance of the seven veils
  Sony SBK 53511, (i) Cleveland O, Szell; (ii) Phd. O, Ormandy $

Exhibit 52 Berlioz: March to the Gallows from Symphonie Fantastique

It was his turbulent passion for an Irish Shakespearean actress, later to become Mme. Berlioz, that inspired the incorrigibly romantic, twenty seven year old Hector Berlioz (1803-1869) to compose the autobiographical *Fantastic Symphony*. Its five movements represent episodes in the life of an artist. A young and desperately lovesick musician has taken an ineffectual draught of opium which brings, not death, but the strangest visions of desires. He plunges into a twilight state of trance where his sensibilities and memories find expression in extraordinary musical imagery. His Beloved One takes the form of a melody, an *idee fixe*, which he hears everywhere, ever returning to haunt his mind. He dreams a full cup of final agonies as he believes that, in a fit of impassioned love, he has slain his Beloved, that he has been condemned, and is now being led to his execution.

This is a death march of unrelieved tension and gloom, complete with the solemn doom of the funereal tramp, the fatal ring of the death-song, and the sad terror of an overwhelmed chorus.[11] Four muted kettledrums set the grueling pace for this sinister procession. The tumbrel starts to roll to the strains of the cellos and basses through a jeering, blood-thirsty crowd that has gathered for the spectacle. The procession advances in measured steps, and the orchestra bursts into a brassy march in an unmatched splendor of sound, with the blaring march tune played by the wood winds, intermittently grim and somber, intermittently majestic and brilliant, interrupted by sudden dramatic outbursts from all the instruments.

161

Presently, as the boisterous outburst from the crowd rises to an ugly climax, the hero mounts the scaffold. The melody of the Beloved appears, an *idee fixe* played by a solo clarinet and followed by the brass. For one brief moment there is a sudden ray of hope for a love that is revived, a flame rekindled . . . the drums roll, only to be cut short by the descent of a sharp chord, followed by a thud of plucked strings as the death-stroke falls. The head bounces audibly to a plucked note in the cellos and doublebasses, and drops into the basket while the rest of the orchestra looks on.[12]

• Symphonie fantastique; Overtures: Le Carnaval romaine; Le Corsaire; Harold en Italie: Symphonie funebre et triomphale
    Ph Duo. 442 290-2 (2) Nobuko Imai; John Aldis Ch. LSO, Sir Colin Davis $

Exhibit 53   Mahler: Andante; Adagio from Symphony No. 10

The image of a song arrested in mid-flight as the pen finally comes to rest in the master's lifeless hand has always clothed a composer's last unfinished work in a powerful ethereal aura.[13] There is a haunting intensity of expression that pervades such music, a tragically moving and noble epitome of farewell that often expresses an exceptional desire to live on, and to enjoy nature and the world to its depths.[14] It was in the midst of life that Gustav Mahler (1860-1911) was told that he had but a little more time to live. And in this final work he poured out his tortured, introspective, sensitive soul. It is a death-song haunted by profound regret and, perhaps, of too conscious an awareness that the past that he had loved, and his values and his sensitivities, were disintegrating with him irretrievably into oblivion.[15] The pages of this manuscript are strewn with marginal notes expressing the agony of leave-taking, the anguish that lurks behind all last farewells. "Have mercy! Oh, Lord! Why has thou forsaken me?" he exhorts. The last tormented fragments he addresses, with remorse, to his much neglected wife, "Almschi, to live for you, to die for you. . ."[16]

Mahler died at the age of 50 and all Vienna mourned. The city that had so cruelly attacked him and driven him away, and had found his music bizarre, now bemoaned belatedly that her noble son and his originality no longer served mankind. Two movements were performed posthumously in Vienna in an orchestral adaptation scored by his then son-in-law, the composer Ernst Krenek (to whom this book is dedicated).[17]

But it was not until 1960 that, at the request of his surviving widow Alma, the symphony was completed by Deryck Cook. The complete version was heard at an unforgettable performance in 1964.

The music begins in an aura of deep regret and soul-searching nostalgia haunted by a feeling of impending doom. Solo violas open the movement with a long, searching, somber theme, a wistful and lonely melody, which forms the unifying base or motto for the entire work. This leads directly to the principal melody, ever more achingly expressive, taken up by the soaring violins. The somber theme is now extended in vibrant and passionate arches, embroidered with anxious-sounding trills and plucked strings. Then it returns in its original solitude, and the whole pattern is repeated. And so the movement continues, the theme and the initial viola motto interacting more closely in an unresolved tension, growing louder until, with the full flood of the orchestra, it explodes into a mighty chorale as if the iron gates had slammed shut!—one of the most vivid evocations of death in all music. It is as if all the instruments have been suddenly transformed into a single organ of solemn and majestic pronouncements, culminating into a deafening outburst, in turn surmounted by a piercing trumpet.[18] The entire orchestra throws itself in distraught into a chorale, with shrieking clusters of instrumental tones pitted against blasting notes from the trumpets. From this great crises emerges a majestic hymn for the brass, unfolded with great splashes from the harp and tripping strings. The movement closes in a state of serene calm, wistful and resigned, with fragments of the main melody disintegrating into a poignant farewell silence.

- Symphony No 10 (Unfinished; Ed. Deryck Cooke);— SCHOENBERG: *Verklarte Nacht*
  Decca Double Dig 444 872-2 (2) Berlin RSO, Chailly $

Exhibit 54 Berg: Allegro - Adagio Concerto for Violin and Orchestra

Alban Berg (1885-1935) was deeply moved when he received the news of the terrible death of his devoted young friend, Manon Gropius, the eighteen year old daughter of Alma Maria Mahler. Throughout her brief life, the beautiful girl had struggled against the ravages of infantile paralysis with heroic calm and courage. Now, a devastated Berg worked feverishly to create for her a fitting memorial, a requiem, expressed in the form of his first and only violin concerto, on which he inscribed "To

163

the memory of an Angel." The composition is in two movements: the first celebrates the happy memories, the natural cheer and gaiety, of the brief life of Manon, while the second depicts, in music, her tragic death and her final deliverance to heaven. The Concerto proved to be Berg's own requiem: he did not live to see it performed.

The second movement expresses the tragedy. The music begins vigorously with frequent fluctuations in rhythm representing the growing struggle with death.[19] A sharply syncopated beat accompanies the death motif that ends in a climax. Now follows the Lutheran chorale *Es ist genug!* which is striking not only for its words ("It is enough Lord, if it be Thy will") that embody the struggle between fear and hope in the face of impending death, but the violin solo seems like an elegy for the loss of Manon. Two variations of this theme follow, and at their end the violin ascends serenely, perhaps symbolically, in a final tranquil statement while the rest of the orchestral strings descend into the depths.[20] In the closing section a folk song, known well to Manon and characteristic of the peasants in the Alps, recurs, cemented by the chorale: the human soul has found eternal peace and salvation.

- Violin concerto; BLOCH: Violin concerto
  EMI CDM7 63989-2, Sir Yehudi Menuhin, BBC SO, Boulez $$

- (i) Violin concerto; Lyric suite: 3 pieces; 3 pieces for orchestra
  DG 439 435-2. (i) Szernyg, Bav BSO. Kubelik (ii) BPO, Karajan $

1   Siegmeister, Elie. *The Music Lover's Handbook* (William Morrow and Co., NY, 1943)
2   Goepp, Philip, *Great Works of Music* (Garden City Publishing Co., NY, 1913)
3   Downes, Edward, *Guide to Symphonic Music* (Walker & Co., NY, 1981)
4   Goepp, Philip, *Great Works of Music*
5   O'Connell, Charles, *The Victor Book of the Symphony* (Simon & Schuster, NY, 1935)
6   Hurwitz, David, *Beethoven or Bust* (Anchor Books, Doubleday, NY, 1992)
7   Siegmeister, Elie. *The Music Lover's Handbook*
8   Goepp, Philip, *Great Works of Music*
9   O'Connell, Charles, *The Victor Book of the Symphony*
10   *Ibid*
11   Moore, Douglas, *From Madrigal to Modern Music* (W W Norton, NY, 1942)
12   The Story of Great Music. *Music of the Romantic Era: A Listener's Guide to the Recordings* (Time-Life Music, 1966)
13   Downes, Edward, *Guide to Symphonic Music*
14   *Ibid*
15   *Ibid*
16   *Ibid*
17   Krenek, Ernst, *Gustav Mahler* (Greystone Press, NY, 1941)
18   Gartenberg, Egon, *Mahler, The Man and his Music* (Schirmer Books, Macmillan Publishing Co. Inc., NY, 1978)
19   Downes, Edward, *Guide to Symphonic Music*
20   *Ibid*

> "Hell is full of musical amateurs: music
> is the brandy of the damned."
>
> — George Bernard Shaw

12 To Hell and Back

The ancient Semites pictured the world as a big, three-tiered house where the lowest part consisted of a great cave, a dark and silent place, that housed the dead and the infernal deities. To the Greeks, the universe was made of concentric spheres where the innermost region, deep inside the ground, was hell. The medieval world saw it as the place of lost souls after death, a huge funnel-shaped pit running down to the center of the earth. Ever since the acceptance of sin and the deepening possibilities of evil within the soul, the vision of man has pictured a place of punishment where sinners remain fixed forever in the depravity that they have obstinately chosen. Here, the soul reduces itself to a condition predicated by its stubborn determination to evil, and suffers the torment of its own perversions.

The sights and sounds of hell where tortured souls must live and cannot die, the stories and legendary personages associated with the netherworld, and the allegorical images that they have invoked about the disordered desires that lurk deep within the hidden places of the self, have inevitably fired the imagination of composers. After all, what can be better suited to resound the sighs, plaints and voices of the deepest woe than the rich tonal tapestry of the orchestral voices. Presented here, in this music, are strange languages and horrid cries, accents of grief and wrath, voices deep and hoarse, with hands clenched in despair, making a commotion that whirls forever through the air of everlasting gloom. Here is the picture in music of a dungeon horrible on all sides round, a great furnace flamed, yet from those flames no light emerges but rather an eternal darkness. Here burns a brimstone sea of unquenchable boiling fire and stinking pitch, where knotted whips of flaming wires, like fiery snakes, strike upon the tortured souls. Here is the music depicting a region of sorrow and doleful shades, where peace and rest can never dwell, and hope never comes; only torture without end from which there is no escape.

165

Exhibit 55 Sibelius: The Swan of Tuonela[1]

Deep in the bowels of the earth, it has been said, lie the measureless caverns of Tuonela, surrounded by the nine sunless seas and a river. Across these dark waters the cursed soul must pass to seek entrance to the cheerless shades of the underworld. And upon the black subterranean river moves the sacred swan, lone and forlorn, singing her strange wild song, floating majestically amidst the deadly craggy banks, flapping her great dark wings above the eternally silent whirlpool. But there is no bitterness in her mournful and pensive music, no glowering rage or rancor; just a sad and brief melancholic lament—chanted loudly, chanted lowly—sung for some passing bloodless soul pausing on his way to Tuonela.

The haunting, blood-freezing strains of the swan's terrible song of loneliness rises cold and clear in the piercing stillness in the dark tones of an English horn, as she floats through the mists and shadows evoked by the strings and the distant rumblings of a bass drum. Now and again, its melody is answered by a phrase from a cello or viola, perhaps a farewell sigh of some poor soul passing on to Tuonela. There is a lull, and then a muted horn echoes fragments of the melody again with an excruciating poignancy. The strings reach soaring heights of soul-wrenching intensity and magnificence only to sink and sigh through the viola and cello. The violins emit an eerie soft brilliance as the swan, with heaving breast, sings once again to bring the short movement to a mystic close in the sighing phrases of a cello.

- Legends: The Swan of Tuonela, Op 22/2; Finlandia, Op 26; Kuolema: Valse triste, OP 44; Tapiola, Op 112
  DG Dig. 413 755-2 , BPO, Karajan $$

Exhibit 56 Liszt: Inferno from A Dante Symphony

Ever since his readings in Dante with Marie d'Agoult during their young idyllic years together, Franz Liszt (1811-1886) drew from the world of the *Divine Comedy* a spiritual sustenance without which his life would have been much the poorer. The *Divina Commedia,* perhaps the greatest Christian poem of all time, embodied the basic human values in the same terms in which he had based his own philosophy of the meaning and purpose of the world—the ideal of love, the guidance of the artist (Dante) through life by the power of philosophy and reason (Virgil), the progress of man through Hell and Purgatory to temporal felicity and spiritual freedom on earth, and a glimpse of the beatific vision and an intimation of eternity.[2] In this music Liszt realized a reality of passion and an agony of remorse akin to the essence of pagan poetry; here is a musical strain that reflects an inner truth rising, from hopeless woe, to a chastened worship of the light.[3] Verse after verse has its precise music in this tonal picture-book: the shrieks of the damned, the dreaded inscription of the infernal portals, and the sad lament of the lovers. The *Dante Symphony* was dedicated to Richard Wagner.

The music begins with an ominous motive blared out loud and dark by the trombone, thrice repeated to announce the dreaded three lines of the inscription on the portals of Hell: "Through me you enter the city of sorrow,/ Through me you pass to eternal pain,/ Through me you reach the people that are lost." A rising phrase in the low brass and strings is accompanied by crashing chords, and still in higher chant the horns and trombones blast out the fatal doom in the last line of the legend of the portal, "Abandon all hope, ye who enter here." Over and over in grim and hope-destroying monotones the crashing chords persist, accompanied by grand descending sweeps of the tremulous strings. A sigh motive rises after the enunciation of the curse, again and again in passionate gusts like a madrigal of woe. In winding sequences it sings a new melody in a more regular pace. The music grows wilder, still following the tune of the song, and rises to a towering height. Furious and barbaric chords, grating dissonance, weird cries, and thundering tones of the brass utter the horror and suffering of the damned, amidst which the curse theme appears with literally "damnable iteration."[4]

Suddenly, in the midst of all this din there is a lull. To the tinkling of harps and the light waxing of strings, and the smoothing tones of flutes and muted horns, a solo clarinet sings expressively the words "There is no greater sorrow than to be mindful of the happy time in misery."[5] To this an English horn replies, and the instruments join in a dialogue which tells the mournful fate of Paolo and Francesca de Rimini. The wood winds question plaintively, the strings and harp answer in another phrase of lament, and then the harp and the mellow English horn sing out the words again together.[6] Other voices join in: the lower strings, a whisper between a harp and two violins, and then, with rising passion, the refrain spreads to the wood winds and the strings, one group answering the other.

Swirling strings usher in a new scene in this world of shades. The blasphemous and mocking laughter resounds in the tones of a harp, the furious frenzy returns, and the sounds rise to a din again. Somewhere there emerges a new sullen note, a dull martial tripping of the drums with demonic growls.[7] The sigh motive returns, but is perverted in humor. The low wood winds and strings utter a chorus of blasphemous mockery, the orchestra falls into its former chaotic song amid demonic cacophony, and the music plunges into a nightmare of groans.[8] And in the sighing strain there arises the chant of inexorable fate. Mockery yields to a tinge of pathos, and the whole orchestra ends the music in a blasphemic climax, with a sense of almost majestic resignation, an apotheosis of grief.[9]

- Dante Symphony; (ii) Dante Sonata
  Teldec/ Warner Dig. 105807 , BPO, Barenboim, (ii) Barenboim (piano) $$

Exhibit 57 Tchaikovsky: Francesca de Rimini

"One day, for pastime, we read of Lancelot, how love constrained him. We were alone, and without all suspicion. Several times that reading urged our eyes to meet, and changed the color of our faces. But one moment alone it was that overcame us . . . That day we read in it no further." So Francesca de Rimini recites to Dante the true story of the fateful lovers, and the cause of her fate in the second circle of Hell where punishment is meted out for sins of the flesh. Just as they were driven by the storms of passion during life, so now must they, she and Paolo, be eternally tormented by the cruelest winds of an infernal tempest under a dark and gloomy air. Moved by his reading of this story in Dante's *Divine Comedy*, and inspired to some degree by Dore's drawings of the eternal tempest, Peter Ilyich Tchaikovsky (1840-1893) conceived an opera. But a poor libretto made him abandon the idea, and he cast his music in the form of this fantasia.

"Leave all hope behind, all ye who enter here." The movement opens grimly, intended to recall the dreaded inscription over the gateway to Hell. Sinister harmonies in the brasses depict the terrors of the underworld. A progressively descending march-like step in the bassoons, trombones and tubas lead, step by step, to the depths of the Inferno. The strings play a complex passage against a background roll of thunder by the timpani. Then an eerie hush falls over the orchestra.

The flutes and the strings stir up the first gusts of the winds. The orchestral sounds increase harshly as the storm builds up and the whole mass of instruments breaks out to paint a terrifying panorama of the Second Circle of Hell. The tempestuous music gives an appalling picture of the cruelest winds and of the spectral figures tossed in their wake. It is an awesome scene with its haunting, driving storms, desolate moans, and dread terror.

There is a lull, and then a solo clarinet merges gently into the horns, cornet and trombone that give out the main theme, a tender and passionate melody, announcing the meeting of the fateful lovers and their tragic tale. The theme is repeated in different guises to evoke the growing passion of the lovers: first by the flutes and oboes, then by muted cellos.[10] Presently, an English horn and harp unfold a second theme, again a beautiful melody that speaks of their sudden love. But it is interrupted by the horrible winds that blow softly at first, and then build up with crashing cymbals and rolling drums to a hideous and wailing tempest of the netherworld, above which is echoed the love-song of Francesca.

• Francesca de Rimini; 1812 Overture; Marche Slav; Romeo and Juliet (fantasy overture)
  EMI Dig. CD-EMX 2152; RLPO, Sian Edwards $$

[1] O'Connell, Charles, *The Victor Book of the Symphony* (Simon & Schuster, NY, 1935)
[2] Taylor, Ronald, *Franz Liszt, The Man and the Musician* (Universe Books, NY, 1986)
[3] Goepp, Phillip, *Great Works of Music* (Garden City Publishing Co., Inc., NY, 1913)
[4] Upton, GP & Bronowski, Felix, *The Standard Concert Guide* (Blue Ribbon Books, NY, 1940)
[5] Goepp, Phillip, *Great Works of Music*
[6] *Ibid*
[7] *Ibid*
[8] *Ibid*
[9] *Ibid*
[10] *Tchaikovsky and his Music: A Listener's Guide to the Recordings* (Time-Life Records, Alexandria, Virginia, 1974)

"The stars move still, time runs, the clock will strike,
The devil will come, and Faustus must be damned."
— Christopher Marlowe

13 Faust

What shall it profit a man if he gain the whole world and lose his own soul? Such is the great story of one of the most precious books ever put together: the legend of Faust. The awful problem of evil is its theme. Man is mortal; that is his fate. Man pretends not to be mortal; that is his sin. And sin corrupts the highest as well as the lowest achievements of human life.

The diabolic legend of Faust is a very old one. A weary old philosopher, Faust, is disillusioned by the limits of knowledge and has given up in despair the hope of ever receiving an answer to his question as to the meaning of life. He is persuaded by Lucifer's disciple, Mephistopheles, to sell his soul in return for a renewal of his youth. This compact lasts twenty four years during which period the Devil satisfies all of Faust's desires, but at the end claims his soul.

It is almost certain that Goethe conceived the idea of a work on this subject before the age of twenty. The first part was completed in 1808 when he was fifty-nine years old, and the second part, published posthumously, he finished just before his eighty second birthday. In the first part, Faust falls in love with Marguerite (Helen of Troy in Christopher Marlowe's play on the same subject, Gretchen in the music of Liszt and Wagner), and the book ends with the devil disappearing with Faust. But in the second part, a remorseful and wearied Faust turns his magical talents into doing good things. He is gradually redeemed through his unselfish love for humanity because it was deemed that no matter how much evil a man may commit, his striving for truth and knowledge must help salvage him. As Mephistopheles tries to claim his soul, it is borne away by angels.

The music of Faust is based upon Goethe's great book. The man who has never exercised his soul amidst the profound abysses and shining peaks of its pages is not to be envied. For if he were to taste but a morsel of its offerings, it

171

will envelope him, and then he will for ever return, as men have done for more than a hundred years, to find new meanings and no meanings, and sometimes, even in the no meanings, sublime intimations of wonder, bewilderment, delight, vexation, disgust and disillusionment.[1] For, in his youthful pride, in his doubts and his self love and selfishness, in his remorse and his strivings, in his disillusionment and discouragement, in his roistering and seductions and satieties, in all his vast learning and patient experimentation, in the regrets of his middle life and in the serenity of his Olympian age—in all that—Goethe was the man Faust, and Faust was, and remains, aspiring mankind.[2]

Exhibit 58 Liszt: A Faust Symphony

That Franz Liszt (1811-1886), the complete Romantic composer and performer, should write a symphony on Faust, the complete Romantic hero, seemed righteous and opportune. Faust, the alchemical mystic, astrologer, charlatan and wanderer, had done it all: he had delved in magic, explored the deepest recesses of knowledge, fought the greatest battles, yielded the supreme power, and had exhausted the pleasures of the flesh. Here was a colossal drama involving Heaven, Earth and Hell that Liszt attempted to encompass in music. That he made it his *magnum opus* said as much for Liszt's influence on Romanticism as it did for Romanticism's influence on Liszt. It was Berlioz who had introduced Liszt to Goethe's *Faust*; appropriately, the symphony was dedicated to Hector Berlioz.

Each of the three movements is devoted to one of the three principal characters. Some have referred to the three movements as three psychological phases rather than three pictures or *tableau*. For Liszt saw himself as Faust and Mephistopheles rolled into one, with Mephistopheles being only the negative side of Faust, or "the spirit one denies in oneself." Throughout the work, certain brief musical motives or themes, instead of full-fledged melodies, form the common text of all the movements. This makes it difficult not to ascribe definite intents of meaning in the music, although Liszt chose not to give any programmatic clues.

The first movement, *Faust*, is a portrait of the tormented and disturbed philosopher, bearing the burdens of all humanity. The music opens with an uneasy introduction played by the cellos and double basses, presently touched by piercing wood winds. It seems to suggest the disheartened and gloomy mood of the restless hero who wonders and dreams of the true life outside that his own narrow quest, within the limits of his cloistered cell, has all but closed to his view. The introduction contains two of Faust's principal themes, the first revealing him as a magician and the other as a thinker. The latter shows Faust in a ponder-

172

ing mood, frustrated and yearning for the lost joys of his youth. The two themes alternate, the first growing more restless, the second ever calming with a sense of answered question.[3] A halting sadness is broken by a quicker, active pulse, and the whole music rushes to a big climax arising from the irresistible drive of the first theme.

The movement proper gets under way with the third of Faust's themes, the so-called *Passion* motive, announced by the horns and clarinets. Here is Faust the lover, with his romantic nature reawakened and his passionate feelings aroused through his recollections of Gretchen. New life is infused into the music as Faust's torments and doubts begin to dissipate. This is the heart of the music, and it exudes an aura of contained bliss that is affirmed with a conclusive finality in a march where the theme is wonderfully changed to a mood of assurance.[4] The melody drives along a freer and more extended course, where all the gloomy tinges appear to be dissolved, to reach a brilliantly joyous height. But the joy is short-lived. Stormy moods and indecision, as Faust dallies with the dreadful notion of selling his soul, mark the further development of the music which surges on in a seamless and energetic flow.

But the inner struggle is not yet over, and an interruption by plucked strings brings on another period of agitation. A final theme completes Faust's complex personality as a series of trumpet calls herald a sense of fatalism with Faust as the hero. This theme forms the musical counterpart for Faust's words in Goethe "In the beginning was the deed." The close of the first movement begins slowly with all four themes prevailing. The wood winds and strings sing the first theme again, accompanied by a trembling of the lower strings. This very accompaniment seems to return the old mood of striving. The theme quickly hurries in pace and begins to darken. The serenity is gone and Faust plunges more deeply than ever into the melancholy mood that had enveloped him earlier: the end of the music seems to recall the dim feelings of its beginning.

The tenderness and passionate love suggested briefly in parts of the first movement are given free rein in *Gretchen*, the second movement. Some have claimed that the Gretchen movement is nothing more than a mere succeeding phase of Faust himself.[5] Others have said that Gretchen was symbolic of his idea of women. There is no individual characterization here; just a subjective drama of a single hero.

A brief melodic duet between a clarinet and flute is followed by a duet between an oboe singing against a tripping figure by a solo viola. This is Gretchen's tender song of love, an unmistakable symbol of the Eternal Feminine permeated with purity and innocence. There are suggestions of unnamed longings and a certain restlessness in the keen and pensive voice of the oboe.[6] Later, the song is heard on a wood wind quartet, and then in an amorous conversation between a quartet of cellos and violins. The theme gives way to a charming musical dialogue between the wood winds and strings evoking the famous scene in which Gretchen plucks off the petals of a daisy, saying, "He loves me, he loves me not, he loves me!" Towards the end, the music almost seems to question parenthetically "*Does* he love me?"[7]

A second love theme associated with Gretchen now makes its appearance on the strings alone. This is a passage of intense beauty in which the music becomes increasingly sensual as Gretchen becomes more and more aware of her overwhelming physical desires. The strings sing of a passion not only awakened, but also returned and realized. In the central part of the movement, the Faust themes are developed in a new web of metamorphosis, rising in an ecstasy of passion and dying away in gentle content, as if he has found in Gretchen all that he had been longing for. Notably, the very first opening theme of Faust is excluded from this reminiscence thus suggesting that this first restless, stirring and wandering music is free of the thought of woman. But the sweetness and purity of Gretchen are victorious in the end. Gretchen's themes are recapitulated without the "flower" episode, and a final section recalls Faust's heroic theme showing Faust's fulfillment in happiness, peace and contentment.[8] The gentle simplicity of both the Gretchen themes belie the fact that they will later become transformed into the great Redemption themes in the Chorus that ends the music.[9]

The third movement, *Mephistopheles*, is the most ingenious. Since the Devil is a spirit that always denies, one that cannot create but can only destroy, this movement has no theme of its own.[10] Instead, the Devil is portrayed in parodies or denials of the Faust themes which are distorted and cruelly mutilated. Invaded by evil, the Faust themes struggle to retain their identity but are torn to shreds: Mephistopheles jeers, distorts, poisons and destroys in a *scherzo* of audacious and sinister power, filled with cynicism and sneers.

Cellos and basses, interrupted by exclamations from the wood winds and cymbals, immediately introduce Mephistopheles. The main theme of this movement turns out to be a mocking echo of Faust's *Passion* theme. A sudden recall of Gretchen's song from the second movement helps to dispel the evil forces, but only temporarily. Presently, all the Faust melodies, representing different aspects of his character, are drawn into the circle of Hell.[11] The *Pride* theme is the last hopeless victim of the assault. There is an outbreak of demonic jubilation from the orchestra as Hell has a feast-day. The only music that the Devil cannot corrupt is the theme of Gretchen; undefiled, her first theme of womanly virtue and selfless love appears at length on the horn and cellos to create a total change of mood. As Faust becomes aware of what is happening to him, a titanic struggle ensues in which the Pride theme descends and disintegrates through an astonishing progression. A Gargantuan climax is reached as the Devil seems to rock from side to side in scornful mirth, and Mephistopheles returns triumphantly to his eternal emptiness. The movement ends appropriately in a fugue ("flight") of the Gretchen theme as Faust's soul is borne aloft to the strains of the first of Gretchen's melodies.

As Mephistopheles leaves the field discomfited, the music passes to purer heights. Now follows the great *Chorus Mysticus* for tenor solo and male chorus which is introduced majestically by a pipe organ. The music given to the solo voice is a rhythmic metamorphosis of the two Gretchen themes that reappear here as if in heavenly transfiguration, with a harp added as accompaniment. What could not be achieved or enjoyed on Earth is here, at last, accomplished in Heaven. The symphony ends in a mystic and triumphant close, a positive and victorious intoning of the last lines of Goethe's *Faust* extolling Woman and Love: "Everlasting womanhood draws us on high."[12]

- A Faust Symphony
  DG 431 470-2; 431 470-4. Kenneth Riegel, Tanglewood Festival Ch, Boston SO, Bernstein $$

Exhibit 59 Liszt: Mephisto Waltz No. 1 (The Dance in the Village Inn)

Franz Liszt (1811-1886) also completed two short works for orchestra based on Nikolaus Lenau's *Faust*. The first, called *Midnight Passion*, is seldom performed today. The second was the *Mephisto Waltz* whose passion, sensuality and dramatics have seldom failed to create an emotional impact. Its languorous and syncopated melody has been called one of the most satanic and voluptuous episodes in all music.

Mephistopheles and Faust, in their wanderings, come upon a dance going on at a wedding feast in an inn. There is much music, dancing and carousing. Faust is irresistibly drawn to a full-blooded village beauty but is timid about approaching her. Mephistopheles is scornful. Is this the man who has sold his soul but shrinks from a rustic woman?[13] Disgusted, he snatches the fiddle from the hands of a lethargic fiddler and plays upon it a passionately seductive and indescribably intoxicating waltz. The amorous Faust whirls about in a wild dance; in mad abandonment, he waltzes the ravishing woman out of the room into the open woods and, together, they disappear into the night.

After a long introduction which contains a suggestion of the tuning of a fiddle, the two waltz melodies are ushered in.[14] The first is a vigorous tune, dazzling in brilliance and energy, that serves as the motive for the music. The second is an expressively amorous melody that adds a sense of urgency and an erotic effect to the music. The second waltz melody is varied in a number of appearances, with each one being more exciting than the last. The music ends with one of the first cadenzas written for a harp in an orchestral piece.

- Mephisto Waltz No. 1; Hamlet; Heroide funebre; Hungaria; Hunnenschlact; Die Ideale; Von der Weige bis zum Grabe
  Ph. Duo 438 754-2 (2) , LPO, Haitink $

Exhibit 60 Berlioz: The Damnation of Faust (Excerpts)

"This marvelous book fascinated me from the very first moment," wrote Hector Berlioz (1803-1869) in his *Memoires*, "I could not put it down. I read it incessantly, at meals, in the theater, in the street, everywhere." The book was a translation of Goethe's *Faust* into French. For some time thereafter, a terrifying symphony that was descriptive of *Faust* kept fermenting ceaselessly in Berlioz's head, but his first attempt at the composition of *Eight Scenes from Faust* remained unperformed. Years later, some of these original ideas were developed differently in a *Dramatic Legend, The Damnation of Faust*. Three orchestral selections from this four-part oratorio-like composition are the best known; one of them, the *Rakoczy March* is presented elsewhere (see Exhibit 76). None of these excerpts correspond to any events in Goethe's book: indeed, Berlioz felt free to invent his own episodes.[15]

In the second part of this work, Mephisto transports Faust to the flowery banks of the river Elbe, where he is lulled to sleep with a song "Voici des roses" ("Here are the roses"). Faust dreams; the song is transformed into a chorus of fantastic gnomes and sylphs who sing, "Sleep, Faust, sleep". Here, he has his first voluptuous vision of Marguerite as an angel in human form. The scene ends with the *Dance of the Sylphs*. The music is strange and eerie. Above a single sustained note by muted cellos and basses that is held throughout this short piece, a waltz floats by on the violins and violas, with occasional interjections by a piccolo, flute, clarinet or harp.[16]

In the third part arises the *Minuette of the Will-o'-the-Wisps.* The fair Marguerite is in her chamber, disrobing while she sings, as Faust watches, concealed by Mephisto behind a curtain. As her pathetic song comes to a close, Mephisto summons the Will-o'-the-Wisps to bewilder the innocent maid and lull her to sleep. This is followed by a minuet played by the wood winds in a soft ethereal strain that seems to float lightly through the orchestra.

* La Damnation de Faust
    Decca Dig 414 680-2 (2), Riegal, Von Stade, Van Dam, King, Chicago Ch. & SO, Solti $$

Exhibit 61 Wagner: Faust Overture

Eine Faust Ouverture was intended to be the first movement of a Faust symphony contemplated by Richard Wagner (1813-1883). The scheme was abandoned, but the music was retained under its present title. According to Wagner's own account, this magnificent music with all its contrasts describes the soul of Faust at the culmination of his weariness of life, before he has met either Mephistopheles or Gretchen.

The music opens slowly, with an introduction given out by a tuba and the double basses in unison, accompanied by soft rolls on the kettledrums. Interrupted by a demoniac yell, it subsides mournfully into a desolate fragment for the violins in which the main theme begins to take form[17]. There is another crash, and a pause; then the quick movement starts with the violins unfolding the main theme, accompanied by a bassoon and horn. Somewhere, an oboe lets out a powerful wailing tune; then the strings continue alone, with slow steps that acquire a majesty of their own.[18] Here is music expressing the restlessness of the soul, its aspirations, and its struggles with destiny. Here, it seems, is life's burdensome and detestable existence, when death is desirable. When the note of salvation has become a thundering note of judgment, and its echoes have died away under another demoniac yell, the fragments of the main theme return softly once more.[19] The music picks up with admirable terseness, and builds up strongly into a mountain of sound that ends in a climax of solemn tragic power.

Presently, a second theme sails in, a quiet angelic figure that is beautifully expressed by the wood winds. It floats and flies, now and again eclipsed by a stormy orchestra, and then it vanishes.[20] The wailing tune of the oboe reappears, given out by the full wood winds as a final cry of despair, and then the orchestra quietens, save only for the strings which pour out the main theme with a lingering sigh.[21] The music ends with the main theme played very loudly, with all the instruments joining in to reach a very dramatic climax.

- "Beecham conducts favorite overtures, vol.2" WAGNER: A Faust overture; BRAHMS: Tragic overture; MOZART: Le nozze de Figaro; Don Giovanni; Die Zauberflote; WEBER: Oberon; Die Freischutz; BERLIOZ: Le Carnaval romaine; ROSSINI: La scala di seta
  Dutton Laboratories CDLX 7009. LPO, Sir Thomas Beecham $$$

1   Bennett, James O'Donnell, *Much Loved Books* (Fawcett Publications Inc., Greenwich, Conn., 1965)

2   *Ibid*

3   Goepp, Philip, *Great Works of Music* (Garden City Publishing , NY, 1913)

4   *Ibid*

5   *Ibid*

6   O'Connell, Charles, *The Victor Book of the Symphony* (Simon & Schuster, NY, 1935)

7   Walker, Alan, *Franz Liszt: The Weimar Years* (Alfred A Knoft, NY, 1989)

8   Watson Derek, *Liszt* (Schirmer Books, NY, 1989)

9   Walker, Alan, *Franz Liszt: The Weimar Years*

10   *Ibid*

11   *Ibid*

12   *Ibid*

13   Moore, Douglas, *From Madrigal to Modern Music* (WW Norton , NY, 1942)

14   *Ibid*

15   Downes, Edward, *Guide to Symphonic Music* (Walker & Co., NY, 1981)

16   *Ibid*

17   Tovey, Donald Francis, *Symphonies and other Orchestral Works* (Oxford University Press, NY, reprinted 1990)

18   *Ibid*

19   *Ibid*

20   *Ibid*

21   *Ibid*

"From ghoulies and ghosties and long-leggety beasties
And things that go bump in the night,"
— Anonymous

14 The Supernatural

A generous acceptance of the supernatural, and a willing suspension of disbelief, has made the genre of sub-literary horror stories and science fiction retain an avid following even to the present day. The love of the supernatural, the strange, and the picturesquely morbid formed one of the strongest motives of Romantic literature. In their pursuit of all emotional sensation, the romantics did not neglect the netherworld of fantasy, dream and nightmare.[1] The early romantics enjoyed trafficking in the macabre, and a deranged preoccupation with horror and strangeness became one of the mannerisms of the movement. From the visions of the "Opium Eater" Thomas De Quincy to the Xanadu of *Kubla Khan*, from Mary Shelley's *Frankenstein* to the *Murders in the Rue Morgue*, from Goethe's demonology to Victor Hugo's revelations, this literary genre allowed readers who could disregard its superficial absurdities to participate in a process of co-creation, by relating the fiction to their own emotional, imaginative and subconscious lives.

The diabolism so dear to the poets found kindred expression in the musical themes of the times. Composers spun elaborate and imaginative tales of ghost ships and spectral crews, of ghastly visions and the Witches Sabbath, and relished in the creation of weird chords, and terrifying and extraordinary orchestral sounds, as their contribution to capture the combination of horror, irrationality and sexuality that characterized this scene.[2] Whether created in jest or seriousness, they represented an attempt to brood upon the mysteries of existence, to forget the unpleasant realities of the mundane, and let loose the great resources of fancy unfortunately dammed up by common life. Blending terror and beauty, they sought to express in their music the dark and unseemingly evil forces that they believed lay at the core of all living things.

Exhibit 62 Saint-Saens: Danse Macabre[3]

Holbien's famous painting *Dance of Death* shows a grim figure playing a *strohfiedel* (xylophone) to imitate the rattling of skeleton bones. Camille Saint-Saens (1835-1921) originally wrote of this picture in a song based on the traditional story regarding the revels of ghosts on All Souls' Day. But the melody proved too hard to sing and so, with grim relish, it was converted into an orchestral piece that shocked and startled all that first heard it. "Horrible, hideous, and disgusting" screamed the *Daily News* after its first performance in London in 1879.

There are three sections to this movement. The music opens softly, a merest whisper. The magic midnight strokes of the clock, the witching hour, are sounded clear and sharp on a harp and on the plucked strings of the cellos and bass to set the scene. Immediately, the stony vaults in the necropolis fling open and a ghastly grinning confederacy of skeletons troops into the night.[4] Death wryly tunes his fiddle, somewhat out of tune, and after a few notes plucked furtively from the lower strings, an obscene dance begins on the flutes with an aptly cheerless first theme, halfway between a wail and a laugh.

Now follows a busy, bustling song set to the rhythm of a rapid and macabre waltz. It is rigid and mechanical, a shadowy counterfeit of gladness where the sob seems to hang on the edge of a smile.[5] The two melodies of this loud second section offer an excellent contrast. The xylophone imitates the clanking of dancing bones against the tombstones amidst the howling of a chilly night wind; at the same time, an ironic warmth from the strings, a brief lyrical melody perhaps reminiscent of happier days gone by, briefly lulls the dance. But the ghastly music picks up again, and the grim dance grows ever faster, louder, and more abandoned. Fleshless feet slap upon the cold stones, empty skulls swing to horrid shrieks and cackles as Death fiddles his mournful chant that is echoed expressively by the wood winds snatching fragments of the *Dies Irae*—part of the requiem of the Catholic Mass.

The opening notes of the first theme are juggled about in quick succession by the oboes and clarinets, each imitating the other, mingled in the demonic bacchanal. As the frenzy mounts to boiling point, the shrill brilliance of a flute and piccolo are added to the ensemble. To this united overpowering chorus, the brass—horns and trombones—blow the full verse of the song. The mad storm of carousing continues until . . . suddenly, out of the whirling darkness as though from a distance, the horns announce the rosy-fingered dawn, sharp and clear, as it breaks the night sky. The oboes imitate, in high shrill reed, the crowing of the cock.

180

A third section now follows, recalling some of the ideas of the opening section. The party's over: the violins shudder as death packs up his fiddle. There is a last fleeting echo of the opening theme, a brief line of wistful rhapsody unifying the whole musical evening. Two chords plucked furtively on the strings bring the ghostly revel to a close, and the departing spirits reluctantly trudge back into their vaults.

- Danse macabre, Op 40; Carnival of Animals; Suite algerienne, Op 60: Marche militaires francaise; Samson et Dalila: Bacchanale. (iii) Symphony No 3 in C min. Op 78.
  Sony SBY 47655 (i) Entremont, Gaby Casadesus, Regis Pasquier, Yan-Pascal Tortelier, Cause, Yo Yo Ma, Lauridon, Marion, Arrignon, Cals, Cerutti; (ii) Phd. O Ormandy, (iii) with E. Power Biggs $$

Exhibit 63   # Mussorgsky: A Night on Bald Mountain

Modeste Mussorgsky (1839-1881) was twenty one years old, and blessed with an imagination rich in fantasy when he was commissioned to write the music to the first act of *The Bald Mountain.* It was to be based on Megden's drama *The Witch,* and it described a gathering of witches as they practiced their mysterious craft with a pageant of sorcerers. In the *finale,* there was a dance in tribute to Satan. The completed work was never played during his lifetime; after his death, it was revised and performed by his friend Rimski-Korsakov in 1886.

The music opens fast and fierce to the subterranean sounds of supernatural voices played turbulently by the strings against which the trombones, tuba and bassoons thunder a Satanic theme. From the great deep the spirits of darkness appear, followed by Satan himself. The music changes into a demonic dance, a "glorification of Satan", punctuated by strongly marked rhythms in the oboes and clarinets that celebrate a black Mass. The opening theme now returns, fast and fierce as before, with the brass weaving the melody against the rapid passages in the wood winds and strings. The Sabbath revelry begins to a new dance theme, starting in a fairly slow tempo but quickly working up to a frenzied climax. At the height of the orgies, the bell of a village church tolls mournfully six times in the distance. Strings and harp announce the coming of dawn, and the spirits disperse as the day breaks.

- Night on the Bare Mountain (orch. Rimski-Korsakoff);—BERLIOZ: Symphonie Fantastique; DUKAS: The Sorcerer's Apprentice
  Sony SBK 46329; Phd. O, Ormandy $$

- (i) Night on the bald mountain (ii) Pictures at an exhibition (orch. Ravel);
  RCA 09026 61958-2. Chicago SO, Fritz Reiner $$

181

Exhibit 64 Schubert: Der Erlkonig (The Erlking)

The great and mysterious Franz Schubert (1797-1828), whom even his daily companions called *Der Einzige* (The Unexplained), had the most remarkable natural flair for setting poetry to music, thus creating the musical genre called a *lied* (an art-song). He could write four to five such songs in a day, finishing one and straight-away beginning on the next, often even failing to remember one that he had written just a few weeks earlier. The weakest poetry was enough to start his golden flow of melody, and it is amazing how many reams of mediocre verse were actually gilded by his music in the six hundred and thirty four songs that he composed.

The Erlking was based on a poem by Goethe retelling a dramatically descriptive German folk-legend that whoever is touched by the King of the Elves must die. The story goes that a friend found the eighteen year old Schubert enthusiastically reading Goethe's ballad aloud. He was pacing the room, book in hand; he then sat down and, writing as fast as he could, put the song on paper practically in its finished form. Some have called it the greatest *lied* ever written.

The poem involves three characters: the Erl King (a symbol of Death), the father and the child. The music opens to the galloping triplets played by a piano against a rumbling figure by the bass to evoke the eerie galloping of horses steaming through the rush and roar of a night storm. The father holds his sick boy close to him, trying to keep him warm. Clashing dissonant music reflects the terror in the child's face as he sees the *Erlking* with his crown and trail. Rounded, soothing tones by the father seek to allay his son's fears—it is only a streak of mist, he says comfortingly. The *Erlking* sings a soft alluring siren-like strain as if from another world. The cries of the child are abrupt and harrowing as he hears the cajoling phantom whispering promises; the father's reassurance is strong and sonorous: "Hush, my child," he says, "It is the wind rustling in the dead leaves." The *Erlking* wheedles and coaxes, now accompanied by his daughters. The child shrieks louder, the father sees nothing. And the horses continue their incessant galloping. As they near their home, the child's terror grows into a final despairing cry as the *Erlking*, with sudden rage, grasps the arm of the child. The music reaches a dreadful climax, and then a sudden hush and pause—"he reaches home with doubt and dread, But in his arms the child is dead!" Two loud and simple chords end the dramatic song.

182

- Goethe Lieder: Erlkonig, etc. SCHUMANN: Lieder
  Decca 436 203-2 , Herman Prey, Karl Engel $$

Exhibit 65   Berlioz: Dream of the Witches Sabbath from Symphonie Fantastique

In this last movement of Hector Berlioz's autobiographical tone novel, the dead hero (see *Exhibits* 36 and 52) sees himself at a witches Sabbath surrounded by a host of fearsome specters, sorcerers and monsters of hideous forms who have assembled for his funeral. The air is pierced by unearthly sounds: dreadful moans and shrieks of laughter. Above this cacophony arises the *Idee fixe* representing his beloved, but stripped off its earlier noble character and now reduced to a vulgar and trivial gro-tesque tune. This is the artist's revenge on his insensitive beloved, parodying her as an old hag who joins in a macabre orgy with the dead. Bells toll, and the creatures dance to a blasphemous burlesque of the *Dies Irae* (a sacred song played only at the solemn Mass for the Dead).

The movement opens slowly to the sounds of muted violins and vio-las to create a satanic infernal atmosphere. A squeaky high-pitched clarinet pipes in the *Idee fixe*, the theme of the beloved, now transformed into a cheap and raucous vulgar tune played over a dull dance of low drums. The love song continues its full course, but with its cheer blighted by uncanny rages and mad cries given out by the basses. A clang of bells, the symbols of doom, ring in the *Dies Irae*, distorted into a mocking rhythm by the bassoons and tubas. A witches dance (*Ronde du sabbat*) kicks off the grim orgy, its driving rhythm started by the cellos and basses and then taken up by various instrumental groups. The music grows fast and furious, the dance theme and the pitiless *Dies Irae* mingle together in polyphony to crown the hopeless terror that ends the dream. For a dream it is, and there is little need to read the story of the young artist whose ineffectual draught brings, not death, but the strangest of visions.

- Symphonie fantastique; Overtures: Le Carnaval romaine; Le Corsaire; Harold en Italie: Symphonie funebre et triomphale
  Ph Duo. 442 290-2 (2) Nobuko Imai; John Aldis Ch. LSO, Sir Colin Davis $

---

1   Kerman, Joseph, *Listen* (Worth Publishers Inc., NY, 1972)
2   *Ibid*
3   Stringham, Edwin, *Listening to Music Creatively* (Prentice Hall, NY, 1946)
4   O'Connell, Charles, *The Victor Book of the Symphony* (Simon & Schuster, NY, 1935)
5   Goepp, Philip, *Great Works of Music* (Garden City Publishing Co., NY, 1913)

"How sour sweet music is,
When time is broke, and no proportion kept!
So is it in the music of men's lives."
— William Shakespeare

15 The Human Condition

The unexamined life is not worth living, said Socrates, and no composer of music has ever lived such a life. Sympathy and empathy, feeling with and feeling into, have been the basis for a search in the sounds of music for the true embodiment of one's sense of things. The story of life is not about revenues and income, or war and peace, but about happiness and wretchedness, success and failure, suffering and freedom. Humankind, said Epitectus, is destined to die, to be enchained, to be racked, or be exiled. The most personal of such human conditions have been the ravages of aging and the certainty of death. Music can be immortal, but mankind is doomed to a timed existence. Transience is the law of human being. Man is the only animal aware of a lack of finish, and not only is he inevitably vanquished by time, but the complexities of his nature thwart him in his efforts to find his true path. Fortunately, fate can have no power over man himself, the inner man; it cannot control human character under which great deeds are done and genuine greatness achieved.

The music presented here expresses the feelings of frustration, misery, regrets and pain—all the still sad sounds—that must be reconciled in the living soul, and that encumber the brief experience called the human condition. Although there is an expression in this music of a monumental and overpowering external doom and of hopeless supplication, there is also a declaration of sacred faith which is typified in the triumphant joy of the undaunted.

Exhibit 66 Liszt: Les Preludes

When Franz Liszt (1811-1886) was thirty years old, he wrote some music for a choral work called *The Four Elements (Earth, Winds, Waves, Stars)*. Disenchanted by its uninspired words, he recast it into a wordless orchestral piece. A decade later he resurrected this composition for a benefit concert at Weimar.[1] While still searching for an appropriate poetic title to frame his music, he chanced upon the *Nouvelles Meditations Poetiques* of Lamartine. From here he usurped the title *Les Preludes* to which he appended a subtitle: *After one of Lamartine's poetic meditations*. And so, the music that had begun by representing the earth, winds, waves and stars ended up, after various revisions, in symbolizing love, human aspirations, nature and immortality.[2]

Liszt was enough of a romantic to know that these images of man pitted against Fate must of necessity be vague rather than follow a story. However, he did preface this symphonic poem with his own free and rhapsodic program which reads: "What is life but a series of preludes to that unknown song whose initial solemn note is tolled by death? The enchanted dawn of every life is love; but where is the destiny on whose first delicious joys some storm does not break?. . . And what soul thus sorely bruised, when the tempest rolls away, seeks not to rest its memories in the calm of pastoral life?. . . but when the trumpet gives the signal, he hastens to danger's post. . . that in the struggle he may once more regain full confidence in himself and in his powers." Here, then, are the contrasting pastoral and war-like elements that dwell loosely in this continuous piece of music—intimations of immortality, an idealization of love, the slings and arrows of outrageous fortune, a longing for the healing balm of pastoral solitude, and the triumphant return to battle.

The music begins, almost inaudibly, with two plucked notes followed by an ascending melodic fragment on the strings. This introduction leads to a solemn three-note musical motive in the wood winds which, evoking a feeling of impending doom, well may be the "unknown song . . . death." This is repeated by the violins and violas, then again by the wood winds, in varying rhythm and pace until the movement proper begins. The main theme is sounded loudly and majestically on the trombones, cellos and basses. It includes the germinal three-note motive which is now framed by the strings in an undulating tripping figure not unlike a wave.[3]

Two melodies arise that seem to sing of love, "the enchanted dawn of every life." The first is played expressively by the violins and cellos with the germ motive embedded in the melody, while the second amorous tune is sung, rich and warm, by muted violas and a quartet of horns to contrast with the first.[4] On closer examination, it, too, turns out to be an ingenious expansion of the three-note germinal motive. The musical fabric of the entire piece is woven out of these three notes by a process of continuous transformation.[5] The melodies build up with the full orchestra to a passionate climax, only to calm down suddenly into a brief dialogue between the strings and wood winds. This segment ends in an ethereal close sustained by bird-like flutterings in the oboe and the tripping chords of a harp that sound like little bells.

Now the storm and fury "breaks. . . the first delicious joys." The music continues fast and fierce, the strings scurry up and down, and the kettledrums rumble to evoke a tremendous whirl-wind of sound as the brasses blare out foreboding chords of thunder and lightning. It is a "storm where violent blasts dissipate. . . fond illusions." In due time, quiet prevails and the germinal motive reappears in the wood winds.

Following the storm comes the romantic and lyrical " rest. . . in the calm of pastoral life", the sweet quiet of a rural existence. The main melody, touched with the freshness of spring, is anticipated by a solo French horn, and then by a solo oboe, before it is voiced by a clarinet. It flirts gaily between the strings and the wood winds to end in a forceful climax in which the musical motive once again makes an appearance. Suddenly, the pulse quickens, tranquillity gives way to agitation, and the military brasses blast out an anticipatory fanfare—something important is about to happen!

In a lively and martial tempo, the two love melodies return but transformed into rousing battle calls. A complex musical structure ensues, with the bass drums, snare drums and cymbals adding to the volume. All is bustle and stir; in the pomp and circumstance of war the hero recovers his individuality and regains possession of his energy. Here is the final triumph of man, in "complete self-realization and with full possession of his forces" and, with trombones and strings recapitulating the early themes, the movement closes grandiosely in that lustily proclaimed victorious spirit so dear to the Romantics.

- Les Preludes; Hungarian Rhapsody No. 2, MUSSORGSKY: Pictures at an exhibition (orch Ravel);
    EMI CDZ7 62860-2 . Philh. O, Karajan $

- LISZT: Tasso, lamento e trionfo; Ce qu'on entend sur la montagne; Festlange; Mazeppa; Orpheus; Les Preludes; Prometheus
    Ph. Duo 438 751-2 (2) , LPO, Haitink $

Exhibit 67 # Beethoven: Symphony No 3 (Eroica)

The story of the *Eroica* symphony of Ludwig van Beethoven is, by now, well known. A dedicated believer of freedom and human rights, he had intended to call it the *Buonaparte Symphony* because he saw in the young Napoleon a true son of the French Revolution, a modern Prometheus who stood as a liberator of all the down-trodden. But when the *Little Corporal*, as Bonaparte had been affectionately dubbed by his men, displayed the human frailties of ambition and personal aggrandizement by crowning himself Emperor, an outraged and bitter Beethoven ripped off the dedication page of this completed symphony, and renamed it the *Sinfonia Eroica: Heroic symphony, Composed to celebrate the memory of a great man.*[6] Any great hero might be celebrated in this noble music, for into it Beethoven poured his own superb vitality to create a work of rare majesty, grandeur and power that has remained unsurpassed in its sheer magnificence and in its breadth and depth of feeling.[7] Years later, when Beethoven was asked which of his symphonies he liked the best of all, he answered, "The *Eroica*, of course." Posterity, too, has agreed with the composer.[8]

With this symphony, the era of simplicity in music ended. With this masterpiece, the symphony itself burst loose from its former bonds, and abandoned its comparative formalism and restrictions to acquire a new heroic stature. For the first time, music became a human experience.[9] To Beethoven, a leading melody was no longer so important in its traditional use as a beautiful theme. Meaning was more important than beauty; indeed, beauty was merely a means to the chief end of music which was to communicate emotional feelings. Feelings, for him, were at the root of all music and, for their expression, he often found it necessary to break the fetters of form, or ruthlessly violate the sacred canons to shock the ears of his audience, and yet fill them with a sense of vital meaning. He also made a great change in the outline of the symphonic form in the third movement which typically should have been an idealized dance. Beethoven made it a humorous phase but with a sardonic humor, and changed its name from a minuet to a *scherzo*.

Two swift, shattering chords open the first movement. Inevitably, it is not enough for just the rafters to tremble; the whole world must tremble too, for here is an announcement that something on a scale of grandeur hitherto unknown is about to unfold.[10] At once the music takes on the main theme, expressed deeply by the cellos. Moments later, it is picked up more boldly by the horns, clarinets and the flutes. This is the famous theme that identifies the hero, a simple tune not unlike a trumpet-call of Napoleon's Legions, and yet, its deceptive simplicity beguiles the torrential edifice of tension that surges and breaks and beats through the music. For, right from the start, this tune never seems to find a resolution, never appears to find the peace it seeks, but is always struggling to find some solution to its pent-up tension: a never-ending battle, as it were, that lingers on to pervade the entire movement. Perhaps this is an expression of heroic striving, the inner workings of human aspirations. Each new attempt by the melody to find an end, to resolve the suspense, only adds to the pressures that build up like a volcano, ready to explode in a Gargantuan cataclysm.[11]

A second contrasting theme, tender and yearning, is presently unfolded, clothed in a new refreshing glow, ushered in divided between the wood winds—an oboe, clarinet and flute—and the violins. It is not a single tune, but a collection of short ideas. Then follows an uncertain whispering of fragments of the themes. Gloomy, reiterated mutterings of the first theme arise in the bass, growing louder, into which fragments of the light-hearted second melody try to break in fitfully. Soon the whole orchestra is striking united hammer-blows in an eccentric rhythm and with an overwhelming power. Six crashing hammer-blow chords herald the end of the first part of this music; they are followed by a delicate sad phrase in the wood winds, with the violins still sustaining the rhythm that slowly evaporates into wisps of the main theme.

The main theme is now developed to celebrate the range of moods, and the course of events, that have marked the life of the valiant hero. Death is, after all, but a small element as an event, of far less importance than the many thoughts or deeds of an eventful day. The predominant mood is one of joy, at times even a careless irresponsible revel: the joy of one who, in his victories over a universal cause, feels a clear right to exultation.[12] The main theme sets off from the security of its home key, just as a living and palpable being would set off on his life's work. And, in one orchestral tone or another, the theme appears in, and dominates, all the elaborate developments of itself.[13] During this journey, the orchestral voices seem to bombard the main theme from all sides, high and low, like the slings and arrows of outrageous fortune, and surround it with little needling accents: First from the violins, then from the oboe, the bassoon, the clarinet, the flute and the basses.[14] Somewhere, the main melody becomes the subject of a jolly duet between the horns and basses with the other strings humming the rhythm, and then the duet is taken up by the flutes and violins.

In the middle of these musical adventures, a new, almost elegiac, melody appears, heard first on the oboes, and then on a flute.[15] It is an apt diversion, serving to foil any premature return home of the main theme. At times, the development causes the music to depart far from the simple form of the basic theme, perhaps even to wander aimlessly, often softening to a mere hush.[16] And when it seems as though the hero may well never return from his peregrinations, back come the fragments of the main theme like a sudden influx of light, in a variety of tuneful guises. Whether it be in the low rumblings of the cellos or basses, or the gentle rounded mellow tones of a horn, or the penetrating accents of the wood winds, it is the same simple utterance of the main theme, the source of all the life and power of this music, that tries to return. In the final stage of the development, as the music weaves its way home through the sustained chords of the wood winds and a tremulousness of the strings, it is a horn, played softly, that impatiently reasserts the simple theme in its home key.

Now follows a recapitulation of the main theme, first by the cellos, then unexpectedly by a horn and a flute, after which the second theme is recalled.

The final part of this movement ushers in a lovely song, perhaps one that might well be the hero's beloved. A lyrical version of the main theme is played by the horns, the music continues in a long crescendo as the violins enter, then the base instruments follow, and finally the trumpets and horn take over. There is a sudden and impressive lull as the new theme of the development section is recalled briefly, and the music ends in a huge climax.

The second movement of this symphony has been described elsewhere (see *Exhibit* 50)

Neither death nor sorrow has the last word in this music. The third movement, coming in the wake of the solemn dirge of a funeral march, is a welcome relief, boisterous and full of electric vitality. There is no note of the somber or the sinister, save perhaps a suggestion of terror in the very vehemence of this mad delight. Here, it seems, are the feasting, the games, and the celebration that followed the burials of the great heroes of Homeric Greece.

The third movement opens as a long subdued whispering by the lightly played strings that blazes out suddenly into a loud and fierce cry of joy. A merry first melody is ushered in by the violins and an oboe, a colorful and tumultuous tune, with a wonderfully elastic rhythm that urges the flying strings along their tangled way.[17] The tripping voices seem to leap hastily, one over the other, overturning the melodies head over heels, loosing their accent in their mad haste, rising higher and higher in the chasing game, until they all fall together in a headlong rhythm.[18] Presently, a trio of horns leaps out above the music, very like a sustained hunting call savoring the chase, and the whole orchestra answers their sonorous cry. Wistfully the horns repeat their engaging utterance, and there is, for a moment, a note of pathos, a brief sigh in a moment's thought, in the responses of the other instruments.[19] But the fierce joy of the movement returns, the instruments are on their feet again and off tripping as before, and all other thoughts are swept aside in the buoyant momentum of the music that ends in a powerful climax.

There can be no doubt about the unrestrained joyous elation of the fourth movement. A preparatory fanfare by plucked strings opens the movement jestingly, and the sounds grow in sonority and brilliance to rest, finally, on a series of mighty chords given out by the whole orchestra.[20] The first melody is introduced simply, plucked note by note by one set of the strings, starting with the violins and progressing to the bass, while the others dance about with snatches and phrases that seem to fit as well above the melody as below it.[21] To this the wood winds respond in a comic echo—flutes, clarinets and bassoons in unison—imitating each note of the strings. It seems clear that the theme has that peculiar quality of a basic motto, that sense of dark and profound groping for a fundamental truth. The theme continues, giving out two variations, and then the joyous main melody unfolds, the *Prometheus* theme, so called because of its occurrence in the composer's earlier ballet music of this name.

Now follows an exhaustive exploration of this melody in eleven variations. After some clownish horseplay by the strings to which the rest of the instruments applaud, all join into a primeval cosmic dance with the simple tune given out by the basses.[22] Sometimes the melody is played without the bass, sometimes the bass without the melody.[23] Every instrument of the orchestra presents its version, and all along the music rings out the spirit of universal and complete joy. Somewhere, the instruments team up into a humorous fugue, building up the music more broadly and fully, with a definite feeling that the momentum and growth are reaching towards a certain climax.

And the climax does come with a sudden and gigantic power, given out vehemently by the whole orchestra. The melody in the basses seems to be exhausted, there is a lull in the volume and the rhythm, and then the orchestral fanfare returns thunderously, with the theme being carried along furiously in various rhythmic guises. The end arrives in a deafening blaze of splendor and overpowering magnificence.

- Symphony No. 3 (Eroica); Symphony No. 5
    Archive Dig. D 106963, Orchestre revolutionnaire et romantique, Gardiner
    $$$

- Symphony No. 3 (Eroica); Grosse Fuge, Op. 133
    EMI CDM7 63356-2 . Phil. O, Klemperer $$

Exhibit 68 Tchaikovsky: Symphony No. 4

Peter Ilyich Tchaikovsky (1840-1893) was a man of morbid sensitivity, with profound leanings towards melancholia and introspection which, carried to excess, contributed heavily to his gloomy and pessimistic outlook upon life. This melancholia first reared its head fleetingly in his fourth symphony. It is not a work of overpowering despair or desolation; in fact, whatever gestures an unkind Fate makes, now and then, are crushed down and thrust aside with contempt by the superb vitality of the music.[24] Some have wondered whether this is not his real tragic symphony in the true sense where the highest tragedy is not measured by the wildest lament.[25] But there is no question regarding its position at the head of a musical cycle that leads to the fifth and the sixth symphonies. In the fifth symphony, there are indeed moments of poignant grief shadowed by the dark wings of melancholy. But there is also a note of defiance, a willingness to battle against the slings and arrows of an unfriendly fate. It is the sixth symphony, the *Pathetique*, completed a few days before his alleged suicide, that expresses the most abject depths of his melancholia, his abysmal hopelessness, and his intolerable sadness.

The chief motive of the fourth symphony is Fate, that fatal power that hinders one who is seeking happiness from attaining that goal. It is mighty and invincible Fate that ensures that peace and comfort do not prevail, and that the sky is not free from clouds. It is Fate that swings, like a sword of Damocles, constantly over the head and poisons the soul. There is nothing to do but to submit and complain in vain. Perhaps it is better to turn away from life's realities and lull oneself in dreams.

The first movement opens with an unmistakable announcement of the menacing Fate theme by the horns, backed by the bassoons. The brazen and somewhat ominous call of the horns is answered, at intervals, by a vigorous warning chord by the full orchestra. Presently, the chords get less insistent, and a passage by the strings ushers in the main melody.

This delicate tune appears first in the violins and cellos, accompanied by the other strings, with faint interruptions by the horn. The rhythm is particularly accented to give the music its vitality and graceful motion. Presently, it becomes more assertive in the wood winds, backed by a strong and insistent accompaniment by the strings. The mood seems to be one of resignation and peace rather than pathos or tragedy. Gradually, its character changes, and the music rises in passion to a swelling torrent of tonal colors. The wood winds and the strings sections enter in a fierce conversation driven by the powerfully accented rhythm. Each section in turn rears a triumphant climax for the other's entrance; the first, lamenting, leads to the soothing aspirations and hopes of the second which, in the very passion of its refrain, loses assurance and ends in another outburst. But through all the triumphs of these climaxes, one feels a subliminal sadness, a tinge of latent melancholy.

Another tune, somewhat pensive yet hopeful, detaches itself sweetly from the main body of the music. It is sung by a clarinet like a joyful and radiant dream beckoning and promising happiness, and is repeated by a dryly humorous, half-pathetic, half-sardonic bassoon.[26] New fragments of melody mysteriously materialize; two, and sometimes three, melodies are created simultaneously, perfectly blended with one another, and move in a somewhat elaborated polyphony through the wondrous fabric of the music. The soul is now wholly enwrapped with dreams. There is no thought for gloom or cheerlessness. All is happiness! A gentle little song appears again on the clarinet to which the strings supply a diaphanous accompaniment while, from above, the flutes shower cascades of glittering notes to the wood wind's song.[27] But it is all a dream, and Fate dispels it. With all its beauty, there is still a shadow over the picture, a certain complete absence of passion. Fate has deemed that man will be tossed hither and thither by the waves of destiny, until he is swallowed by the sea of life.

Now follows one of the most charming and strange episodes in the music, a hymnal kind of duet involving a solo for strings and the kettle-drums, with contrasting wood winds providing the accompaniment. The definite pitch, the velvety tone, and the inimitable rhythm of the timpani create an aura of almost mesmeric calm, which is soon rudely shattered.

The trumpets begin with a bright tongue of tones, the horns repeat the figure ominously, the rhythm picks up swiftly and, with a rising emotional intensity, all the rhythmic and melodic elements of the music that had been introduced so far blend together to reach a compounded, awe-inspiring climax forged, so it seems, from the combined might of a hundred instruments.[28] Thunderous basses urge the orchestra forward, fragments of melody are reviewed and discarded and then rediscovered in a whirling mass of musical terror and strife. From this chaos, the horn and trumpet leap defiantly out and cast aside all unbidding thoughts; presently, the peaceful and pensive song of the wood winds returns.

As the movement approaches its end, the strange duet between the strings and kettledrums returns, complete with the accompaniment by the wood winds. But the music is more restless now, as if it were heralding some disturbances to come. And come they do, in a sudden and compelling burst of flooding sound and strongly accented rhythms. There is a brief rehearsal of the joyous themes, and the music closes fast and fierce in a climax.

The second slow movement has been described elsewhere. (see *Exhibit* 11)

There are no determined feelings, no exact impressions in the third movement. The mood is intermittently gay and mournful. Here are capricious arabesques and vague figures such as those that slip into the imagination when one is slightly intoxicated with wine, and has forgotten all the cares of life. At first the plucked strings play alone with a gaiety that is just short of exuberance. Then an oboe and bassoon, and presently a clarinet, join in to form a Trio to play a merry tune suggestive of folk-music. Dainty bits of melody are lightly flipped about just like bubbles tossed in the hands of woodland sprites at play.[29] This is interrupted by the brass, except for the tuba, and they play a *pizzicato* theme that is struck by the plucked violins slowly and with very short notes. It seems suggestive of toy soldiers marching across the grass, accompanied by a miniature fanfare by a piccolo. With the wood winds and bass competing for attention, the strings make several false starts and finally run through the whole *pizzicato* (plucked) section again.[30] Finally, all sections of the orchestra join in the revel, competing with each other, tossing fragments of melody among themselves, creating an interesting effect of sounds and colors, with the strings winning out by a shade. The overall mood is brilliant and happier; this time there is no interruption by the summons of Fate, and the plucked strings bring the movement to a close in a light-footed rush of tones.[31]

Mighty cymbals clash, strings and wood winds swirl, and the brass blares to open the loud *finale*. The entire orchestra bursts into a barbaric and vehement display of force, with each instrument bringing out its utmost in dynamic contrast and sheer power. Nowhere in music is there a more magnificent and overpowering beginning. Strings and wood winds rush fiercely, and the brass and drums sound their boldest. After a brief interlude by plucked strings and basses, a first theme is given out by a flute, clarinet and bassoon. It is an old Russian folk-tune that is well-known to the peasants: *In the Fields there stands a Birch Tree.* Go to the people, the music seems to say, see how they enjoy themselves, how they surrender themselves to gaiety, how happy they are.

A little minor tune appears tentatively in the strings, but it is brushed aside by the all-powerful sounds that opened this movement. Presently a new theme enters, rudely altering, by its accents, the current rhythm of the music. It grows more powerful and soon leads to a climax of stupendous power.

The little minor tune soon reenters, and this time the orchestra holds its breath and listens. It is presented in various guises, first by an oboe, then a flute and a horn in sequence, then by a sonorous trombone, the mighty bass, and finally the tearful oboe once again. And all along the strings sneer and make good sport, and presently convert into a musical phrase that leads directly into another overwhelming repronouncement of the mighty music that began this movement.[32]

For a moment, a sadness engages the thoughts of the strings, but the melancholia grows more lyrical as it becomes ornamented with glittering cascades by a flute. There is a pause, and forthright the music breaks into the loud noise of the beginning. First it is the horns that inject a joyous phrase, then a few instruments join in, the phrase is repeated, and then the whole orchestra responds. Rejoice in the happiness of others, the music seems to say. There is a recollection of the revelry of the third movement that plunges deliriously into a furious joy and exultation as the movement closes to the same music that opened this movement.

- Symphonies Nos. (i) 2 (Little Russian); (ii) 4 in F min
  DG 429 527-2; (i) New Philh. O, (ii) VPO, Abbado $

Exhibit 69   Brahms: Tragic Overture, Op. 81

"Brahms is becoming more and more like Beethoven. His latest work is magnificent, although one must perhaps hear it several times before being able to grasp it completely." The great Viennese surgeon and Brahms' confidante, Dr. Billroth, was referring to the Tragic Overture. The composer had confessed to him that he could not resist giving satisfaction to his melancholy nature by writing an overture for a tragedy, one "that weeps" and "can only be called dramatic."

It is not known whether Johannes Brahms (1833-1897) had any special tragedy in mind when he wrote this piece, but it is clearly one of his most moving works. The tragedy in this music is subjective, and not of the world. There is no story here, no program based on any Greek masterpieces; just pure emotion bent into an intelligible and moving form abstracted from material life. Indeed, there is no need of a program for this powerful theme in which the pathos is expressed so majestically, and in which the tragedy has the character of inevitability.[33] Here is Brahms the philosopher, displaying the power of a great mind and the warmth of a great heart, as he considers the endless tragedy of life in the soul-language of the music that he knows so well.[34] In this work, it has been said, one sees a strong hero battling with an iron and relentless fate, passing hopes of a victory that cannot alter an impending and inevitable destiny.[35]

Two sharp chords, and the music launches into an unaccompanied stern and noble main melody stated by the strings. It is filled with an intense yearning and, simultaneously, mingled with an unspeakable terror. This is a song reflective of a great and brooding sorrow. The music rises swiftly in an up-rush of great energy to which the whole orchestra replies in chorus. A dramatic dialogue ensues, with the basses presenting a fragment of the main theme in a progressively loudening series of questions to which the wood winds reply with passionate answers.[36] A slow and sustained dark passage of utter dejection follows, with a lonely oboe sobbing as a solemn horn looks on.[37] But through the solemn darkness a light seems to break in the serene tones of the trombones.

Presently, a sanguine second theme is introduced, an aspiring melody full of passion and comfort, more lyrical and more free-flowing to provide an antidote for the tragedy. Here is, perhaps, the hope for a possible ultimate triumph. It rises to a magnificent and defiant climax, and then the opening music returns, complete with the two chords and the first theme. A short but poignant development of the themes now follows, in which two oboes take up the plaintive rhythm and transform it into a slow and sad little march tune of indescribable pathos. Upon this descends, in muted violins, the solemn message of peace that was earlier imparted by the trombones.[38] Conflict and crisis, calamities and weaknesses, are expressed along epic lines, and seem to beguile the listener into circumstances from which there is no escape. The impassioned second melody follows again, and it rises anew to another proud and defiant climax that paves the way to the conclusion. The music ends quietly, with the trombones silent and the more brighter themes prevailing, as if to say that tragedy is more deeply pathetic in its magnificence than in its gloom.

- "Beecham conducts favorite overtures, vol.2" BRAHMS: Tragic overture; MOZART: Le nozze de Figaro; Don Giovanni; Die Zauberflote; WEBER: Oberon; Die Freischutz; WAGNER: A Faust overture; BERLIOZ: Le Carnaval romaine; ROSSINI: La scala di seta
  Dutton Laboratories CDLX 7009 . LPO, Sir Thomas Beecham $$$

- Symphony No. 1; Tragic Overture; Academic Festival Overture
  EMI CDM7 69651-2, Philh. O, Klemperer $$

Exhibit 70   Liszt: Tasso, Lamento E Trionfo (Tasso's Lament & Triumph)

For over three centuries, as the distant rays of a fading sun have reflected long stripes over the blue waters, the gondoliers of Venice have sung a song by the fourteenth century Italian bard Torquato Tasso. Many had heard this song, as did a young Franz Liszt (1811-1886) when he passed through the city in the autumn of his romance with the Countess d'Agoult. This tragic tune, to which the gondoliers gave a special plaintive quality, deeply impressed upon him the suffering and final redemption of the great poet, whose stormy bouts of insanity had often been manipulated by his enemies to imprison him. Indeed, he had suffered much in his beloved Ferrara. As a genius, he had been misjudged during his brilliant life, but he was eventually redeemed at Rome where he was crowned as poet-laureate. Though his words live on in the songs of Venice like an eternal halo surrounding his spirit,[39] it was Byron's reverential and pitiful picture of Tasso in prison, the poignant grief so nobly and eloquently uttered in his *Lament of Tasso,* that moved the composer to celebrate in music this unfortunate poet's destiny of tragedy and triumph. When Goethe's play *Tasso* was performed at Weimar to honor the centennial of Goethe's birth, Liszt used an early version of this music as a prelude.

The music expresses eloquently the striking contrasts of Tasso's life: his inseparable grief during life compensated by a posthumous glory.[40] It opens with just a strain of the single portentous melody of this musical piece, vaguely reminiscent of an Hungarian folk-song. Uttered painfully by the cellos and double basses, it virtually seems to call up the august spirit of the departed poet that still haunts the warm waters of Venice. There is a tearing anguish in this song, an intense and hopeless grief, that seems to bare the very soul of Tasso's lament. Those smooth and false smiles, the base coquetry that had wrought such dreadful catastrophe in his life, become overtly palpable in the tune. The music quickens as the secret grief of the hero moves towards a fierce revolt, and in full tragic majesty, the bass clarinet and bass cello, accompanied by strings and harps, ushers in the whole dark and noble theme in a panoply of woe. It is repeated by the violins. Here is the very soul of Tasso, his great theme in the old gondoliers' song, tinged in this music with melancholy colors.[41] There is a hint of martial grandeur in the tune, perhaps a latent acclaim of our hero-poet, mingled with the sighs of underlying descending musical tones.

Presently, a new melody sails in on the cellos and horn, an imploring tune with descending chords, that is soon picked up by the violins.[42] The main theme reappears, richer and fuller than before, carried by the brass in stately festivity. Somewhere, the theme opens expressively in delicate harmonies, carried by the wood winds with contrasting broader and more sentimental phrases in the strings. It rises to a full-blown exaltation, much like one that Tasso probably received at the height of his fame when he entered Ferrara.

Suddenly, the music takes a fanciful turn and strikes up a festive dance, a minuet, with its vibrant and enchanting melody joined intermittently by the majestic strains of the heroic theme. From here on, the *Lamento* has closed, and the *Trionfo* claims its rights. One can almost picture in this music our proud and melancholy poet, laurel-crowned, meditating over his masterpieces at the center of a festival feast, while agile dancers flit about him in homage.[43] The noble theme becomes more prominent, the music grows louder and more brilliant, and the former lament returns, but this time blending with the joyous musical moods and motives. Finally, with herald calls from the brass and fanfare by the running strings, the whole song bursts out in a brilliant celebration. Here is the final victory of the poet in Rome, a magnificent exaltation expressed in majestic peals of the main theme played by the wood winds, as the strings and basses echo its transformation from a theme of lament into a song of triumph. The music ends in a revelry of jubilation.

- Tasso, lamento e trionfo; Ce qu'on entend sur la montagne; Festlange; Mazeppa; Orpheus; Les Preludes; Prometheus
    Ph. Duo 438 751-2 (2), LPO, Haitink $

Exhibit 71 Beethoven: Symphony No. 9 (Choral)

Beethoven's last symphony is truly one of the most indestructible masterpieces in the entire realm of art. Nowhere before was his poetic speech so pregnant with meaning; indeed, it is not improbable that he set about composing this work with a conscious effort to surpass even himself. The idea of composing music to Schiller's *Ode to Joy* had occurred to him when he was only twenty two years old. He was forty nine when these early sketches reached their final form. The orchestral instruments, those wordless singers of his earlier symphonies, proved to be pitifully insufficient to express his demonic inspiration and his gigantic energy and power—he was forced to turn to the human voice to unfold the final expression of the cosmic thoughts and emotions that surged within him.[44] Beethoven himself conducted the first performance and, story has it, he was still beating time after the music had come to an end. With tears in her eyes, one of the soloists took the Master gently by the arm and turned him around to the audience to receive a mighty ovation that he could not hear. For, he had been deaf these past twenty years.

This last great work begins with softly played fragmented pieces of music, in particular a much repeated two-note fragment. This is ushered in by the first violins, violas and basses, while the second violins and cellos keep up a soft tremulous accompaniment. There is a feeling of confusion and restlessness, as if the sounds were groping and trying to express something that persistently defied utterance.[45] In this music, it seems, is the great chaos and void before the Creation, that prepares the listener for the vastness of the design that lies ahead.[46] Fragments of melody are snatched hastily from the strings, and seem to fly about like a series of beginnings in search of an ending. Miraculously, these shattered pieces suddenly fall together into place like nebulae condensing to an orb and, in a mighty unison, a bold and austere first theme is shouted joyously forth like a flash of orchestral lightning.[47] The full orchestra strikes an emphatic, brutal chord with brusque impatience to announce that all is finally well in the universe.

The opening fragments are repeated again, and so is the theme. The song is magically different now, a new expression of passion and manly jubilation that seems to celebrate the joy of life and living. And that joy is explored in the music in all its varied depths. Before long, a second theme is ushered in by the wood winds. It consists of a large number of different lyrical melodies that are grouped together in paragraphs of every imaginable size and shape.[48] Somewhere, quite by accident and very superficially, arises a resemblance to the forthcoming theme of the *Ode to Joy*.

A highly concentrated development of the mysterious opening material now follows. The music remains intensely quiet without crescendo, its periods marked by a distant boom of drums and flashes of light from the very low-pitched trumpets.[49] Slowly the main theme gathers shape in a hesitant waxing and waning dialogue between the wood winds. It is a sort of repetitive and frustrating musical pattern of pushing ahead and then pulling back to slowly muster the forces. Presently, the strings, now rather angry and quite determined, start a new drive that they are able to sustain. The music passes to the wood winds that now accelerate the pace. Then all at once, the energetic rhythm bursts out on the full orchestra, led by the timpani with a fierce discord. The music builds up savagely and angrily to a thrilling climax. The energy now abates progressively, until it subsides into an exquisitely plaintive passage played by the whole mass of wood winds, that develops almost happily in its own touching way, like a ray of musical sunshine.[50]

Four abrupt bars of music, and the whole great development, the hitherto almost happy conversational course of events, becomes at once a thing of the past—a tale that has been told. A recapitulation of the entire opening section follows. So far, the opening has been a softly played episode with subtle manipulations of tone to project a feeling of vast and spacious sound. Now the music is plunged in its midst and, instead of resembling a distant nebula, the very heavens seem set on fire.[51] The orchestra crashes angrily into the main theme, no longer in unison, but with the bass rising in answer to a fall in the melody. Each phrase given out by the strings is echoed by the wood winds. All at once, with childlike pathos, the main melody of the joyful second theme reappears. But there is something very terrible about its joyous facade, like the pathos of the messenger in a Greek tragedy who has come with what has the appearance of good news, but which really portends a calamity.[52] In this way, the recapitulation continues, in one of the most flowing and elaborate passages ever written in music. Instead of any abrupt modulation at its close, the music flows on quietly, in a gentle vein of melancholy, carrying a conversation between the fragments of the mighty first theme.

Gradually, the tragic dialogue rises to an impassioned crescendo and bursts into a storm. The whole mass of strings stands hushed and overawed, while the horns softly recall the main theme. The strings take up the tune again as the isolated wood winds respond. The strings continue in a menacing crescendo; neither in numbers nor in tone do the wood winds make the slightest effort to be heard. Indeed, there is something peculiarly fascinating in the very effect of their disappearance behind this rising granite mass of sound, and in their quiet emergence again as the sound subsides.[53]

But no sooner has the mass subsided than it bursts out again, with a final tragic passion, in a most dramatic muttering of the whole corpus of strings, beginning with the basses and rising until it is high in the violins. The rhythm, alluded to by the trumpets and drums, recalls the opening, but the melody that is sung now is new and has never been heard before. Here, at the very last moment, is introduced a new theme! Perhaps this occurrence is nothing but a reflection of life itself, where the best often comes least awaited in the humblest places.[54] The movement closes as it should, in a mighty unison of the first main theme, and thus ends the tragic mood abruptly with its own pregnant motto.[55]

After the tragedy comes the satiric drama.[56] If the first movement were to reflect the tragic irony of the superficial facade that is constructed by man to present the joys of maturity, then the second movement may be imagined to represent the endless round of worldly pleasures, the childish cycle of superficial things with which man distracts himself and which, ultimately, brings him back to the point where he departed.[57] The beauty of the second movement, with its rare and irresistible rhythm and high-spirited melody, is so clear and perfect that no one can escape it.

A short introduction by the strings, with the timpani answering forcefully, marks the rhythm and opens the satiric drama. Tripping along in a dazzling filigree, like a mystic dance of the will o' the wisps, the main melody of this apparently happy movement is introduced by the second violins. It is then picked up, and experimented upon, by the various strings, horn, wood winds and bass. The light-footed and rollicking tune accelerates and reaches climax after climax with ever growing assertiveness, with the timpani renewing the rhythm of the orchestra when it appears to flag.[58]

A second melody appears softly on the wood winds, a sweet tune with an overt ecclesiastical turn, almost like a bucolic parody of a hymntune.[59] However, the first theme jostles it aside and maintains its hegemony, and continues to dominate in one continuous raucous romp. Somewhere, the bassoons take up the main melody in comic relief, joined by the flutes, oboes and clarinets. A drum is presently heard to which the orchestra replies softly, and this dialogue is repeated four times. The entire section is now restated, with the melody assigned initially to the wood winds, then to the cellos and violas. The horns reenter with a counter-theme in the strings; and the subject is once more taken up by the bassoons with an accompanying tune by the oboe. In this way, the sprightly music trips along, and the full orchestral chorus joins in with a pure free dance to close the movement. But the joy in the music is superficial. There is an intimation of impatience and dissatisfaction with this type of pleasure, and in the exasperated chords that terminate this movement, one feels a seeking for a different type of joy.[60]

The slow third movement, skillfully positioned here to contrast with the mighty *finale,* explores the idea of melody to its innermost depths. Its quality lies in the luxurious tunes that move with restless whim, scarce touching one enchanting lullaby before leaving it for another. It is made up of two related sections with different speeds and tones that alternate with each other. The one sets off the other, but there is no striking or disturbing contrast between them. Bassoon, clarinet, oboe and strings intone a brief introduction, and then the moving and tender melody of the first section flows in exquisitely on the strings. The horns, bassoons and clarinets take up the last notes of each strain, and finally the wood winds usurp the tune while the strings provide a tripping accompaniment. Complacence, passionate yearnings, wistful melancholy—all have their full expression here.[61] With a distinct increase in speed and tone, the second violins and violas introduce a deeper and more intense, but still calm and pastoral, melody of the second section, accompanied by the bassoons and lower strings. What joys are contemplated here? Those of peace, perhaps, or of the assured and sanctified love of an immortal beloved?[62]

The first section returns, with the first violins embellishing its tune to the plucking of the second violins and basses, evoking an image of a gently flowing brook, with the bassoons and clarinets echoing the strain. The second section is now recalled by the flutes, oboes and bassoons. And so the melodies alternate with variations, the scenes and rhythms being broken by a prolonged pealing from the trumpets, but with a distinct feeling that something significant is brewing. Somewhere a solo horn is heard, to the expressive plucking of the strings, in a new and strange wistful tune, like the voice of one crying from the wilderness. A grand and beautiful final section follows, and the movement dies away in comparative serenity.

Only words, not instrumental sounds, can fully express the lofty heights of emotion reached in the fourth movement. However, there is first a period of preparation, reflection, consideration, and anticipation that is paved by the wordless orchestra.[63]

A wild discordant explosion by the timpani and the wood winds, and a chaotic and strident fanfare from the whole orchestra launches in the last movement. After a momentary silence, the double-basses reply. The fanfare is repeated even more harshly, and once again the basses reply. The first three movements are briefly recalled, interviewed and discarded. The opening theme of the first movement with its tragedy of life is recalled by tremulous strings and sustained chords in the wood winds but it is quickly cut short by a declamatory passage by the cellos and basses. The scurrying second movement with its reaction from tragedy to a superficial humor that cannot be purely joyful except perhaps during childhood, and then the lyrical beauty of the third movement which is devoid of action because it is of an order too sublime for a world of action are likewise fleetingly passed into review. Each reminiscence is once again strongly disapproved and terminated by the lower strings.[64] None has passed the test for being an expression of untainted joy. Instead, a new melody, a revelation, is required.

Such a theme is now introduced: a grand melody that took half a lifetime to evolve before it was emancipated from all influences of fashion and vagaries of taste, and which now arises to represent a pure and enduring humanity.[65] The wood winds indicate the forthcoming theme over the horns. The cellos and basses respond and take the lead to guide the oboes, clarinets and bassoons into new and sacred ground. Now we hear and feel the surge of the great underlying conception of the work, the mad exaltation that is presently to come.[66]

There is a soft and distant voice in the cellos and basses. The voice grows stronger as it rises in an uplifting and unadulterated joy. Here is the word, the phrase, the ultimate musical pronouncement that the world has been seeking and waiting for.[67] The higher strings join in as if they have been shown the way by their lower counterparts, the melody grows stronger and richer as the other instruments add their voices and finally, an unrestrainable full orchestra bursts out the theme valiantly. It is the mighty hymn to joy! The joyous strings take up the strain, then the whole orchestra breaks in with trumpets soaring. Now follows a chaotic dissonance of the opening musical fragments, impatient and restless, confused and frenzied. A great turmoil ensues, until a mighty and awesome voice of authority speaks out loudly to calm the upheaval.

"Freude (Joy)," cries a solo baritone voice, gargantuan and magnificent. "Freude" responds the massive chorus basses. The voice recites the great three lines supplied as an introduction to Schiller's *Ode to Joy*, with the repeat of the second half given by the whole chorus without sopranos, and then loudly by the whole orchestra. Here is the great moment toward which the entire work has been striving. Throwing off compunction and hesitation, all instrumental standards are flung aside: there is an open desertion by the music to the cause of verbal song. The resources of instrumental tones are abandoned for words, and all the voices break in. To joy is added jubilation and exaltation as the voices reach out ecstatically to touch all humankind.[68]

The instrumental music from this point on, though it be gloriously apt, overpoweringly rich, and movingly beautiful, takes the second place. The words of the poem, and the human voice, come first. At best the two may be wedded in a marriage of equal dignity; but as to meaning, the instruments can no more than reinforce or enrich the words.[69] The whole function of independent music loses its *raison d'être,* giving way to the definite tenor of words.

As the strings follow the singers in the first verse, a counter-melody appears high in the oboes, to which a choir of wood winds rears a new song of beauty. Now the voices themselves, of which a solo voice quartet and the chorus sing alternate strains, weave a fuller harmony to which the oboes and clarinets give answering phrases. As one voice ends the phrase of greeting, another instantly catches on at a higher or lower plane, or two voices chant it in duet, while yet another two sing a dance of joy in polyphony. At its densest, at least six independent voices could be singing their sweetly clashing madrigals. The instruments either follow and echo the voices or spur them on with trills and other rhythmic tricks. As the vocal climaxes are reached, the whole orchestra joins in, either in redoubled melody or in enlivened rhythm.

In this way, the voices and verses continue. In the seventh verse, the blaze of glory vanishes. A solemn silence is broken by grotesque sounds, so it seems, in the depths of darkness, much like a veil covering the terror of things too exalted for human understanding.[70] The sounds, begun by a bassoon, contrabassoon and bass drum, gather hesitantly into a rhythm. Then, out of the depths of the starry spaces emerges a modification of the principal theme, transformed into a military march complete with piccolos, flutes, cymbals, triangle and the big drum, along with distant sounds from the wood winds and trumpets. Nowhere has the terror of war been so simply and so adequately presented! Schiller had compared the paths of heroes to the stars in their heavenly courses, and so it is with this military note. A solo tenor voice forcefully sings "Froh!

(Glad!)"—"Glad as suns, His will sent flying, Through the vast abyss of space" sings the magnificent voice, supplemented by the male voices of the chorus.

Then the orchestra breaks out triumphantly, flying dizzily with great energy. Gone are the deadly march and the clouds of war. After a moment's respite, the chorus returns to the opening lines of Schiller's Ode. Above the sounds of gleeful dance and high voices, and above the long tones of altos sustained by clarinets and brass, "myriad countless chant the greeting." The whole loud music is a completed paean of universal profound joy, uniting all individual rejoicing and love, acme of the perfect state of art where Greek paragon meets Christian ideal in simple and spontaneous joy.[71]

The final chorus is an expression of almost frenzied exultation, interrupted by a brief calm, and then an overwhelming conclusion, a final cosmic appeal, in which heaven and earth and all between vie with each other in a tumultuous climax of rejoicing and pure glee, struck again and again by all the instruments in a careless and deafening abandon of mighty celebration.

- Symphony No. 9 in D minor (Choral)
  EMI Dig. CD-EMX 2186; TC-EMX 2186; Joan Rodgers, Della Jones, Peter Bronder, Bryn Terfel, RLPO Ch. & O, Sir Charles Mackerras $$

- BEETHOVEN: Symphony No. 9 in D minor (Choral)
  DG 447 401-2 Janowitz, Rossl-Majdan, Kmentt, BPO. Karajan $$

[1]   Stringham, Edwin, *Listening to Music Creatively* (Prentice Hall, NY, 1946)
[2]   *Ibid*
[3]   Machlis, Joseph, *The Enjoyment of Music* (W W Norton , NY, 1984)
[4]   *Ibid*
[5]   *Ibid*
[6]   O'Connell, Charles, *The Victor Book of the Symphony* (Simon & Schuster, NY, 1934)
[7]   *Ibid*
[8]   Downes, Edward, *Guide to Symphonic Music* (Walker & Company, NY, 1981)
[9]   O'Connell, Charles, *The Victor Book of the Symphony*
[10] Bernstein, Leonard, *The Infinite Variety of Music* (Simon & Schuster, NY, 1966)
[11] Downes, Edward, *Guide to Symphonic Music*
[12] Goepp, Philip, *Great Works of Music* (Garden City Publishing Co., NY, 1913)
[13] O'Connell, Charles, *The Victor Book of the Symphony*
[14] Bernstein, Leonard, *The Infinite Variety of Music*
[15] *Ibid*
[16] Hurwitz, David, *Beethoven or Bust* (Anchor Books, NY, 1992)
[17] O'Connell, Charles, *The Victor Book of the Symphony*
[18] Goepp, Philip, *Great Works of Music*
[19] O'Connell, Charles, *The Victor Book of the Symphony*
[20] *Ibid*
[21] Goepp, Philip, *Great Works of Music*
[22] *Ibid*

23 Downes, Edward, *Guide to Symphonic Music*
24 O'Connell, Charles, *The Victor Book of the Symphony*
25 Goepp, Philip, *Great Works of Music*
26 O'Connell, Charles, *The Victor Book of the Symphony*
27 *Ibid*
28 *Ibid*
29 *Ibid*
30 Spaeth, Sigmund, *A Guide to Great Orchestral Music* (The Modern Library, NY, 1943)
31 Jacobs, Arthur, *Lend Me Your Ears* (Avon Books, NY, 1987)
32 O'Connell, Charles, *The Victor Book of the Symphony*
33 Ewen, David, *Music for the Millions* (Arco Publishing Co., NY, 1944)
34 O'Connell, Charles, *The Victor Book of the Symphony*
35 Ewen, David, *Music for the Millions*
36 Tovey, Donald Francis, *Symphonies and other Orchestral Works* (Oxford University Press, UK, reprinted 1990)
37 *Ibid*
38 *Ibid*
39 Goepp, Philip, *Great Works of Music*
40 Downes, Edward, *Guide to Symphonic Music* (Walker & Co., NY, 1981)
41 O'Connell, Charles, *The Victor Book of the Symphony*
42 Upton, GP & Borowski, Felix, *The Standard Concert Guide* (Blue Ribbon Books, NY, 1940)
43 Goepp, Philip, *Great Works of Music*
44 O'Connell, Charles, *The Victor Book of the Symphony*
45 *Ibid*
46 Downes, Edward, *Guide to Symphonic Music*
47 Tovey, Donald Francis, *Symphonies and other Orchestral Works*. The finest discussion of the *Choral* symphony is presented in Tovey's book from which this paragraph has been put together
48 *Ibid*
49 *Ibid*
50 *Ibid*
51 *Ibid*
52 *Ibid*
53 *Ibid*
54 Goepp, Philip, *Great Works of Music*
55 Tovey, Donald Francis, *Symphonies and other Orchestral Works*
56 *Ibid*
57 O'Connell, Charles, *The Victor Book of the Symphony*. This paragraph is based on the description of the second movement in O'Connell's book.
58 *Ibid*
59 *Ibid*
60 *Ibid*
61 *Ibid*
62 *Ibid*
63 *Ibid*
64 Tovey, Donald Francis, *Symphonies and other Orchestral Works*
65 Newmarch, Rosa, *The Concert-Goer's Library of Descriptive Notes, Vol. 4* (Oxford University Press, London, 1934)
66 O'Connell, Charles, *The Victor Book of the Symphony*.
67 *Ibid*
68 *Ibid*
69 Goepp, Philip, *Great Works of Music*
70 Tovey, Donald Francis, *Symphonies and other Orchestral Works*
71 Goepp, Philip, *Great Works of Music*

"One man with a dream, at pleasure,
Shall go forth and conquer a crown;
And three with a new song's measure
Can trample a kingdom down."
— A.W.E. O'Shaughnessy

16 Struggling Heights: The Fight for Freedom

The nineteenth century saw the beginning of an intellectual movement focused on the attainment of national freedom. The movement was spurred by the Napoleonic ambitions, and the French success story served to arouse the long-suppressed feelings of national consciousness in the many lands that had been encumbered, not only by political tyranny, but also by cultural domination. It stirred hopes of revolt against subjugation, and a freedom from foreign subjection. For the most part, these may well have been nothing but a magnification of the consciousness of the individual living in bondage.

In this volatile age, music became a vehicle for nationalistic feelings. As states became composed of citizens rather than subjects, and as kings became dethroned and small duchies overthrown, the new consciousness of rights and privileges affected the music of those peoples and races that were the most nationalistic in spirit. It was a natural development both of the romantic movement and of the growth of democracy, since romanticism and democracy both favored regional stories, provincial scenery and local characters. Chopin filled his works with sorrow for the tribulations of his native Poland, and the melodies of Schubert were aimed directly at the hearts of the people around him.

The symphony and its freer offshoot, the symphonic poem, became a free voice that was developed to radiate a sense of the soil, and a feeling for a nation's culture. Reacting to a sterile Western dominance, and striving to foster their own spiritual resources, composers in Bohemia and Moldavia, Russia and Norway found refuge in folk-like elements and ideas. They turned to their native half-forgotten folk songs and colorful legends, their own heroes and histories, and to the beauty of their own lands and the magnificence of their own heritage to seek the grist for a nationalistic musical mill. In some cases, this music was inextricably interwoven with their native songs and dances that gave to symphonic music a colorfulness and individuality, and a type of vigor and vitality, not found in earlier orchestral writings. Others added to their powerful music a strong sense of the epic. The true significance of this music lay in the cause, the unexpressed national idea, that pressed irresistibly towards fulfillment; the concrete elements of the folk song were less important.

Exhibit 72 Tchaikovsky: Overture Solennelle 1812

Peter Ilyich Tchaikovsky (1840-1893) was a Russian through and through. From his earliest childhood, he had grown up saturated with the miraculous beauty of the Russian landscape: The forests, the steppes, the narrow river, the faraway village, and the modest little church.[1] Quite unexpectedly, one or another popular Russian folk song would find its way into his compositions. This intense nationalism grew as he became the foremost representative of Russian music. For the average Russian, the year 1812 had an awesome significance: Napoleon's back had been broken in Russia, not by cavalry or cannonballs, but by the deadly Russian winter. It was as if the very soil had been raised by the saints to rid the land of his shadow. And it should come to us as no surprise that the 1812 Overture became his most overplayed work.

The music is introduced by a loud, fairly fast yet solemn chorale played by the violas and cellos that seems to be supplicating the Gods for assistance during the impending crisis.[2] "Save, O God, Thy People" are the words from a Russian hymn intoned by the melody. The flutes, clarinets, horn and bassoons briefly take over the prayer. Wood winds and strings alternate the plea before they invoke the appeal in unison. The liturgy is shattered by a single blast from the timpani, and the mood changes as the combined voices of the strings and wood winds grow angrier. There is another loud blast, and now the oboes sing a plaintive chant, and the strings sweep upwards. To the combined rattle of military drums, the sounding of the wood winds and the horns, the blaring of trombones, and the clashing of cymbals, there arises a grand and dignified martial call to arms. Suddenly, for an instant, the world stands still; then forthright, the bassoons, cellos and bass take over.

From the distance now arises the thunder of hoof beats—the famous Cavalry Charge. The snare drums roll, and the wood winds and horns loudly announce the clarion call. The violins and violas join in to provide a peaceful contrast, and simultaneously heighten the galloping war cry of the horns. So all day the noise of battle rolls, on a cold strait of barren land beneath the winter skies, as man by man the goodly warriors fall. Then, as the fight subsides, the music fades out and comes to a complete halt.

The movement proper now begins with a grim motive, call it the Strife theme, reminiscent of strife and anger, played loud and fast by the strings with abrupt runs and fierce accents, and with mounting upward and downward sweeps.[3] This melody represents the Russian side in the music. The enemy is sighted and announced vigorously by the trumpets and cornets through the opening strains of the *Marseillaise* which is the melody representing the French side. It is supported by a turbulent accompaniment by the strings and wood winds. After a chaotic and stirring climax, the music subsides and a second theme emerges, a lyrical happier song of hope and love for the homeland, call it the Hope theme, played by the violins and violas. Wood winds take over this melancholic strain, growing ever softer with each passing phrase. Nationalistic feelings are perpetuated through a bohemian Cossack dance that follows, led in quietly and imperceptibly by a flute, horn and the tambourines. The oboe, clarinet, bassoon, violas and cellos each strike up the dance melody briefly in their turn before the music fades away.

Now comes the development of the three themes. Echoes of the Strife theme are woven with nervous fragments of the *Marseillaise* by the horns and wood winds. The former soon emerges stronger as the Russians gain the edge in battle, interrupted by a series of explosions like distant cannons, to lead the fiery music to a breath-taking climax. The sequence of the Hope theme and the Cossack dance, and the opening Russian hymn reflecting God and the fatherland, are repeated in an abridged form. This is followed by a transitional string segment that grows progressively softer in anticipation of the grandiose *finale*.

Victory spreads her radiant wings in the grand celebration that follows. The entire initial musical section, from the loud chorale onwards, returns with renewed vigor, complete with the upward and downward sweeps of the strings, but this time with clanging bells and clashing cymbals. The mood is unmistakably one of festivity and thanksgiving instead of impending doom. The *Marseillaise* fades away, defeated by the victorious Russian Cavalry March which serves as a countermelody. The blaring brass and straining strings pour out a jubilantly played Russian national anthem, *God Save the Czar*. Booming cannon and pealing bells continue with ear-splitting joyous abandon to bring the celebration to a bombastic and triumphant close.

- 1812 Overture; Francesca de Rimini; Marche Slav; Romeo and Juliet (fantasy overture)
    EMI Dig. CD-EMX 2152; TC-EMX 2152, RLPO, Sian Edwards $$

- 1812 Overture; Capriccio italien, Op 45; Marche slave Op 31; Romeo and Juliet (fantasy overture)
    Naxos Dig. 8.550500; RPO, Adrien Leaper $

Exhibit 73 Beethoven: Egmont Overture, Op 84

This incidental music to Goethe's tragedy *Egmont* deals with the religious oppression of the people of the Netherlands by Spain in the sixteenth century. The leader of the Dutch Protestants was the martyr-hero Count Egmont who brought about their victory over the Spanish yoke, but only after he himself had died for the cause. Beethoven's music, as also Goethe's tragedy, introduces an additional romantic aspect that plays no part in the true historic scenes. This is the simple love and devotion of Clara for Egmont which, despite its humble surroundings, splendidly evokes the heroism of this patriot-soldier. Terrible and sudden in his wrath, his dark star has destined him to tread a deep and dangerous path that brings him to the scaffold. It has been said that even the callous Spanish soldiers wept for the brave Count who commended himself to God ere he laid his head on the block. And tears were seen on the iron cheek of Alva, the Spanish leader, as he looked down upon the fateful scene from a window in a house opposite.[4]

The introduction opens on a somber note auguring the tragedy to come. Emphatic and gloomy chords, suggestive of brutal strength, alternate with a strangely wistful and compassionate musical phrase: the crushing power of oppression pitched against the cry of the oppressed.[5] The main theme, audacious and impetuous, is announced slowly on the violins, to which a new tender and poignant melody replies in the wood winds. The musical idea is now stated by a cello, and continues with a progressively descending pitch to give a feeling of resolution and strength.[6] Stronger voices protest; mightier utterances crush them down—the violent brutality of the cellos, violas and bassoons alternates with the outcries of the violin.[7]

There is a pause; then the wood winds sound a cheerless chord, and the agitation grows and takes bodily form to end in a powerful climax. Here is the "Symphony of Victory", announced fast and fierce by the full orchestra with much fanfare by the brass. Out of this apotheosis arises Egmont's last dream—the figure of Freedom arises, bearing the features of Clara, holding a wreath of victory above the hero's head. The music seems an echo of his dying words as the hero envisions the triumph that his death will inspire.

- Overtures: Egmont; Coriolan; Creatures of Prometheus; Fidelio; Leonora No. 1; Leonora No. 3; The Ruins of Athens
    RCA Navigator 74321 21281-2. Bamberg SO, Eugen Jochum $

Exhibit 74 Sibelius: Finlandia

Finland—the cradle of the Vikings! Here is a land of low, reddish granite rocks emerging from the pale blue sea, solitary islands of hard archaic beauty inhabited by hundreds of white seagulls, icy winter winds, lashing gales, bleak pines and lonely Arctic clouds. The fine dusky harshness and dark colors of the earth and skies blend imperceptibly in the music of Jean Sibelius (1865-1957). Here are gnawing bassoons and austere horns, shattering trombones and lashing waves of strings, and the icy glittering of the harp.[8] From this musical tableaux emerged an awakening Finland at the turn of the century, smoldering to break the chains of the Russian government on the Finnish press. The grand tone poem that the world knows now as *Finlandia* so aroused a nationalistic populace that its public performances were banned by the Czar. After a victorious struggle for independence, a grateful nation chose the famous melody of the chorale in its middle section as its national anthem.

There is a menacing recalcitrance in the grim, snarling chords played by the brass in the opening music, to which the sad and soothing wood winds and strings reply in short, appealing supplications. Trumpets and trombones blare out a call to action, and the full orchestra leaps ahead with brilliant and powerfully accented rhythms. The wood winds and violins sing a defiant melody, confident of the certainty of victory, that is reiterated by the cellos and double basses. The music soars up to a jubilant climax, and subsides at once.

Now emerges a serene hymn-like chorale, the famous theme that had touched the limits of the emotions of patriotism. It is intoned softly, first by the wood winds and then by the cellos and violins. Here is a great mourning for those fallen in battle for the birth of a nation. Conflict and defiance return with a renewed vigor, the wood winds proclaim the chorale aloud and, with a growing feeling of triumph, the music ends in a huge climax of terrific power and awesome eloquence.

- Finlandia, Op 26; Kuolema: Valse triste, OP 44; Legends: The Swan of Tuonela, Op 22/2; Tapiola, Op 112
    DG Dig. 413 755-2 , BPO, Karajan $$

Exhibit 75 Weber: Der Freischutz (Overture)

From the middle of the eighteenth century, most of the great courts in Germany had shown an unequivocal preference for Italian art over the German, and the court of Saxony was no exception.[9] The life of Carl Maria von Weber (1786-1826) at Dresden had become one long struggle against these Italian cultural invaders who had on their side not only the royal family, but most of the aristocracy and a fair number of the general populace. In this effort, he had been hindered and humiliated in every conceivable way as director of the despised German opera, and it was only his unquenchable German patriotism that had sustained him.[10] It came from the same impulse that had stirred the first beginnings of a German literature in Herder and Goethe, which culminated eventually in an united burst of nationalism after the downfall of Napoleon.

Der Freischutz (freely translated as *The Enchanted Marksman*) struck the great first blow to the Italian musical influence in Germany, a blow from which it never recovered. This new opera was freshly Teutonic in its language, title, legends and characters. Everything was thoroughly German from start to finish, no less in its settings than in its words and music: The *Lindenbaum* in the village square, the shooting contest, the ghostly Gothic props, the very clothes of the foresters, and the folk and fairy tales.[11] The German people recognized themselves and their country at every point in the music. It summed up for them all their aspirations towards an art of their own, and its colossal success was more to its being a symbol of a great nation's cultural awakening than anything else. The music of this overture is one of the earliest examples in opera in which the chief material of the opera itself is incorporated in the orchestral prelude, to set the atmosphere and suggest the action to come. The whole overture was a striking novelty at its time, and still remains one of the world's great masterpieces.

The story itself is full of the romance and magic that comes from an enchanted world. Certain individuals, says a saga, were accustomed to make a pact with a sinister figure known as the Black Huntsman. In return for their souls, they received from him seven magic bullets that were forged at midnight in a ravine, the grisly Wolf's Glen. These bullets could bring down anything that walked or flew. Six of them followed the will of the possessor, but the destination of the seventh one rested with the Black Huntsman himself.[12]

The overture begins with a slow prelude that breathes the very spirit of a romantic German forest. The strings and wood winds play a mysterious and arresting musical fragment that is answered by an expressive figure on the violins. Here is a magical mood of wonder and expectancy, the very essence of romantic music. A lovely and tranquil main melody, a quiet hunt theme, is then sung by four horns which seem to breath the spell of the forest. It is accompanied by a soft rustling in the violins which are supported by solid harmonies in the lower strings.[13] Suddenly the mood darkens. As this tune dies away, the violins and violas break into a tremulous shuddering to which the clarinets add their own deep color. Plucked double basses and the timpani strike in with sinister reiterated notes, and the cellos break into a poignant wail. The terror rises to a fast and breathless climax, and then fades away almost into silence.

The main music now begins with a brief fragment of very spirited and dramatic music. After a loud triumphant assertion by the whole orchestra, a solo clarinet sings out a magnificent melody against an accompaniment of violins and violas, describing the dark powers made dangerous by man's villainy in the wild Wolf's Glen. It is a song that goes straight to the heart, like a distant wail that the winds have dispersed throughout the depths of the woods. The hero cries out his terror at the evil around him in the words "What evil power is closing around me?" Tremulous strings accompany the tune which leads into a contrasting and melodious second theme given out first by the clarinets and the first violins, and then repeated sweetly by the flutes, clarinets and bassoons. It is a melody of appealing loveliness, trustful and innocent, a song of hope and desire, which the virginal heroine of the opera announces as her pulse beats wildly and her heart throbs with expectation. This section is brief, and is followed by a reappearance of the first theme, then a reminiscence of the heroine's song by the violins, after which the music changes to the introductory cello solo, but this time played by the violins and bassoon.

Now the full orchestra bursts in, the wild upward and downward rushes in the strings, flutes and clarinets are followed by another sinister tremulousness by the strings as the villain agrees to deliver his soul to the devil. The brilliance of the music and its headlong pace become irresistible. This is interrupted, for a moment, by four imperiously arresting chords by a horn. Then, like a shaft of light suddenly piercing the darkness created by the continuing *tremulo*, a solo clarinet piercingly sings

213

out a haunting tune to the tragic words "Ah! horrid darkness lies before me." The struggle is over, and the heroine's theme returns exultantly on the clarinets and flutes to illuminate the gloom, sweeping away all sadness and fear to carry the music to a magnificent orchestral climax, vindicating the final triumph of simplicity and goodness.

- "Beecham conducts favorite overtures, vol.2" WEBER: Oberon; Die Freischutz; BRAHMS: Tragic overture; MOZART: Le nozze di Figaro; Don Giovanni; Die Zauberflote; WAGNER: A Faust overture; BERLIOZ: Le Carnaval romaine; ROSSINI: La scala di seta
    Dutton Laboratories CDLX 7009. LPO, Sir Thomas Beecham $$$

Exhibit 76 Berlioz: Rakoczy March

A few days before he left Vienna for a concert tour of Budapesth, Hector Berlioz (1803-1869) came across a collection of old Hungarian melodies. One of the tunes, allegedly composed at the court of Prince Rakoczy as a *Marche Hongroise*, was based on a wild gypsy folk song. Its stirring rhythm and nationalistic folk air caught the composer's attention and, with Hungary being deep in its struggle for independence, Berlioz quickly wrote a brilliant concert march in which he used this air as its main theme. The effects of the provocative theme, the thrilling climaxes, the stirring use of kettledrums, and the gradual and skillful crescendos from very soft to very loud, were electrifying on the Hungarian audience. "The theater was shaken by a tumult of shouting and stamping," wrote Berlioz in his *Memoires*, "their overcharged souls burst with a tremendous explosion of feeling that sent a thrill of fear right through me. I felt as though my hair were standing on end."

The March opens in a marked rhythm with military fanfare from the brass and wood winds. After a momentary pause, the trumpets give out the brisk rhythm, and the theme of the old folk-air is announced softly by the flutes and the clarinets, accompanied by simple harmonies in the oboes and horns, with a plucking of the strings. The main theme develops a quick crescendo and climax, and the whole section is repeated.

The second section begins with a bold and tripping musical phrase given out by the wood winds, and accompanied in a typical "gypsy" manner by sharp sweeping clusters of tone by the plucked strings. A tiny musical fragment, consisting of three notes with an accent, is repeated between instruments, and in sequence.[14] Drums and triangles are heard; indeed, there is not a sound that does not enhance the martial mood of the music. Presently, the main theme is heard briefly, with the shrill piccolos lending brilliance to the stirring melody, and the orchestra lets itself
214

go in a cataclysm of sweeping thunder and fury in a long crescendo. The rolling of drums, the brilliant and deafening rhythms sounded from the tambourine and triangle, the unison passages in the melody with new rhythmic developments, and the massive chords from the accompanying instruments, broken by the dull beats of a bass drum like the sound of distant thunder, all bring the gorgeous music to an electrifying climax.

- Marches: BERLIOZ: Rakoczy March; WAGNER: Tannhauser March; TCHAIKOVSKY: Marche slave; SOUSA: The Stars and the Stripes; JOHANN STRAUSS I: Radetsky March; ELGAR: Pomp and Circumstance, No 1; SAINT-SAENS: Marche militaire francaise; RIMSKY-KORSAKOV: Procession of the nobles; MENDELSSOHN: War March of the Priests; BAGLEY: National Emblem March

  RCA Victrola 7863-57881-2 , Boston Pops O, Arthur Fiedler $

Exhibit 77   Rossini: William Tell (Overture)

The story of William Tell, based on the familiar play by Schiller, is well known. The freedom loving Swiss had, for long, been overruled by the Hapsburg Dukes who had placed the hated tyrant Gessler in their land to represent the Emperor. Gessler's cruelty became so unbearable that the patriotic Swiss leaders met one night in a lonely meadow, and vowed to overcome the Hapsburg yoke. The famous trial of archery at Altsdorf where William Tell was forced to shoot an apple placed on his son's head has been retold for generations in every Swiss school. Eventually Tell did kill the tyrant, and lead his country's revolution against the foreign rule. Today, a grateful Swiss nation remembers William Tell and his son in a statue erected in the village square at Altsdorf, and in a beautiful William Tell Chapel that stands in his memory on the shore of Lake Lucerne.

William Tell (Guillamme Tell) was the last opera that Gioacchino Rossini (1792-1868) wrote before he retired at the age of thirty seven. Perhaps influenced by the patriotic piano pieces of his younger contemporary Chopin, Rossini's characteristic tunefulness and brilliance struck a deeper note in this music, carrying it to a dignity and loftiness of expression, and a feeling for true patriotism, that was entirely different from anything else that he had composed.[15] The Overture has become one of the most popular operatic overtures ever written.

High in the Alps in the heart of Switzerland were three Forest Cantons, and in one of these lived William Tell. The Overture, which is written in four parts, is a faithful description of the Alpine life that was so dear to the heart of its countrymen. The music opens with a short melody unfolded by a solo cello depicting the awakening of *Dawn*. A dreamy melody by the cello continues throughout the movement, lost in the unfolding of beautiful harmonies by four other cellos. All along, an extremely quiet timpani rolls in the distance. These rumblings get louder and closer, the cello holds the music on a high and sustained note, and suddenly, a tempest breaks in fury in one of the most forceful musical descriptions of *The Storm* in the mountains.

Tremulous violins and violas scurry like racing winds; the piccolos, flute and oboe, and then the clarinets and bassoons, play a short repetitive musical fragment evoking the first big raindrops, and the timpani rumbles in the distance.[16] With explosive blasts combined from the horns, trumpets and trombones, and the deep pounding of the bass drums, the storm breaks out. It rages on angrily, in the shrieking tones of the wood winds and the howling blare of the horns, with the bass drums pounding relentlessly.[17] Presently, the music quietens, and the raindrops patter again in the wood winds. A solo flute sings high in the air as the birds peek out cautiously to check the waning rumblings and, as the atmosphere clears, the song of birds continues, alone in the flute, in a lovely musical phrase to end this section.

After the storm comes *The Calm*, a musical pastoral depicting the quiet life of a mountain shepherd. A solo English horn unfolds a peaceful scene on the mountain top as the melody plays the Swiss shepherd song (*Ranz des Vaches*) which is taken up by the flute. Here are the sounds and echoes of a Swiss shepherd blowing his long mountain horn. A pretty duet follows, to which a triangle adds a charming chime.[18] Suddenly, the calm air is pierced by a fanfare of trumpets and, to the blare of horns and the roll of the timpani, a clarion call to arms is raised that ushers in the patriotic main theme. This is the revolutionary call to revolt for the Swiss patriots. There is a thrilling excitement in the air: The game's afoot!

A brief pause, and forthright the strings, horns, clarinets, bassoons and timpani plunge into the theme. The music is quiet at first, but grows quickly louder as the piccolos, flutes and oboes join the fray. Fast and fierce the music flows; the cymbals clash, triangles ring, the violins sweep through their phrases with incredible agility, a tiny piccolo shrieks out in the air, and as this pounding mass of sound builds up to an inevitable explosive *finale*, there is a split second complete silence, as the orchestra catches its breath.[19] A loud explosion, and the music ends in a spectacular climax.

- Overtures: William Tell; Il barbiere di Siviglia; La Cenerentola; La gazza ladra; La scala di seta; Il Signor Bruschino
  BMG/RCA 60387-2-RG, Chicago SO, Reiner $$

1   Downes, Edward, *Adventures in Symphonic Music* (Farrar & Reinhart, NY, 1944)

2   Stringham, Edwin, *Listening to Music Creatively* (Prentice Hall Inc., NY, 1946)

3   *Ibid*

4   Downes, Edward, *Adventures in Symphonic Music*

5   O'Connell, Charles, *The Victor Book of the Symphony* (Simon & Schuster, NY, 1935)

6   Moore, Douglas, *From Madrigal to Modern Music* (WW Norton , NY, 1942)

7   O'Connell, Charles, *The Victor Book of the Symphony*

8   Rosenfeld, Paul, *Musical Portraits: Impressions of twenty modern composers* (Harcourt Brace & Co., Inc., NY, 1920)

9   Newmann, Ernest, *Stories of the Great Operas* (Garden City Publishing Company, NY, 1930)

10   *Ibid*

11   *Ibid*

12   *Ibid*

13   *Ibid*

14   Kinscella, Hazel Gertrude, *Music and Romance* (RCA Manufacturing Co., Inc., NJ, 1941)

15   Ewen, David, *Music for the Millions* (Arco Publishing Company, NY, 1944)

16   Rudel, Anthony, *Classical Music Top 40* (Fireside Book, Simon & Schuster, NY, 1995)

17   *Ibid*

18   *Ibid*

19   *Ibid*

"There's sure no passion in the human soul,
But finds its food in music."

— George Lillo

17 The Human Comedy

A sense of humor is one of the great assets of mankind, for it denotes not only cheerfulness and friendliness, but also a lack of egotistical self importance. Comedy laughs *at* man, not at his misery or unhappiness, but at the things that can genuinely bring forth a smile—his mistakes, his follies, his minor misfortunes, his antics, and his enjoyments.[1] Comedy also laughs *with* man when he finds life happy and pleasurable.

The effect of comedy in music has been achieved through situation and sound. The comedy of situation depends upon characterization, and upon sets of circumstances which, at their end, leave the listener happy and satisfied. Few can resist laughing at others, or at themselves, when laughter is called for. If the laughter seems to be malicious or cruel, and the world appears to be turning bitter, it is only temporarily. This musical world of comedy is peopled by a wide variety of beings: sophisticated beings whose humor is intellectual, boisterous ones whose wit is rough and ready, and slow-witted ones who provide humor unknowingly.[2] And all along, the music seeks to show that human nature, with all its faults, is essentially good and deserving of happiness.

Exhibit 78 Haydn: Finale: Presto-Adagio from Symphony No. 44 (Farewell)

The noble family of Esterhazy, like so many of the European nobility, were great patrons of music. They maintained a symphony orchestra at their splendid palace on the family estate at *Esterhaza,* built in the wild and remote Hungarian marshes near Vienna. Here, far from distrac-

219

tion and care, and cut off from communication with the outside world, the newly promoted *Kappelmeister* Franz Josef Haydn had full opportunity to pour out his ideas in composition, and satisfy the endless demands of his music-loving prince for new scores. Prince Nikolaus loved the palace and gardens which he had modeled after Versailles and, as the years went by, he began to spend less and less time in Vienna. This became particularly hard on the team of resident musicians who could not bring their families to stay with them at *Esterhaza,* and who could leave to be with their kin only when the Prince himself left for Vienna. In 1772, the Prince stayed on at his palace longer than usual, and the desperate musicians pushed "Papa" Haydn to approach the Prince for the leave that would allow them a visit to their homes and dear ones. And so, the story goes, Haydn composed this symphony as an innocent trick to make his good-natured patron aware of the plight of his players.

The last movement of this symphony opens briskly with a vivacious and light melody. But halfway through the music, the tempo changes and the mood becomes slow and melancholic. One by one, as the Prince and his court looked on, each musician blew out the candle on his music stand that held his score and, with his instrument tucked under his arm, quietly left the hall. Oboes and horns began their exit after a prominent turn in the music: The first oboe and the second horn snuffed their candles and departed. The bassoonist exited after four more bars of music, then the second oboe left, followed promptly by the first horn. Slowly the room grew darker as more candles became extinguished and, as the orchestra thinned out, the music turned slower and more poignant. Here, indeed, was being played a long and reluctant farewell. Now only the strings remained; the double bass player had a comic solo before he, too, departed. The violists and assistant violinists soon were done. Presently, in the gloomy shadows, only two remained, the devoted concert-master Tomasini and Haydn himself. And, if they were to blow out their candles, the music would have come to a silence in the dark.

Prince Nikolaus could take a hint. The following day the court left for Vienna and the musicians departed for their homes.

- Symphonies Nos. 45 in F sharp minor (Farewell); 48 in C (Maria Theresa), 102 in B flat
     Naxos Dig. 8.550382; Capella Istropolitana, Barry Wordsworth $

Exhibit 79 Strauss: Till Eulenspiegel's Merry Pranks

Till Eulenspiegel (Till Owlglass), that popular medieval hero of every German schoolboy, is a sort of personification of the triumph of nimble wit over bourgeois dullness and empty custom. An impish and amoral rogue, Till yet manages to ingratiate himself with everybody by his hail-fellow-well-met gusto.[3] There is a likable turn to his folly, for he is of the soil as none of the other heroes of trickery. When he is eventually grabbed by the collar and hauled along to the gallows, he goes as a matter of course, without knowing why.

Richard Strauss (1864-1959) was thirty one years old when he applied his creative imagination and the available orchestral resources to make this music not only an apotheosis of this likable folk character, but also a running commentary on life in general. It speaks for the individual who dares to stand out against generally accepted opinions.[4] In more than one spot, the mocking laughter and sarcasm of this eternal rebel seems to echo Strauss' own contempt for the fellow musicians who had tried to ridicule the pioneering efforts in his own art, and had put down his own music.

The entire music stems from two main themes which are continuously developed, either singly or in combination, to form virtually inexhaustible sources of new patterns. This is a difficult piece of music for the novice listener. Even Strauss had remarked that in *Till Eulenspiegel's Merry Pranks,* he had given his critics a hard nut to crack! It is suggested that at its first listening, the reader use the printed program on the CD jacket to note exactly the transition from one scene to the next.

The first four notes of the orchestra, as the music begins, vividly presents the first theme. This is followed, almost immediately, by a rising and quickly repeated second theme played by the horn. Keep these two *Till* themes in mind, for out of them will be fashioned the fabric of the whole piece. There is a fine ancient humor pervading this work, distilled from the dregs of folk-lore; even a demonic quality that is inherent in the subject. The humor is the thing, not the story of each of the pranks of our jolly rogue; indeed, the two themes at the very opening appear to prepare us for a wondrous tale that seems to say "once upon a time there lived a wag named Till Eulenspiegel."[5]

Violins announce softly a tender melody that becomes progressively low pitched, setting a mood of long ago and far away. This is the rogue theme, reminiscent of the pure innocent lovableness of the rogue. A humorous and mischievous second theme played by a horn arises almost immediately, call it the horn or the mischief theme, and this tune symbolizes the wayward side of Till's nature. It is repeated in quick succession by different instruments in a rapid crescendo, and ends furiously in a loud climax proclaimed by the entire orchestra. The first theme is again picked up merrily by a quick-piping clarinet, its tender innocence appearing a little more jaunty and clownish than before but still rather honest. But a mischievous scream by the high flutes transforms the music into a roguish mood, and sets the stage for Till's first merry prank in the market place.

It is market day and the women sit at their stalls and prattle. We hear the click of horses as Till approaches, the jogging market tune being a variant of the second mischief theme. Suddenly, Till springs his horse right into the crowd. There is a terrific din and confusion, the two themes leap about maliciously as all Bedlam breaks loose in an enormous orgy of orchestral noise. In haste the rascal rides away to safety to the loud blare of the trombones. All at once there arises, in the midst of this whirling music, a straightforward German folk tune, announced by the clarinets and bassoons, and the scene changes suddenly to set the stage for the second prank.

Till is now disguised as a priest. However, interpolations by the clarinets of Till's first theme over the bourgeois folk song reveal Till's true identity and his mocking, grinning face. A veiled proclamation of the mischief theme, and little shuddering triplets, suggest Till's qualms at mocking religion and, throwing aside his disguise, he becomes himself again.

A short shuddering phrase on a solo violin, followed by a long, gliding wail sends a clear message without any doubts that Till is in love. The two Till themes languish and grow sick with longing. The horn theme represents Till himself, not the demon rogue possessed to tease mankind, but a forlorn man suffering in passion. The infatuated violins, clarinets and flutes declare his devotion zestfully and with great ardor, but all is in vain. Till's advances are rejected and, to a tremendously loud development of the first theme by the brass that is several times repeated, the rogue reappears to swear vengeance on all mankind. But just a moment later, the carefree undulations of the mischief theme on the clarinets show that all has been forgotten and, typical of our restless hero, the moment is ripe for the next prank.

The cellos, accompanied by a persistent plodding rhythm by the wood winds, announce the professors and the pompous mediocrity of academia, the very pedants against whom any upstart genius finds himself in perpetual revolt. The mischief theme adjusts to the new rhythm as if to suggest that Till has fallen in line with his new boring companions. But now the mocking begins; fragments of the mischief theme from different parts of the orchestra are pitched in defiance, and in quick succession, against the dull plodding rhythm of the academia. An exuberant orchestral colloquy follows, but the joke soon ends, and a disinterested Till leaves the dry professors and doctors behind in stupefaction.

A happy, naive street song follows as a contented and conventional world goes by. Fragments of the two themes are bandied around by the wood winds as our hero struggles, with some soul-searching, about a perennial dilemma: whether to submit to the accepted order of things and mend his ways, or continue his wayward life.[6] A wave of tenderness passes over the orchestra.[7] But the arch villain gets the upper hand. Slowly, the mischief theme is unfolded again by the horn, it grows louder, gathering strength until, with a boundless insolence, the two themes dance with profane glee to a rhythmic augmentation by the French horns and trombones to triumph in an unholy orchestral climax.[8] At the height of the festivities the brass sound a prophetic warning.

A drum rolls a long hollow roll and, with heavy menacing chords on the wood winds and lower strings, the jailor drags our rascal into the court room. An impudent clarinet responds indifferently with Till's theme in mocking defiance of the solemn and somber thundering of justice. But the court means business, the clarinets panic, and the lower strings and brass pronounce the sentence.[9] Tubas and contrabassoons snarl a stark and brutal realism as the trap-door opens, and the clarinets and flutes wail piteously. There is a last orchestral convulsion, and Till is dead.

A long pause. The main theme now emerges dream-like, in full melody and beauty, to the plucking of strings, awakening a new understanding of life and its humor, a new realization of the joy and tenderness of life, as if to announce nostalgically once again "Once upon a time there was a wag named Till . . ." The full orchestra breaks into a gallant farewell, as if in a final outburst of demonic laughter on the triumph of the spirit over material obstacles.[10]

- Till Eulenspiegel; Also sprach Zarathushtra; Salome: Salome's dance
  DG 415 853-2; BPO, Karajan $$

- (ii) Till Eulenspiegel; (i) An Alpine Symphony. Op. 64; (ii) Also sprach
  Zarathushtra, Op. 30; Don Juan, Op 20; (iii) Ein Heldenleben, Op 40.
  Double Decca 440 618-2 (2) . (i) Bavarian SO; (ii) Chicago SO; (iii) VPO,
  Solti $

Exhibit 80 Wagner: A Siegfried Idyll

It has been said that Richard Wagner (1813-1883), that most German of Germans, was a gigantic musical force who wrote music, not only for the German nation, but for the whole human race. With grand majesty, he commanded kings and Gods, and bent the powers of nature and magic to his bidding in his music. There is something, therefore, almost humorous that this Titanic spirit should be reduced to the stature of a common man, and write a private instrumental piece of unusual beauty and quiet loveliness for his personal family. This music was written to celebrate the happiness of domestic, albeit illegitimate, felicity. Wagner had much to be thankful for, because in Cosima, he had found a tender haven of love and understanding. His imagination caught fire at the idea of putting to music his great love for his destined wife and their infant son Siegfried, and there was no staying it until the fire had completely burned itself out. For months Wagner composed in secrecy, and rehearsed at a nearby inn.

On early Christmas morning, Cosima's birthday, local musicians assembled for the first time at *Triebschen*, Wagner's villa in Lucerne. They set up their music desks on its broad stairs, and after quietly tuning their instruments, they took their places. Wagner, standing at the top of the stairs, conducted. Then came the violins, violas, wood winds, and horns, and at the bottom, out of sight of the conductor, the cello and bass.[11] As she lay with her little son in the netherland that exists between sleeping and waking, Cosima thought that she was dreaming. But as consciousness gradually returned, she realized the intimate and affectionate meaning of the music, and the inner gratitude that was being expressed to her. When the music was over, Wagner came to her bedroom and presented her with the score. "I was in tears", she wrote in her diary, "but so was the rest of the household."[12]

He had inscribed it as the *Triebschen Idyll, a Symphonic Birthday Greeting from Richard to Cosima.* Years later, the children still referred to the work as the "Stairway Music." The *Idyll* remained a secret and personal document, never intended for the ears of the outside world. It was only when the family came upon desperately hard times that the document was sold, and the music was published under its present name.

The music opens with an introductory building-up of the first theme, a beautiful love melody, which then unfolds leisurely in its own way. A soft, tender continuation leads to a popular German cradle song "Sleep, Little Child, Sleep" (*"Schlaf, Kindchen, schlaf"*) which is sung in its bare simplicity by a solo oboe, and then quickly joined by the first theme played by the muted strings, interrupted by mysterious mutterings by the horns.[13] The two melodies are blended, and to them are added new themes and motives which are the roots from which the music grows. The violins lisp the cradle song to a close, and then a new and strange light appears, the rhythm becomes faster, and the wood winds bring out the theme "Siegfried, Hope of the World"—perhaps a wishful father's prophecy for his infant son's destiny.[14] After some development, the first theme returns; this love theme dominates through all the music, weaving in its many forms a background for the whole piece.

At last a climax is reached. The violins dash down in a torrent, a solitary horn is heard with an energetic new theme that is played quietly, perhaps a song of youthful manhood, while a clarinet and flute break in, now and then, with a song of the forest birds.[15] The many melodies combine and blend, and then a trumpet rises triumphantly. Presently, the trumpet is silenced, the music winds down in a poetic recapitulation, and the horns croon the cradle song even more tenderly as the Hope of the World snuggles safely in his sleep.[16]

- (i; ii) Siegfried Idyll, (iii, iv) Overture: Der fliegende Hollander. (i, v) Gotterdammerung: Siegfried's Rhine journey; Lohengrin: (i; ii) Prelude to Act 1; (vi; iv) Prelude to Act 3. Die Meistersinger: (vi; iv) Overture; (vii; viii) Prelude to Act 3 (ix; viii) Parsifal: Prelude and Good Friday Music. Overture (vi; iv) Rienzi; (vii; x) Tannhauser. Tristan: (iii; iv) Preludes to Acts 1 and 3; (vi; iv) Death of Isolde: (i; v) Die Walkure: Ride of the Valkyries.
  DG Double 439 687-2 (2) (i) BPO; (ii) Kubelik; (iii) Bayreuth Festival O; (iv) Karl Boehm; (v) Karajan; (vi) VPO; (vii) Deutsche Oper, Berlin, O; (viii) Jochum; (ix) Bav. RSO; (x) Otto Gerdes. $

Exhibit 81 Strauss: Don Quixote

"Come, once more before I die I will read *Don Quixote*." said George Gissing, as he made the last rounds in his library to bid farewell to the friends of a lifetime. So, too, may it be said of this music of Richard Strauss (1864-1949). For, this music is so alive that it charms the hours of youth and renews the youth of old.[17] Always merry, at times searching and plaintive, it fills the heart with sunshine, and in the warmth of it the mists of time seem to fade away. Here is a song whose sounds never grow old; men find it good to be alive, and the glory of morning streams all over the world. *Don Quixote, Fantastic Variations on a Theme of Knightly Character* is not a work to sit down to, but music to set out upon. Let the listening of it's three sections be a pleasure journey: interrupted, indeterminate, delayed, and full of loitering and surprises.[18] It is a grand wandering through life, with all its cities and inns, the wayside and the square, duels, fantasies, woeful obsessions, forlorn homecomings, a clearing of the vision, and a lying down for the long sleep.[19]

The mature refinement and sheer incandescence of this music have made some believe that this is Strauss' masterpiece. There is not a single excess or error of taste; every note in its complex structure counts for something, every detail makes the point of its program brilliantly.[20] The lovable and mad Don is represented by a solo cello, while Sancho Panza, the Don's devoted squire, is depicted first by a bass clarinet and tenor tuba, and subsequently by a solo viola.

The *Introduction* begins with a high-spirited statement by a flute and oboe. It is a debonair little tune, knightly and gallant, and from it will spring the theme of knightly character of the Don himself. The music is picked up by the violins and then by the violas, and conveys a placid and rambling mood, a little stiff-jointed and absurd, suggesting, perhaps, the reclining Don meditating of fantastic visions over his readings of ancient and chivalrous tales. Presently, his thoughts turn to the fair Dulcinea, and a lovely song by an oboe, accompanied by muted strings and a harp, unfold her theme.

Suddenly, muted trumpets blare out an excited martial call in ponderous clusters of tone, over gigantesque mutterings by the tubas and bass strings. All is absurd and chaotic: The lady is surrounded by giants and hostile warriors, and our gallant knight rides to her rescue! The confusion rises as the music progresses. Snatches of musical fragments, terrifying chords, and rushing incoherent passages prevail, and the thematic phrases continue to be heard in an increasingly complex and dense musical structure.[21] Several loudly proclaimed discordant clusters of tone, and a final loud empty note by the trumpets and trombones tell us that the Don's mind has cracked, and that the gentleman has become quite mad.[22]

There is an orchestral silence, and then the music formally introduces the main theme. The knight of melancholy countenance, the gaunt Don himself, is wonderfully delineated by a solo cello, though the melody seems to be curiously distorted compared to that played in the *Introduction*.[23] Then follows, down the road, the lumbering theme of Sancho Panza, uttered by a bass clarinet and a tenor tuba, coarse yet somewhat ingratiating, to which a solo viola adds a few marvelously contrived fragments of homely platitudes.[24] Perhaps, there is even a suggestion, now and again, of the trotting feet of the rickety Rosinante and the donkey that bear our knight and his squire.

226

And now the two set out on their musical journey in the *First Variation* of the theme, the solo cello jogging in front of the bass clarinet. A tender strain from the flute, oboe and muted violins, reminiscent of Dulcinea, elicits chivalresque thoughts from the solo cello, and down-to-earth mutterings from the bass clarinet and the solo viola.[25] Suddenly, the music stops: a slowly circling progression by the clarinet, bassoon, violins, and violas describes the circling of the distant windmills.[26] The solo cello grows louder as it gallops forward for a closer look. Convinced that they are giants, the cello charges to give battle. A harp trips loud and strong, and a high sustained note on the cello reveals a prostrated Don, while the music of the windmills continues to circle on.

A vigorous martial variant of the main theme opens the *Second Variation* as the solo cello prepares to charge an imaginary army made up of all the nations of the world. The wood winds protest frantically that it is nothing but a flock of sheep, now heard in the bleats of the muted brass. Notwithstanding, the cello marches into battle, a bold fanfare strikes up as the muted brass cry out piteously, and the music ends in a triumphant statement of the martial theme proclaiming our Don's victory.

The *Third Variation* finds the Don and his squire in deep argument about the ways and means of chivalry. A waxing Don, now voiced by the violins, duets with a garrulous and questioning bass clarinet and tenor tuba. The violins grow impatient, the wood winds object persistently, their thoughts expressed in a long and homely statement put forward by a solo viola.[27] The violins interrupt, and begin an impassioned melody that soars and shimmers with the nobility of chivalrous thoughts and the rapturous dreams of Dulcinea. The orchestra glows as the transfigured voice of the Don rises to a radiant climax.[28] The bass clarinet ventures another protest, but the violins force it into a permanent silence.

The *Fourth Variation* finds the solo cello and the wood winds jogging along the road again. A doleful ecclesiastical chant announces a band of penitent pilgrims. Thinking them to be bandits, the Don attacks and is knocked out senseless. A bass clarinet, tenor tuba and viola utter a horrified wail; the solo cello hesitatingly awakens, and an exuberant bass clarinet and tenor tuba rejoice at his recovery.[29]

In the *Fifth Variation*, the music is meditative. As Sancho sleeps, a pensive solo cello keeps vigil. And in the night our errant knight's fancy lightly turns to thoughts of love. A tender rippling in the harp, and tremulous murmurings in the strings, overlay the warmer tones of the cello as the image of Dulcinea lingers in his mind's eye.

The musical pair are on the road again in the *Sixth Variation* when a coarse parody of Dulcinea's theme is given out by an oboe, with punctuating strokes from a tambourine. It is a rough peasant girl riding on an ass. Sancho playfully identifies her as Dulcinea; the Don is convinced that some foul magic has transformed his beloved, and he swears vengeance.

Soaring strings, a rippling harp, the rolls of a kettledrum, and chromatic scales on the flutes all combine to evoke a ride through the air, blindfolded, on a wooden horse fanned by a great bellows.[30] This is the *Seventh Variation*, and though the Don believes that they are soaring through the empyrean blue, a long-held note on a bassoon indicates that they are squarely planted on earth.

A lilting *bacarolle* transformed by a solo violin and oboe, with fragments of the theme spaced out by a trombone, English horn and strings, describes the episode of the ride in an oarless boat in the *Eighth Variation*.[31] The Don is certain that the deserted bark is a gift from some enchanted spirit, left for them to use to embark upon new adventures. The boat capsizes; they barely manage to struggle ashore, and a flute, clarinet and horn offer thanks for their deliverance.

A dry, theological wrangle between two bassoons describes the pair of Benedictine monks on mules that our jogging duo encounter along the road. Believing them to be magicians, the violins rise to the occasion and rage up and down the scale in a triumphant rout. For once the Don is victorious in this *Ninth Variation* which blends imperceptibly into the next.

In the last and *Tenth Variation*, the Don is challenged to single combat by the Knight of the White Moon. But he is no other than a townsman from La Mancha who, to save the mad Don from further injuries, sets up a condition that the vanquished man must return home for a year. Vigorous sweeps of the low-voiced strings, and interjections from the wood winds, confirm the Don's quick defeat.

The countless incoherences and half-finished thoughts that have plagued the story right from its beginning now start to come together. To the desolate throbbing of the kettledrums, the long and weary homeward march begins. Here is a mighty dirge for a broken hero with lost ideals and shattered illusions.[32] Through this most beautiful of all music, despair gives way to resignation, and from bewilderment arises understanding.[33] Pastoral fragments echo in the wood winds as our hero contemplates an idyllic life as a shepherd, and a lasting and comforting peace.

For the time has come in the *Finale* for the music to move on, from the frolic of Don Quixote to the essential spirit of the Don, the spirit that makes him that "Ingenious Gentleman, Don Quixote de La Mancha." It is a spirit that comforts and delights those who are no longer boys. In this final grand music, the knight and his squire touch life and live life from remotely separate points of view: Sancho is comfort, the Don, aspiration.[34] Sancho's soul dwells in the valley of content; the Don, for the discipline and enlargement of his soul, will not avert his eyes from the heights, nor spare himself the weary struggle thither.[35]

The voice of the cello grows fainter as the Don's strength ebbs away. Wisps of the original theme flit through the orchestra. The music ends in a bright cluster of tone, as serene and as ineffably bright as the smile that lingers on the face of the happy dead.[36]

- (i) Burleske for piano and orchestra, (ii) Don Quixote
  BMG/RCA 09026 61796-2 , (i) Byron Janis (ii) Janigro, Chicago SO, Fritz Reiner $$

- (i) Don Quixote; Death and Transfiguration
  DG 429 184-2, (i) Fournier, BPO, Karajan $$

1 Marx, Milton, *The Enjoyment of Drama* (Appleton, Century, Crofts, Inc., NY, 1961)
2 *Ibid*
3 McKinney, Howard, & Anderson, WR, *Discovering Music* (American Book Company, NY, 1934)
4 *Ibid*
5 *Ibid*
6 Stringham, Edwin, *Listening to Music Creatively* (Prentice Hall, NY, 1946)
7 *Ibid*
8 McKinney, H, & Anderson, WR, *Discovering Music*
9 *Ibid*
10 *Ibid*
11 McKinney, Howard, & Anderson, WR, *Discovering Music*
12 Sabor, Rudolph, *The Real Wagner* (Sphere Books, Penguin Group, NY, 1987)
13 Tovey, Donald Francis, *Symphonies and other Orchestral Works* (Oxford University Press, NY, reprinted 1990)
14 *Ibid*
15 *Ibid*
16 *Ibid*
17 O'Donnell, Bennett, *Much Loved Books* (Fawcett Publications, Inc., NY, 1965)
18 *Ibid*
19 *Ibid*
20 Hagin, BH, *The New Listener's Companion and Record Guide* (Horizon Press, NY, 1978)
21 O'Connell, Charles, *The Victor Book of the Symphony* (Simon & Schuster, Inc., NY, 1935)
22 Hagin, BH, *The New Listener's Companion and Record Guide*
23 O'Connell, Charles, *The Victor Book of the Symphony*
24 *Ibid*
25 Hagin, BH, *The New Listener's Companion and Record Guide*

26   *Ibid*
27   *Ibid*
28   Downes, Edward, *Guide to Symphonic Music* (Walker & Co., NY, 1981)
29   Hagin, BH, *The New Listener's Companion and Record Guide*
30   *Ibid*
31   *Ibid*
32   Downes, Edward, *Guide to Symphonic Music*
33   O'Connell, Charles, *The Victor Book of the Symphony*
34   O'Donnell, Bennett, *Much Loved Books*
35   *Ibid*
36   O'Connell, Charles, *The Victor Book of the Symphony*

"I'll sing thee songs of Araby,
And tales of wild Cashmere,"
— H.G. Wills

18   The Enchanted World

Music begins where speech ends, and many fantastic and fanciful stories have been more artistically and eloquently related in the sound of music. This has been especially true in the case of instrumental music, in which the absence of a narrative allows the imagination of the listener to supply the many charming details which are often the most fascinating elements of a story. Whether it be the horns of elf-land gently blowing, or the fate of a fairy princess transformed under a magic spell into a beautiful swan, or the sight of a firebird with flaming plumage plucking at the golden fruit from a marvelous silver tree in Baghdad, or even the simple flight of a bumble bee, the power of the imagination to suggest has been far greater in music than in the most expressive statements of the written or spoken word.

Exhibit 82   Dukas: The Sorcerer's Apprentice[1]

Paul Dukas (1865-1935) based this very familiar orchestral *scherzo* (a "joke") on Goethe's story of a young apprentice who had often watched his master utter a charm to make a broomstick sprout limbs and follow the magician's bidding. He now proceeds, in his master's absence, to order the broomstick to fetch water for his bath. When he tries to stop it, he realizes that he has forgotten the formula to halt the spell. The stick continues to haul water; the panic-stricken apprentice seizes an ax and splits the stick in half, whereupon two painfully obedient sticks proceed to fetch even more water. The sorcerer returns fortuitously just as a mounting flood threatens to engulf the hapless lad and, with a brusque command, sends the broom back to its corner. The characterizations in this music

231

are gems of brief and accurate description and, once the story is known, its progress can be followed easily as it unfolds with much gusto and gay merriment in the vivid musical portrayals.

A slow mysterious opening by the violas and cellos sets the stage for a world of enchantment. The muted violins, descending gradually in a series of little leaps, softly chant the high-pitched plaintive melody of the magic spell. The broom responds with a grotesque, low-pitched brisk tune, recreating the sorcerer's incantations, played brilliantly by the brass and wood winds. To a sharp thwack of the kettledrum, the apprentice utters the fateful formula.[2] There is an ominous silence. The broom stirs with a faint grunt from the bottom of the orchestra; the grunts multiply, acquire a rhythm, and then the uncanny business begins.[3]

A curiously hobbling, very low-pitched rhythm by three bassoons and a contrabassoon, reminiscent of the awkward gait of the broom, gets going, and bounces forward with relentless energy as the broom scurries back and forth under the spell. The rhythmic pulsation gets faster; the melody of the magic spell returns with whimsical glee, and is tossed fleetingly between the giggling clarinets, bassoons, horns and trumpets as the tension is built up feverishly by a shuddering orchestra. Horns and trumpets blare out the apprentice's panic-stricken screams which grow louder and louder to reach a deafening climax as he desperately splits the stick in two! There is a breathless silence . . . and then the plagued activity begins again, fast and furious, as the bassoons and contrabassoon pick up with a renewed vigor, and an uproarious orchestra, as if possessed by the flood, builds up to a zany crescendo. A dreadful series of blasts by the brass announce the sorcerer's return. The spell is promptly dispelled and the room is still. With a final blast, the broom is relegated to its corner. The themes of the beginning return quietly, simply, and the work ends, as it began, clothed in mystery.

- The Sorcerer's Apprentice; MUSSORGSKY: Night on the Bare Mountain (orch. Rimski-Korsakoff);—BERLIOZ: Symphonie Fantastique;
  Sony SBK 46329; Phd. O, Ormandy $

Exhibit 83   Mendelssohn: Overture to A Midsummer-Night's Dream

That a boy of seventeen should have written so full a masterpiece is one of the marvels of music history. With this single exquisitely wrought work, a hitherto immature composer stepped unfalteringly from experimentation to greatness. In a beautiful and serene garden setting at his family's affluent Berlin house, Felix Mendelssohn-Bartholdy (1809-1847) introduced his first overture to a small family audience. Elfin in the delicacy of its atmosphere, diaphanous in its instrumentation and buoyant in spirit, the music is not only a brilliant interpretation of the spirit of Shakespeare's wonderful fantasy but is also a mirror of the composer's own personality.[4]

It is not necessary to be familiar with the play to enjoy this music. ". . . Once I sat upon a promontory, And heard a mermaid on a dolphin's back, Uttering such dulcet and harmonious breath That the crude sea grew civil at her song . . ." Thus speaks Oberon in the play, and in such a faery delicacy is this music pitched, full of the subtlest tints and hues touched with an almost effeminate grace and gentleness. Here is true love and black magic, pathos and pleasantry, pranks and clowning, set to an ethereal quality compounded of dew and honey and nectar, the scents of summer flowers on warm midnight airs, and the rhythm of happy revelry as elfin feet dance gaily beneath the diaphanous blades of grass.[5]

Four lovely chords, faint and mysterious, played by the wood winds summon in the magic dream-world of Oberon and Titania. The soft, intangible, and delicately wavering music of the woodland fairies follows in the violins, with occasional plucking sounds by the violas. These must be the gay swirls of tiny feet in fairyland, for no mortal could dance to this aerial rhythm! The whole orchestra joins in the joyous revelry, and the music grows louder and firmer. A slow romantic theme floats briefly in the air, reminiscent of the mortal lovers in the play, and it offers a perfect contrast to the tripping opening melody. The dance is momentarily interrupted by a march-like theme as the Duke and his hunting train pass by to the sound of the horns. The dancing resumes, and blends into the jolly tuneful rhythm of a rustic peasant dance. A curious braying, first heard in the strings and then in the low tones of a tuba, bovine rather than brazen, signifies Bottom who, by fairy magic, has been turned into an ass in the play.

The themes are now exquisitely developed with much fantasy and zest. As in the play, the lovers wander together deep into a darkening forest where sudden sounds, at first startling, grow fainter. And the fainter they grow, the more terrifying they become until at last, in a mournful key, poor Herminia of the play—"never so weary, never so in woe"—lies down exhausted to sleep in the glade.[6] The rest of the movement continues in a lively and colorful mood, replete with dainty witchery and full of wonderful new sounds. Suddenly, the four lovely chords that opened the music dispel the midsummer night's dream, just like the magic juices that mischievous Puck had placed on the eyes of Shakespeare's sleepers. To a final drum-roll, the fairy sounds float away, higher and higher into the dream world of enchantment, to end the music.

- Overtures: A Midsummer Nights Dream, Op 21; The Hebrides (Fingal's Cave), Op 26; Athalia, Op 74; Calm Sea and Prosperous Voyage, Op 27; The Marriage of Camascho, Op 10; Ruy Blas, Op 95.
    BMG/RCA Dig. RD 87905 [7905-2-RC}. Bamberg SO, Flor $$$
- (ii) A Midsummer Night's Dream Overture (i) Symphonies Nos. 4 in A (Italian); 5 in D minor (Reformation);
    Erato/ Warner 2292 45932-2, (i) ECO, (ii) LPO, Leppard $

Exhibit 84 Weber: Overture to Oberon

In a bosky dell at the foot of a tiny glen, at the bottom of which flows a tripping stream overshadowed by leafy trees, lies the magic realm of Oberon, the king of the elves.[7] No one has spun a more gossamer tune of the horns of elf-land faintly blowing, or evoked the creatures of a joyous fantasy world, more romantically than Carl Maria Von Weber (1786-1826) in the overture to his opera *Oberon*. Every picture of drama is mirrored in it. Here is a world of fairies and sprites, the pomp and majesty of chivalry and romance, the anguish of separation and death, all blended together in a nostalgic ambiance of pure enchantment. Knowing that his health was failing swiftly, and with the clouds of impending doom hanging overhead, Weber put all that he could into this music which he personally conducted at its first performance. About three weeks later, he passed away in his sleep.

The story is about Oberon and Titania who have quarreled, and cannot be reconciled until two lovers can be found whose passion can survive the ordeals of temptation. In a vision, Huon, the chosen lover, succumbs to the beauty of Rezia, and goes through a series of trials and adventures to seek his loved one. Oberon provides him with a magic horn which, when blown, would summon the elf-king and his troops to his aid. Huon survives the ordeals to unite with Rezia, and the fairy monarchs, too, are reconciled.

The overture opens to the voice of a poetic horn, twice sounded as if from the ends of the earth, that announces a group of three notes which form the magic spell that would summon the elf king. Here is a mortal's music brought under a fairy spell, probing the immense remoteness of one's inmost soul for its sounds. It seems that space has become annihilated, and everything has become exquisitely clear and tiny.[8] A rush of

234

little sounds follows immediately, played by muted strings and a spar-kling flute and clarinet, suggestive of the pattering of little feet as the fairy folk trip lightly along. After a pause and a sharp crash from the whole orchestra that dispels, for the moment, the visions evoked by Oberon's horn, a lively rush of gay music begins. All is bustle and pag-eantry, and the adventure starts.

Again the magic horn sounds, and then a clarinet sings about a gentle ray of light that has broken sweetly on life's broader stream.[9] Rushing violin figures seem to spur on the escaping lovers. An unforgettable tune sung by a clarinet now emerges, evoking a distant vision of Rezia on a desert island, spying the sail of an approaching ship. She hails it with her scarf, to which the violins reply with an exultant passage. Somewhere, a lusty stamping rhythm caused by the two elves, Puck and Droll, enrich the development. Rezia's bewitching melody returns, and the distant vi-sions gather together into a climax of the most irresistible charm, though quite an unfairylike and unsentimental brilliance.[10] This, it has been said, is not the music of a learned composer, but that of a poet!

- "Beecham conducts favorite overtures, vol.2" WEBER: Oberon; Die Freischutz; BRAHMS: Tragic overture; MOZART: Le nozze de Figaro; Don Giovanni; Die Zauberflote; WAGNER: A Faust overture; BERLIOZ: Le Carnaval romaine; ROSSINI: La scala di seta
  Dutton Laboratories CDLX 7009 . LPO, Sir Thomas Beecham $$$

---

[1] Stringham, Edwin, *Listening to Music Creatively* (Prentice Hall Inc, NY, 1944)
[2] Downes, Edward, *Guide to Symphonic Music* (Walker & Co., NY, 1981)
[3] *Ibid*
[4] Ewen, David, *Music for the Millions* (Arco Publishing Co., NY, 1944)
[5] O'Connell, Charles, *The Victor Book of the Symphony* (Simon & Schuster, NY, 1935)
[6] Tovey, Donald Francis, *Symphonies and other Orchestral Works* (Oxford University Press, NY, reprinted 1990)
[7] Kinscella, Hazel Gertrude, *Music and Romance* (RCA Manufacturing Co., NJ, 1941)
[8] Tovey, Donald Francis, *Symphonies and other Orchestral Works*
[9] *Ibid*
[10] *Ibid*

"Of arms I sing and the hero..."
— Virgil

19 Myth and Legend

Ever since the world began, the telling of tales has been one of the happiest ways in which the people of the world have entertained each other. Perhaps, in the beginning, the stories served to fulfill an effort to seek order and unity in the universe, or to comprehend the indiscriminate powers of nature. Unbounded by the laws that governed human behavior, the multitudinous and anonymous powers of the natural world seemed to remain the unseen partners in the struggle for human existence, from the first wail of an infant to the final disappearance into the grave. The myths provided an explanation, or an attempt to grapple with the question of origins, of the sky and earth, of night and day, and of the human condition.

The music of the world of legend abounds with motion: The wind is always blowing, as the sea is always heaving, the rivers are always rushing, and the tall trees are trembling to their tops.[1] The sounds embody moving creatures, animals and humans, and Gods who slide from snowy peaks or rise from foaming waters.[2] The men themselves appear great and swift, fiery and proud, of exalted stature and magnificent dress; melody flows from them like honey, and the dark orchestral chords through which they are heard seem to stream away from them like their long hair.[3]

From the time that Homer sang his great epic of the tragic consequences of the wrath of Achilles, the effects of human moral and emotional choices, the very stuff of human experiences, have remained great musical themes. Hope and fear, caprice, brutality and amorousness, and a dozen other such conceptions have formed the motifs of the innumerable legends and myths on which this music has been based. And naturally so, for in them are rooted deeply the dual nature of man, created half to rise and half to fall, the sole judge of the glory, jest and riddle of the world.

237

Exhibit 85 Wagner: Lohengrin (Prelude: Act 1)

High above the mists on a mountain in Spain stands the castle of Monsalvat, within whose revered walls, a company of holy knights have made their home. Only the perfectly pure in heart can form this chosen order, for they have been entrusted by the angels to guard the Holy Grail (*San Graal*) , the Chalice from which Christ drank at the Last Supper, and into which His blood was collected while on the Cross. One of this select band is Parzival, that noble Knight of the Round Table, and Lohengrin is his son.

The old anonymous German epic of *Lohengrin* had captured Richard Wagner (1813-1883) in a vice.[4] Even though his physician had ordered complete quietness during his prescribed therapy at the baths and the volcanic soils of Bohemia, the excited composer found it impossible to relax. The desire to write this legend of the Grail as an opera had become maddening; The music was impatiently swelling up in his mind, crying out to be expressed, and Wagner could barely remain in the baths before running out to put it on paper.

It would be hard to imagine a more dazzling or fervid musical vision in all Romantic music than that of the Grail in this prelude. The scene is a hate- and strife-filled world, a land from where love has vanished. Like the pale blue aromatic vapors ascending in an unearthly landscape, a strange and enchanted music begins lowly, as a delicate long drawn-out chord is played by the strings and the softly blown wood winds. Slowly, the violins warm up and color more deeply into richer and stronger tones as a barely perceptible, yet magically attractive, vision seems to condense out of the pure blue ether of the sky. It seems like an infinitely delicate outline of a host of angels, floating down from Monsalvat and bearing the sacred vessel. Equally imperceptibly, the music begins to flow into a serenely beautiful melody, the Grail theme, sung by the violins in a stately and deliberate fashion. The theme is now repeated by the oboes and clarinets to add a slightly richer color, with the violins presenting a syncopated accompaniment.

As the vision moves closer to earth, the music begins to rise to a crescendo. New instruments are added, horns and bassoons prepare the way for the trombones and trumpets, the theme grows louder and more impassioned, until it breaks into an awesome and majestic climax, drawing upon the mightiest golden voices from the brass and wood winds, sustained by a roll of the kettledrums, and embellished by a metallic clash of the cymbals.[5] Here is the apparition of the Holy Grail, long lost to sinful man, now vouchsafed for a brief and brilliant moment. Its blazing glory enfolds the enchanted beholder who is struck blind and numb in awe and worship by its fiery beams of golden light, as the most intimate recesses of one's heart tremble with sacred emotions.[6]

The flood light, with its solar intensity, now dies swiftly away, like a celestial gleam. The music seems to float heavenward, growing lighter and more transparent, as the heavenly host withdraws upwards into the vast ethereal blue, followed by its empyrean choirs.[7] The music ends, as it began, in the disembodied sound of four soft violins evoking the spiritual atmosphere that had enveloped the Grail.

- Lohengrin: (i; ii) Prelude to Act 1; (vi; iv) Prelude to Act 3. (i; ii) Siegfried Idyll, (iii, iv) Overture: Der fliegende Hollander. (i, v) Gotterdammerung: Siegfried's Rhine journey; Die Meistersinger: (vi; iv) Overture; (vii; viii) Prelude to Act 3 (ix; viii) Parsifal: Prelude and Good Friday Music. Overture (vi; iv) Rienzi; (vii; x) Tannhauser. Tristan: (iii; iv) Preludes to Acts 1 and 3; (vi; iv) Death of Isolde: (i; v) Die Walkure: Ride of the Valkyries.
  DG Double 439 687-2 (2), (i) BPO; (ii) Kubelik; (iii) Bayreuth Festival O; (iv) Karl Boehm; (v) Karajan; (vi) VPO; (vii) Deutsche Oper, Berlin O; (viii) Jochum; (ix) Bav. RSO; (x) Otto Gerdes. $

Exhibit 86 Wagner: Ride of the Valkyries from Die Walkure

The Valkyries, say the ancient Scandinavian myths, were the fierce and militant daughters of Wotan, and it was their task to snatch the fallen brave from the field of battle and bear them to Valhalla to join their father's hosts. Tall, lusty and fair-headed, these cold and inhuman warrior maidens stormed through the high air amidst thunderclouds and lightning, astride their great steeds, shrieking horse-laugh jokes about the dead heroes that they carried on their saddles.

Richard Wagner (1813-1883) opens the third act of his opera *Die Walkure* with this electrifying music: The nine Valkyries clad in full armor, sisters all, ride through the air on horseback. Callous and uncomprehending, utterly devoid of soft and tender feelings, they regard human suffering and death as a joke, and can understand nothing else but their unquestioned obedience to their Godly father, and their total dedication to their allotted task. They have come to assemble on a lofty mountain peak, before taking off again in a band to Valhalla with their catch for the day.

Nowhere in the annals of music has there been a tone-picture of such superb and detailed suggestiveness, and of such incredible power, as this marvelous musical description of the aerial flight of the Valkyries. Here is the stormiest, the roughest and fiercest, untamed music to evoke the swift and vivid rhythm of the bounding ridden horses, and the unearthly wild cry of the screaming riders. Closer and closer the thundering band approaches; the orchestra summons up its mightiest forces to sway and move to the compelling leaping music of the mighty chargers.[8] The wood winds blare out the gigantic neighs of the steeds, and a great upward-leaping rhythm roars through the brass and explodes in the timpani.[9] Swiftly the Gargantuan spectacle passes by, and then fades from view along a steep mountain pass, the wild cries and echoing hoofbeats lingering briefly behind.

- (i; v) Die Walkure: Ride of the Valkyries. (i; ii) Siegfried Idyll, (iii, iv) Overture: Der fliegende Hollander. (i, v) Gotterdammerung: Siegfried's Rhine journey; Lohengrin: I; ii) Prelude to Act 1; (vi; iv) Prelude to Act 3. Die Meistersinger: (vi; iv) Overture; (vii; viii) Prelude to Act 3 (ix; viii) Parsifal: Prelude and Good Friday Music. Overture (vi; iv) Rienzi; (vii; x) Tannhauser. Tristan: (iii; iv) Preludes to Acts 1 and 3; (vi; iv) Death of Isolde
    DG Double 439 687-2 (2) , (i) BPO; (ii) Kubelik; (iii) Bayreuth Festival O; (iv) Karl Boehm; (v) Karajan; (vi) VPO; (vii) Deutsche Oper, Berlin O; (viii) Jochum; (ix) Bav. RSO; (x) Otto Gerdes. $

Exhibit 87 Saint-Saens: Omphale's Spinning Wheel (Le Rouet d'Omphale)

The story of Hercules, the strongest man who ever lived, occupies a unique place in Greek mythology. He was the favorite son of Zeus who took special measures in his schooling by arranging that he should live among the mortals, much of it in servitude, so that he could gain a knowledge of the real world and a special insight into the human condition. Thus educated, he could aid the Gods in their councils when he took his place on Mount Olympus. This charming though short symphonic poem by Camille Saint-Saens (1835-1921) relates a story of Hercules when he had to disguise himself as a woman to avoid being involved in certain unpleasant circumstances, and was put to work at the spinning wheel as a serving maid by Omphale, the queen of the Lydians. This "musical myth" was first composed as a piano solo, but was received with greater enthusiasm by the Parisian audience in its orchestral form.

The subject of this music is female witchery and seduction, and the triumphant struggle of weakness.[10] Hercules is degraded to female drudgery, clothed in soft feminine raiment, while the queen assumes the lion skin and club. The spinning wheel is but a mere pretext, chosen to create the rhythm and the general atmosphere in this tone poem.

240

The music opens to the whirring sounds of a busy spinning wheel played quietly by the muted strings alternating with the flutes. The clever sounds gradually attain a livelier motion to set the rhythm which is accented by a horn, while the higher wood winds add graceful arabesques to the main theme. A chain of alluring harmonies played by the wood winds above the humming strings represents the laughter of the queen's maidens as they watch the disguised hero in his awkward attempts to use the wheel.

Presently, a lovely song emerges in full chorus, played by the wood winds and occasional strings. The tune is repeated, a harp adds its touches of exquisite harmony to that of the horn, and a drum taps lightly in the background. Later, a single note of a trumpet is answered by a silvery laugh in the wood winds. And all along, the strings hum ceaselessly to the turning of the wheel.

Hercules' theme is now heard, a heroic air, played by the lower strings and the sonorous basses of the wind and brass instruments, accompanied by a low roll of a drum and a soft clash of the cymbals.[11] The song grows intense as the trumpets clang and the drums increase their rolling. A lighthearted phrase for a solo oboe, accompanied only by two soft clarinets, marks Omphale's efforts to mock the proud hero.[12] At last, the full effort of strength battling vainly with weakness reaches a single heroic height, and sinks away with dull throbs.[13]

The whir of the spinning wheel resumes its lively characteristic rhythm with a renewed buoyant spring, mockingly aimed, with railing triumph, at the discomfiture of the mighty hero. Once again the laughter of the maidens is heard in the light voices of the flutes, and once more the cooing horns and the soft rippling harp return with the murmuring strings. The spinning continues until, at the close of day, the workers stop, one by one, and the vivacious and ingenious music slows down to silence.

- SAINT-SAENS: Le rouet d'Omphale; BERLIOZ: Overtures: Le Carnaval romaine; Beatrice en Benedict; Benevuto Cellini; Le Corsaire; Romeo et Juilette: Queen Mab scherzo; Les Troyens: Royal hunt and storm BMG/RCA 9026 61400-2. Boston SO, Munch $$

Exhibit 88 Beethoven: The Creatures of Prometheus (Overture)

The story of Prometheus is well known among the Greek myths. He was the rebellious young hero who defied Zeus and brought the gift of fire to the earth to warm and enlighten mankind. For daring to oppose the

Gods, he was chained to a snowy crag where he was tossed ceaselessly by the winds while two vultures tore at his belly, devouring his liver. But being an immortal he could not die. It seemed that he was destined for eternal torture, when another great hero, Hercules, who, too, had defied the Gods, came to his rescue and unchained him. When the heroic and allegorical ballet *The Creatures of Prometheus* was choreographed in Vienna by a leading dancer, Ludwig van Beethoven (1770-1827) was invited to compose the music. The score for the ballet was divided into an overture, sixteen pieces of incidental music, and a finale.

The music is introduced by an oboe that unfolds a solemn and tender melody that leads into the Overture itself. The main section of the music is a vivacious and carefree piece, based on a dashing theme played softly at first by the violins, and echoed forthright by the whole orchestra. A second melody, serene and lilting, is introduced by the wood winds, and after some rich and very lyrical development, the violins unfold a third theme. Presently, the basses strike a stronger and more dramatic note. The rest of the movement involves a recapitulation of the themes, and the music ends in a stirring *coda* appropriate for a breezy and brilliant classical ballet.

- Overtures: Coriolan; Creatures of Prometheus; Egmont; Fidelio: Leonora 1, 3; The Ruins of Athens
  RCA Navigator 74321 21281. Bamberg SO. Jochum $

1 Van Doren, Mark. *The Noble Voice* (Henry Holt and Company, NY, 1946)
2 *Ibid*
3 *Ibid*
4 Newman, Ernest: *Stories of the Great Operas* (Garden City Publishing Company Inc., Garden City, NY, 1930)
5 Downes, Edward, *Guide to Symphonic Music* (Walker & Co., NY, 1981)
6 O'Connell, Charles, *The Victor Book of the Symphony* (Simon & Schuster, Inc., NY, 1935)
7 Downes, Edward, *Guide to Symphonic Music*
8 O'Connell, Charles, *The Victor Book of the Symphony*
9 *Ibid*
10 Goepp, Philip, *Great Works of Music* (Garden City Publishing Co. Inc.,NY, 1913)
11 Kinscella, Hazel Gertrude, *Music and Romance* (RCA Victor Company, NJ, 1930)
12 Downes, Edward, *Guide to Symphonic Music*
13 Goepp, Philip, *Great Works of Music*

"Heav'n, that but once was prodigal before,
To Shakespeare gave as much; she could not give him more."
— John Dryden

20 Shakespeare

The plays of William Shakespeare lack less than a score of years of being five centuries old. Yet they are as alive today as are certain present questions that occupy the lives and minds of men and women everywhere. Almost all the phases of human existence and human problems are between the covers of these volumes, and though it is a show full of sound and movement, it is, nonetheless, full of the unforgettable.

The plays move on, not act by act, but speech by speech. They voice heroic conflicts of the soul of man in clash with doom. They release, as one generous opening of the hand, the wisdom of the ages. They paint pictures that are fresh and eloquent today because the pigment used was everlasting truth. Into his world you can go intimately, and from it you can learn things singularly applicable to your daily coming and going. There is no past when he writes, because he touches the past with such urgency and intimacy that it becomes our present.

Reading Shakespeare, as Shakespeare wrote it, is the finest game in the fields of literature.[1] A child can enjoy the tales; an old man can, by means of the game, make himself a scholar in our language. Read him not with the eye, but with the lips. Read him valiantly aloud, not in a murmur, but with full-bodied stress. And you will read in him the common and authentic language of the highest and the lowest. He was, at once, the voice of a profoundly articulated spiritual vision as well as that of domestic and popular melodrama. In the pitch and splendor of his lines, and the torrential yet compact eloquence of his long speeches, he caught the very fire that continues, for one reason or another, to appeal to audiences to this very day. Perhaps, the greatest tragedy of Shakespeare is that the generality of mankind, in their mass of maundering commentaries, lectures and essays, have smothered him nearly to death!

And so it has come to pass that in the astounding panache and brilliance of his heroes, and from the splendid dramas that threw open heaven and hell and all in between, endless composers of music have drawn inspiration, or have thought that they have done so, and it is to their spirit that this final chapter pays homage.

Exhibit 89   Berlioz: King Lear (Le Roi Lear)

The inspiration for this overture, a story goes, came after a romantic crisis in the life of the over-imaginative Hector Berlioz (1803-1869), when he allegedly rushed off to slay his beloved, but instead wound up committing an ineffectual suicide by drowning. Coincidentally, Berlioz claims to have completed this piece about four weeks after he had read *King Lear* for the first time. Both these stories are probably as apocryphal as the connection of this music to Shakespeare's *Lear*.[2] Neither any particular passages in literature, nor any particular events in Berlioz's passionate life, formed the origin of this work. Rather, it has been proposed, it was his innate ability to control the vivid tone colors of the orchestral instruments that was the natural inspiration for this magnificent and unmistakably tragic piece of music.[3] Years later, when the composer was asked to conduct his own music during a tour, he was so amazed and overwhelmed by the power of this composition that he found himself unable to hold back a tear.

The music begins with short phrases in the bass strings that are repeated by muted violins. Perhaps this is the commanding figure of Lear himself. After two pairs of such phrases, with each pair repeated in its entirety, a beautiful melody is unfolded by an oboe accompanied, in the background, by plucked strings. This must surely be Cordelia, for no other song can claim to sound the depths of Cordelia's heart, revealing the tenderness that her father could not find. The tune is taken up by a soft chorus of wood winds together with the first violin in polyphony, and then four French horns and trombones sing the whole song softly for a third time, gorgeously accompanied by the whole orchestra.

Now a storm breaks, reminiscent of Lear's wild storm scenes on the heath. It is a recapitulation of the opening Lear theme of the basses, but this time accompanied by the majesty of a full orchestra and backed by a furious, invariable, rhythmic thunder by the kettledrums. Two echoing chords bring the introduction to an abrupt end.

The main section of the overture opens with a violent main theme recalling the opening Lear motive, accompanied by an expressive and sweetly lyrical phrase played by the first violins. A second melody, wearing its heart on its sleeve, unfolds on an oboe, this time bringing out a far

244

more impassioned aspect of the music's pathos.[4] The movement continues smoothly, with a development of the first and second themes, merging into ever more violent and raging outbursts. The music grows louder and more furious and, in a final outburst of rage, ends in a startling and shrill plucked chord, as if something has snapped in the mad king's brain![5]

- Overtures: Le Roi Lear, Op 4; Le Carnaval romain, Op 9; Harold en Italie; Sony MPK mono 47679-2. William Primrose, Viola; RPO, Sir Thomas Beecham $$

- Overtures: Le Carnaval romaine; Le Corsaire; Les Francs-juges; Le Roi Lear; Waverly
  Ph. 416 430. LSO. Sir Colin Davis $$

Exhibit 90 Tchaikovsky: Romeo and Juliet (Overture Fantasia)

The tragic memories of his only true love, the beautiful French singer Desiree Artot, who had left him for another, were still fresh in his heart when Peter Ilyich Tchaikovsky (1840-1893) composed his first important work, based upon Shakespeare's play of family conflict and doomed love. He dedicated *Romeo and Juliet* to his friend and mentor Balakirev who had not only proposed the idea, but had also provided Tchaikovsky with a detailed musical program and outline. The composer added the word "fantasia" to emphasize the freedom of form in which he chose to work.

The music opens in slow, hymn-like fragments that recall the sympathetic Friar Laurence whose ministrations lead indirectly to the tragedy of the lovers. Soon a somber and prayerful melody, reminiscent of a medieval chorale, unfolds in the clarinets and the bassoons, enhanced by ethereal chords plucked by a harp.[6] It is the theme of the holy friar. But beneath its serene veil lurks the dark and sinister ancient feud between the star-crossed families. Serious tones and swift scales in the plucked strings, at times bold and menacing, at times dark and furtive, soar upward in deceptive piety only to sweep down again to darker and lower shadows against the calm of the friar's song.[7] Fragments of lovely melodies try to rise in the strings, but they are foiled by an ominous rumbling on the kettledrums: Something evil is about to begin!

Now the family conflict, brusque and aggressive, bursts into an open conflagration in the full orchestra. Deafening masses of tone are hurled across the orchestra as the instruments rage in a torrent of malice, with upward and downward sweeps on the violins. But it is a brief outburst; as suddenly as it came, it recedes into the deep recesses again as the music

245

winds down almost to nothing, its volume decreasing because of a gradually diminishing number of instruments.

Presently, out of a tremulous background, the muted violins and an English horn unfold the main theme, a caressing and tender love song that is perhaps the most poignant music written by this composer. It is really an eloquent duet between two intensely beautiful melodies that represent the two lovers. The first is woven as an unforgettable, gentle yet melancholic, tune from the tonal voices of the English horn and muted violas with a soft accompaniment by the horns.[8] The other is played by the muted strings that reply with brief and sweet embraces in lovely chords. Here is sweetly expressive music, richly poetic, capturing the mood of the enraptured pair as they watch the coming of dawn in Juliet's chamber.[9] The melody soars to a climax in the muted strings to the words: "Oh, tarry night of ecstasy! Oh, night of love, stretch thy dark veil over us." Then the whole orchestra, sighing and aching, plays the love theme again.

The tender union of the lovers is rudely interrupted by a furious street brawl between their families. Deafening masses of tone are hurled once again through the orchestra as a terrifying and ugly picture of bitterness drowns the lovers' song. The seething tension builds up, and even the friar's plaintive tune, echoed in the horns, is without effect in soothing this chaotic and fierce struggle. Presently, the love theme emerges, more magnificent than before, with wave upon wave of ingratiating sound, striving forward, accumulating.[10] But its sheer beauty is now clothed in a new vehemence and tension that builds up into a secondary climax. The glow fades, and the melody of love gradually dissolves into the conflict theme: Once more the sound grows in force and passion, and once again gigantic forces crash through the orchestra as the music rises to a mighty climax.

There is a pause, and then the love music returns in the low strings, clothed in somber colors, transformed into a sad lament, a dirge for the dead, by the cellos, violins and bassoons, accompanied by a low beating of the timpani. The music mourns briefly for the eternally faithful lovers, and the end comes with sharp tragic chords, reminiscent of the conflict theme.[11] Romeo is dead, and Juliet lies dead beside him.

- Romeo and Juliet (fantasy overture); Francesca de Rimini; 1812 Overture; Marche Slav.
  EMI Dig. CD-EMX 2152; TC-EMX 2152, RLPO, Sian Edwards $$
- Romeo and Juliet (fantasy overture); 1812 Overture; Tempest; Marche slave Op 31;
  Sony SK 47179 Chicago SO, Abbado $$

Exhibit 91 Nicolai: The Merry Wives of Windsor (Overture)

"My new opera has, in its composition, made me very happy. The happiest hours of an artist are those which he spends in creation." So wrote Otto Nicolai (1810-1849) of his sprightly comic opera based on Shakespeare's play of the same name. This little masterpiece, overflowing with lyrics, wit and pure happiness is, perhaps, one of the most popular of all operatic overtures.

It is moonrise over Windsor Forest. From the shadowy depths of the orchestra arises a shimmering melody, a genial air announced by the basses and cellos, and then played high by tremulous violins until it is picked up by the gleaming tones of a flute.[12] Presently, the main theme appears in the strings and the wood winds. It is a vivacious and prankish tune with a slower counter theme, as children disguised like forest fairies and fanciful insects punish the fat knight Falstaff for his attempted sins.[13] A subsidiary passage leads to the second theme, an ingratiating melody of irresistible charm and grace, played by the first and second violins. Other sprightly airs enter, a fragment of this tune returns in the first violins in a dance tempo, and the whole orchestra plays, very loudly, a fantastic medley, amidst much merriment and gales of musical laughter, to end in a brisk and rollicking climax.

- Favorite Overtures: NICOLAI: The Merry Wives of Windsor; MENDELSSOHN: The Hebrides (Fingal's Cave); Ruy Blas; SUPPE: Morning noon and night in Vienna; ROSSINI: La Scala di seta; William Tell; La gazza ladra; Semiramide. Michael Dutton Laboratories mono CDLX 7001 . LPO, Sir Thomas Beecham $$$

Exhibit 92 Berlioz: Romeo and Juliet (Excerpts)

". . . love swift as thought, burning as lava, imperious, irresistible, immense, pure and beautiful as the smile of an angel; the furious scenes of vengeance, the delirious embraces, the desperate struggles between love and death were too much for me. . . . Ah! I am lost!" Two forces drove the impetuous Hector Berlioz (1803-1869) to compose this dramatic symphony. One was his discovery of Shakespeare's *Romeo and Juliet* as these words in his *Memoires* amply indicate. The other was his passion for the Irish Shakespearean actress Henrietta Smithson, later Mme. Berlioz, whose most successful role was that of Juliet. His *Romeo et*

Juliette is divided into three parts of discontinuous scenes. The music is distributed between the orchestra and a chorus, interspersed with vocal solos, with the most dramatic and passionate moments of the play being entrusted to the orchestra alone. The music has a profound intensity and philosophic depth, with an occasional touch of spiritual beauty, that seems to sing to humanity as a whole.[14] The two most popular excerpts are the *Love Scene* and the *Queen Mab Scherzo*.

Some have called the incandescent *Love Scene* the most beautiful music in the world. It is Berlioz's embodiment of a consuming love, perhaps a reflection of his own feelings when he fell in love with his own first Juliet.[15] Soft flutes and softer strings, and the soft tones from a distant horn, unfold the breath-taking enchantment of Capulet's still and deserted garden. Fragments of melody unveil a delicate series of moods: The sadness of solitude, and the feverish thrill of the ball whose last gay strains of singing music are dying away ominously in the distance. Murmurings of muted strings are heard underneath the balcony, over which arise the sighs of an English horn and clarinet. Exclamations from the violins rise in intensity, then subside and break off into agitated figures on the strings.[16] Now emerges a mournfully impassioned love idyll, poured out by the muted cellos and reinforced by a horn. The passion of Romeo shines in its purity, and in its sustained flow are reflected his sincere sentiments. The murmurings of muted strings, the sighs of the English horn and clarinet, and the exclamations of the violins are heard again, and lead to an even more intensely impassioned statement of the cello's melody.[17]

From the balcony, the wood winds now reply, agitated, and their response is interrupted twice by the cellos below. Here is a clear dialogue of wistful lovers, complete with the delicate bliss and pure ardor of early love. As the lower strings hum an urge of desire, the higher wood winds add touches of ecstasy, the melting violins sing a wooing song, and all break into an overwhelming rapture as though transfigured in the brightness of their own passion.[18] The restless spirit starts again, the violas sing a soothing answer from below, the agitation works up to a point of great intensity and then breaks off abruptly: The enchanted night has reached the graying dawn. Halting fragments from the wood winds, and the last sighing exclamations from the cellos, end the music.

"I talk of dreams Which are the children of an idle brain, Begot of nothing but vain fantasy; Which is as thin of substance as the air." From the words and spirit of Mercutio's speech arises *Queen Mab, The Fairy of Dreams,* a musical gem that portrays the airy flight of Mab and her fairies. The music seems to soar, beyond all concrete limits, to the magical realms of dreams.

A play of alternating wood winds and muted strings leads to a rush by the muted violins. The rush subsides, the preliminaries are repeated, and then the rush unfolds the main theme played by the wood winds. It is a fairy rhythm, alternating with the rushing and chattering strings.[19] Here is a fairy dance with a skipping, mincing step followed by a gentle swaying, as the main figure, Mab, leads her troops on a gossamer thread in a dreamland journey.[20] Imps they are, these flitting sprites, almost like little insects with a personality!

The first section ends on a sustained trill of the violins, and then the main song unfolds in a flute and English horn, accompanied by an aerial harmony by the violins and violas and the highest tones of a harp. Soon the skipping dance and magic rush resumes, faster and brighter than before. Presently, a horn is blown in the distance, the golden call of fairyland, punctuated by comments from the strings and wood winds. For a moment the call is tinged with sadness, but it rings out brightly again, like a cheery hunter's lay. There is a lull, and then the kettledrums begin a soft drumming, almost as if they were hailing the fairies. The music grows louder and fuller as the whole orchestra joins in to a huge crescendo, complete with the crash of drums and the clang of brass. The sounds break off abruptly to a mere trembling of the violas, fading ever softer in evocative clusters of tones from the muted violins and the wood winds.

A new melody now dances joyously in the clarinet over the tinkling of a harp, accompanied by the sparkling strokes of the cymbals and the long-blown tones of a horn: The very essence of fairy life.[21] Additional instruments join in to reach another climax of breath-taking splendor. Suddenly, there is a slowing down, like the beginning of the end of a dream. The air hangs heavy with dim romance: hushed chords sound from muted strings, then the strings alternate with wood winds, then arises the silvery tones of cymbals, the strings lead to staccatos of wood winds, plucked strings and harps follow, and finally there is a long sustained note on the cellos.[22] Once again there is a frightening pause, and then the music ends in a huge crash, like a glad awakening to daylight and to reality.[23]

- Overtures: Romeo et Juilette: Queen Mab scherzo; Le Carnaval romaine; Beatrice en Benedict; Benevuto Cellini; Le Corsaire; Les Troyens: Royal hunt and storm; SAINT-SAENS: Le rouet d'Omphale
  BMG/RCA 9026 61400-2 . Boston SO, Munch $$

Exhibit 93 Tchaikovsky: Hamlet
(Overture Fantasia)

The whisper of conspiracy along palace stairways and corridors, haunting specters over moonlit ramparts, defections, deceit and rebellion, crisp equivoke and venomous railing, weak women and mocking devils, and youth—preening, pitiless, wavering youth, fluent in swift word-play and pert turns of speech: All this, and more, did Shakespeare put into this great melodrama.[24] Peter Ilyich Tchaikovsky (1840-1893) dedicated this piece to Grieg.

The music opens slowly in the cellos and violins, grim and full of pathos, as Hamlet grieves his father's untimely death. A dramatic theme unwinds gradually, progressively building up power and volume to end in a climax. Now strikes the midnight hour in the muted horns, and the ghost theme follows, played by the horns, trombones, tuba and double basses accompanied by trumpet calls and tremulous strings.[25]

The main theme of the music presently unfolds, somber and agitated, reflecting both Hamlet's indecision and his resolute purpose. It is followed by the graceful song of Orphelia, given out with a sense of impending doom, first by the wood winds with a string accompaniment, and then picked up by the strings.[26] A march rhythm in the brasses follows, it is repeated by the strings and the wood winds, and then the main theme returns transiently.

Gradually, the music grows in volume and intensity. First the main theme is worked up with great agitation with a phrase played by a solo oboe, followed by Orphelia's melody. Fragments of the two themes are tossed in a long and strenuous development, the march rhythm recurs and predominates, and the whole orchestra works itself up into a frenzied climax. There is a lull, and the music comes to a close, very softly, with echoes of the main theme.

- (i) Fatum (symphonic poem); (ii;iii) Francesca de Rimini; (ii;iii) Hamlet (fantasy overture); (iv;v) Romeo and Juliet (fantasy overture); (i) The Storm; The Tempest; The Voyevodas (symphonic poems); (iv;iii) Overture 1812
  Ph Duo 442 586-2 (2) (i) Frankfurt RSO, Eliahu Inbal (ii) New Philh O (iii) Igor Markevitch (iv) Concg O (v) Bernard Haitink $

---

1   O'Donnell, Bennett, *Much Loved Books* (Fawcett Publications Inc., NY, 1965). This essay is put together from O'Donnell's book

2   Tovey, Donald Francis, *Symphonies and other Orchestral Works* (Oxford University Press, NY, reprinted 1990)

5   *Ibid*

6   Stringam, Edwin John, *Listening to Music Creatively* (Prentice Hall Inc., NJ, 1959)

7   O'Connell, Charles, *The Victor Book of the Symphony* (Simon & Schuster, NY, 1935)

8   *Ibid*

9   Stringam, Edwin John, *Listening to Music Creatively*

10   *Ibid*

11   Downes, Edward, *Guide to Symphonic Music* (Walker & Co., NY, 1981)

12   *Ibid*

13   *Ibid*

14   Ewen, David, *Music for the Millions* (Arco Publishing Co., NY, 1944)

15   Downes, Edward, *Guide to Symphonic Music*

16   Haggin, BH, *The New Listener's Companion and Record Guide* (Horizon Press, NY, 1978)

17   *Ibid*

18   Goepp, Philip, *Great Works of Music* (Garden City Publishing Co., NY, 1913)

19   Haggin, BH, *The New Listener's Companion and Record Guide*

20   Goepp, Philip, *Great Works of Music* (Garden City Publishing, NY, 1913)

21   *Ibid*

22   Haggin, BH, *The New Listener's Companion and Record Guide*

23   Goepp, Philip, *Great Works of Music*

24   O'Donnell, Bennett, *Much Loved Books*

25   Upton, GP, & Borowski, Felix, *The Standard Concert Guide* (Blue Ribbon Books, NY, 1940)

26   Ibid

An

Appendix

Postlude

You have just completed an exciting overview of a broad world of music from many lands and over many centuries, composed by the masters of the art and played by skilled musicians. There is a lot of music discussed in this book; yet it is but a mere fraction of what is available. There are many favorites that one would have liked to see included here, but to make this introductory book a manageable listening companion of sensible length required that the number of pieces be limited to the present collection. The historical approach in Part 2, and the thematic approach in Part 3, also determined the choice of music selected, so that the novice listener could be offered as enjoyable a listening experience as possible the first time around.

Where can one go from here? For those brave hearts who wish to venture forth on their own, pursuing a particular composer or a special theme, The *Penguin Guide to Compact Discs and Cassettes* (Edited, Ivan March, Edward Greenfield, Robert Layton, Penguin Books, NY, 1994) is an outstanding guide to excellence in recorded classical music. This freely available paper-back volume has served many an *aficionado* for over a decade, and deserves purchase and perusal by any serious classical music buff.

For others who need guidance to more great music, *Beethoven or Bust* by David Hurwitz (Doubleday, Anchor Books, NY, 1992) is a marvelous compendium. An interesting feature of this slim volume is that it provides a list of 88 Listening Groups, each consisting of four compositions, which, when compared and contrasted, take the listener further through the web of classical music. There are well over 500 musical pieces mentioned in this book and, combined with the *Penguin Guide*, the listener can look forward to a lifetime of enjoyment of great recorded music.

Bibliography

This bibliography should be seen and used as something more than just a collection of books on music. The unity of this set goes beyond the fact that each member of it is a great book worth reading; rather, the unity is shown by the continuity of discussion of the common themes and problems of listening to good music. All the works are significantly related to one another and, taken together, they adequately present the ideas and issues, the terms and topics, that has made the music appreciation tradition what it is.

Abraham, Gerald, *The Music of Sibelius* (W W Norton & Co.,Inc., NY, 1947)

Altschuler, Eric. *Bachanalia, The Essential Listener's Guide to Bach's Well Tempered Clavier* (Little, Brown & Co., Boston, MA, 1994)

Apel, Willi, & Daniel, Ralph, *The Harvard Brief Dictionary of Music* (Pocket Books, Simon & Schuster, NY, 1960)

Barzun, Jacques, *Classic, Romantic and Modern* (Doubleday Anchor Books, NY, 1961)

Berger, Melvin, *Guide to Chamber Music* (Anchor Books, Doubleday, NY, 1990)

Bernstein, Leonard, *The Infinite Variety of Music* (Simon & Schuster, NY, 1966)

Carter, Harman, *A Popular History of Music* (Dell Publishing Co., NY, 1956)

Copeland, Aaron, *What to Listen For in Music* (The New American Library, NY, 1959)

Peter, Conrad, *A Song of Love and Death* (Poseidon Press, NY, 1987)

Crompton, Louis (Ed.), *The Great Composers: Reviews and Bombardments by Bernard Shaw* (University of California Press, Los Angeles, 1978)

Downes, Edward, *Guide to Symphonic Music* (Walker & Co., NY, 1981)

Drew, Elizabeth, *Poetry, A Modern Guide to its Understanding and Enjoyment* (Laurel Editions, Dell Publishing Co., NY, 1959)

Evans, Edwin, *Tchaikovsky* (Avon Books, NY, 1960)

Ewen, David, *Music for the Millions* (Arco Publishing Company, NY, 1944)

Ewen, David, *Romain Rolland's Essays on Music* (Dover Publications, NY, 1959)

Forbes, Elliot, *Thayer's Life of Beethoven* (Princeton University Press, NJ, 1979)

Gartenberg, Egon, *Mahler, The Man and his Music* (Schirmer Books, Macmillan Publishing Co., NY, 1978)

Geiringer, Karl, *Haydn* (Anchor Books, Doubleday and Company, NY, 1963)

Goepp, Philip, *Great Works of Music* (Garden City Publishing Co., NY, 1913)

Grove, George, *Beethoven and his Nine Symphonies* (Dover Publications, NY, reprinted 1962)

Gutman, Robert, *Richard Wagner, The Man, His Mind, and His Music* (Harcourt, Brace Jovanovich, NY, 1968)

Hagin, BH, *The New Listener's Companion and Record Guide* (Horizon Press, NY, 1978)

Hill, Ralph, *The Symphony* (Penguin Books, NY, 1949)

Hurwitz, David, *Beethoven or Bust* (Anchor Books, Doubleday, NY, 1992)

Jacobs, Arthur, *Lend Me Your Ears* (Avon Books, NY, 1987)

Kamien, Roger, *Music: An Appreciation* (McGraw Hill Inc., NY, 1982)

Kerman, Joseph, *Listen* (Worth Publishers Inc., NY, 1972)

Kinscella, Hazel Gertrude, *Music and Romance* (RCA Manufacturing Co., Inc.,NJ, 1941)

Krenek, Ernst, *Gustav Mahler* (Greystone Press, NY, 1941)

Landon, H.C. R, *The Symphonies of Josef Haydn* (London, 1955)

Le Mee, Katherine, *Chant* (Bell Tower, NY, 1994)

Machlis, Joseph, *The Enjoyment of Music* (W W Norton & Co., NY, 1984)

McKinney, H & Anderson, WR, *Discovering Music* (American Book Co., NY, 1934)

MacDonald, Calum, in *The Symphony, Past, Present, Future.* BBC Music Magazine, Summer Special, 1995

Marx, Milton, *The Enjoyment of Drama* (Appleton, Century, Crofts, Inc., NY, 1961)

Moore, Douglas, *From Madrigal to Modern Music* (WW Norton & Co. Inc., NY, 1942)

Newmann, Ernest, *Stories of the Great Operas* (Garden City Publishing Company, NY, 1930)

Newmann, Ernest, *Wagner as Man and Artist* (Garden City Publishing Co., NY, 1941)

Newmarch, Rosa, *The Concert-Goer's Library of Descriptive Notes* (Oxford University Press, London, 1931)

257

O'Connell, Charles, *The Victor Book of the Symphony* (Simon & Schuster, NY, 1935)

Peter, Conrad, *A Song of Love and Death* (Poseidon Press, NY, 1987)

Robertson, Alec (Ed.) *Chamber Music* (Penguin Books, NY, 1957)
Rosenfeld, Paul, *Musical Portraits: Impressions of twenty modern composers* (Harcourt Brace & Co., Inc., NY, 1920)
Rudel, Anthony, *Classical Music Top 40* (Simon & Schuster, Fireside Book, NY, 1995)

Sabor, Rudolph, *The Real Wagner* (Sphere Books, Penguin Group, NY, 1987)
Seigmeister, Elie, *The Music Lover's Handbook* (William Morrow and Company, NY, 1943)
Spaeth, Sigmund, *A Guide to Great Orchestral Music* (The Modern Library, NY, 1943)
Stringham, Edwin, *Listening to Music Creatively* (Prentice Hall, NY, 1946)
Sullivan, JWN, *Beethoven. His Spiritual Development* (Mentor Books, NY, 1937)

Taylor, Ronald, *Franz Liszt, The Man and the Musician* (Universe Books, NY, 1986)
Thomson, Oscar, *Debussy, Man and Artist* (1937, reprinted 1967, Dover Publications Inc., NY)
Tovey, Donald Francis, *Symphonies and other Orchestral Works* (Oxford University Press, NY, reprinted 1990)

Upton, GP & Borowski, Felix, *The Standard Concert Guide* (Blue Ribbon Books, NY, 1940)

Vallas, Leon, *Claude Debussy, His Life and Works* (Oxford University Press, 1933; reprinted 1973, Dover Publications, NY)
Van Doren, Mark, *The Noble Voice* (Henry Holt and Company, NY, 1946)
Vienus, Abraham, *The Concerto,* (Doubleday, Doran and Company, NY, 1944)

Walker, Alan, *Franz Liszt: The Weimar Years* (Alfred A Knoft, NY, 1989)
Watson Derek, *Liszt* (Schirmer Books, NY, 1989)

Index

Adagio 8, 82, 162
Agnus Dei 78
Alhambra 43
Allegretto 8,45
Allegro 8, 82, 163
Allemande 72
Andalusia 43
Andante 8,49, 82, 162
Apres Midi d'un Faun (Debussy) 134
Archduke Trio (Beethoven) 109
Arpeggio 9

Bacchanale 180, 181, 183
Bach,JS 48, 67-71
Badinerie 74
Baroque 63
Bassoon 30
Beethoven, Ludwig von 30, 45, 51, 158, 188, 199, 210, 241
Berg, Alban 163
Berlioz, Hector 10, 20, 121, 126, 161, 172, 176, 183, 214, 244, 247
Billroth, Theodore 195
Bolero (Ravel) 3
Bonaparte, Napoleon 188, 208
Bouree 74, 75
Brahms, Johannes 95, 99, 195
Brandenburg Concertos (Bach) 67, 69
Brass Choir 33
Byron, Lord 20, 126

Carnival of the Animals (Saint-Saens) 22
Celesta 39
Cello 22
Chamber Music 105

Chopin, Frederic 130
Choral Symphony (Beethoven) 199
Chord, Musical 9
Classical style 81
Coda 10
Concertino 64
Concerto 64, 65
    Concerto Grosso 64, 65, 67, 69
Concerto for piano & orchestra No 21 (Mozart) 102
Concerto for violin & orchestra in E major (Bach) 70
Concerto for violin & orchestra (Berg) 163
Concerto for violin & orchestra in E minor (Mendelssohn) 18
Contrapunctal Music 44
Cordelia 244
Corsair, The (Berlioz) 126
Courante 72
Credo 43, 77
Crucifixus - Mass in B minor (Bach) 77

D'Agnoult, Maric 166, 197
Danse Macabre (Saint-Saens) 180
Dante 166
    Dante Symphony (Liszt) 166
Death 157
Death and Transfiguration (Strauss) 159
Debussy, Claude 146, 149
De Falla, Manuel 135
Development 54, 55
Dies Irae 42, 180, 181, 183
Don Quixote (Strauss) 225
Double bass 23

Dukas, Paul 231
Dvorak, Antonin 28

Egmont Overture (Beethoven) 210
Ein Heldenleben (Strauss) 123
Eine Kleine Nacht Musik (Mozart) 16
Emperor Quartet (Haydn) 112
Enchanted world, The 231
English Horn 28
Epitectus 185
Eroica Symphony (Beethoven) 158,
    188
Erl King, The (Schubert) 182
Esterhazy 13, 49, 219
Exposition 47, 53

Falla, Manual de 135
Falstaff 247
Farewell Symphony (Haydn) 219
Faust 171
Faust, The Damnation of (Berlioz) 176
Faust Overture (Wagner) 177
Faust Symphony (Liszt) 172
Fingals Cave (Mendelssohn) 150
Finlandia (Sibelius) 211
Fireworks Music, Royal (Handel) 75
Flute 28, 134
Flying Dutchman, Overture
    (Wagner) 153
Fountains of Rome (Respigi) 137
The Four Seasons (Vivaldi) 65
Francesca de Rimini (Tchaikovsky)
    168
Freedom 207
Freischutz Overture, *Der* (Weber) 212
Fugue 47
Fugue in G minor (Bach) 48
Funeral March (Beethoven) 158

Gigue 73
Glockenspeil 147
Goethe, Johann W von 171, 172, 177,
    182, 186, 210, 231
Gregorian Chant 42, 43
Gretchen 171, 173, 177
Gropius, Manon 163

Hamlet overture (Tchaikovsky) 250
Handel, George Frederic 75

Harmony 9
Harold in Italy (Berlioz) 20
Harpsichord 67
Haydn, Franz Josef 13, 49, 84, 112,
    219
Hebrides Overture (Mendelssohn) 150
Heiligenstadt 86
Hell 165
Hercules 240
Hiawatha 28
Holst, Gustav 37
Holy Grail 117, 238
Homophony 45
Human comedy 219
Human condition 185
Hungarian Rhapsody No. 2 (Liszt) 127

Idee fixe 20, 21, 121, 122
Impressionism 134
Instruments, Musical 13
Italian Symphony (Mendelssohn) 128

Kettledrums 39
Keys 54
    Dominant 54
    Home 54
King Lear, overture (Berlioz) 244
Krenek, Ernst 162
Kyrie 43, 76

Largo, 8
    New World Symphony (Dvorak) 28
Liszt, Franz 127, 166, 172, 175, 186,
    197
A Little Night Music (Mozart) 16
Lohengrin, Prelude (Wagner) 238

Mahler, Gustav 162
Marche Hongroise-Rackoczy (Berlioz)
    214
Mars- The Planets (Holst) 37
Marseillaise 208, 209
Mass 42, 76
Mass in B Minor (Bach) 76
Melody 9, 10
Mendelssohn, Felix 18, 128, 150, 232
Mephistopheles 175, 176
Mephisto Waltz No. 2 (Liszt) 175
Merry Wives of Windsor, Overture

(Nicolai) 247
Midsummer Night's Dream, Overture
   (Mendelssohn) 232
Military Polonaise in A Major (Chopin)
   130
Minuet 74, 75
   and Trio 16, 57
Modulation 54
Moldeau, The (Smetana) 118
Monophony 41
Motive 9
Mozart, Wolfgang Amadeus 16, 55,
   102
Mussorgsky, Modeste 33, 181
Myth 237

Nationalism in Music 207
New World Symphony (Dvorak) 28
Nicolai, Otto 247
Night on Bald Mountain (Mussorgsky)
   181
Nights in the Gardens of Spain (Falla)
   135
Nocturnes (Debussy) 149
Norway 211
Nutcracker Suite (Tchaikovsky) 27

Oberon Overture (Weber) 234
Oboe 31
Ode to Joy 199
Oedipus (Sophocles) 99
Omphale's Spinning Wheel
   (Saint-Saens) 240
Orchestra, its beginnings 13
Orphelia 250
Overture
   Corsair, The (Berlioz) 126
   Creatures of Prometheus
      (Beethoven) 241
   Der Freischutz (Weber) 212
   Egmont (Beethoven) 210
   Faust (Wagner) 177
   Francesca de Rimini (Tchaikovsky)
      168
   Flying Dutchman (Wagner) 153
   Hamlet (Tchaikovsky) 250
   King Lear (Berlioz) 244
   Merry Wives of Windsor (Nicolai)
      247

Midsummer Night's Dream
   (Mendelssohn) 232
Oberon (Weber) 234
Roman Carnival (Berlioz) 10
Romeo and Juliet (Tchaikovsky)
   245
Tragic (Brahms) 195
William Tell (Rossini) 215

Passacaglia 95
Pastoral Symphony (Beethoven) 90
Percussion Instruments 39
Piano concerto No. 21 (Mozart) 102
Piano Quintet in A Major- Trout
   (Schubert) 106
Piano sonata in C Major - Waldstein
   (Beethoven) 51
Pizzicato 16
Plainchant 42
Planets, The (Holst) 37
Pictures at an Exhibition (Mussorgsky)
   33
Polonaise 130
Polonaise in A Major (Chopin) 130
Polyphony 44
Prelude 72
   Afternoon of the Faun (Debussy)
      134
   Lohengrin (Wagner) 238
Preludes, Les (Liszt) 186

Quintet 13
   Piano in A Major- Trout (Schubert)
      106

Rakoczy March (Berlioz) 214
Ravel, Maurice 3, 33
Recapitulation 55
Renaissance, The 61
Respigi, Ottorino 137
Rhapsody 127
   Hungarian No 2 (Listz) 127
Rhythm 7, 10
Rimski-Korsakov, Nicolai 151
Ripieno 64
Ritornello 65
Roman Carnival Overture (Berlioz) 10
Romance 17
Romantic Period 117

Romeo and Juliet (Tchaikovsky) 245
Romeo et Juliette (Berlioz) 247
    Love scene 247
    Queen Mab scherzo 247
Rondo 51
Rossini, Gioacchino 215
Royal Fireworks Music (Handel) 75

Saint-Saens, Camille 22, 180, 240
Saltarello 11
Sanctus 78
Sarabande 72, 74
Scheherazade (Rimski-Korsakov)
    The Sea & The Ship of Sinbad 151
Scherzo 82
    Queen Mab (Berlioz) 247
Schiller, F 199
Schubert, Franz 23, 182
Sea, The 145
Sea, The (Debussy) 146
Senta 153
Sibelius, Jean 166, 211
Siegfried Idyll (Wagner) 224
Sirenes (Debussy) 149
Shakespeare, William 243
Smetana, Bedrich 118
Socrates 185
Sophocles 99
Sorcerer's Apprentice (Dukas) 231
Sonata form 52-54
Sonata, Piano in C major (Beethoven)
    51
Strauss, Richard 123, 159, 221, 225
String Choir 15
String Quartet No. 3, Op 76 (Haydn)
    112
Suite 72-73, 75
    Orchestral No. 2 (Bach) 75
Supernatural 179
    Surprise Symphony (Haydn) 49
    Swan, The (Saint-Saens) 22
    Swan of Tuonela (Sibelius) 166
Symphony 82-85
    No. 3 (Beethoven) 188
    No. 4 (Beethoven) 30
    No. 5 (Beethoven) 85
    No. 6 (Beethoven) 90
    No. 7 (Beethoven) 45
    No. 9 (Beethoven) 199

    No. 1 (Brahms) 95
    No. 4 (Brahms) 99
    No. 9 (Dvorak) 28
    No. 44 (Haydn) 219
    No. 94 (Haydn) 49
    No. 10 (Mahler) 162
    No. 4 (Mendelssohn) 128
    No. 40 (Mozart) 55
    No. 8 (Schubert) 23
    No. 4 (Tchaikovsky) 192
Symphonie fantastique (Berlioz) 121

Tarantella 21, 130
Tasso's Lament & Triumph (Liszt) 197
Tchaikovsky, Peter Ilyitch 27, 31, 168,
    192, 208, 245, 250
Tempo, Musical 8
Theme and Variations 49
Till Eulenspiegal (Strauss) 221
Timbre 8, 13
Titania 232, 234
Tragic Overture (Brahms) 195
Triebschen Idyll 224
Trout Quintet (Schubert) 106
Trumpet 33, 37
Tutti 64

Unfinished Symphony (Schubert) 23

Valkyries, The Ride of the (Wagner)
    239
Viennese School 81
Viola 20
Violin 15
Violin concerto in E major (Bach) 70
Violin concerto (Berg) 163
Violin concerto in E minor
    (Mendelssohn) 18
Vivaldi, Antonio 65

Wagner,
    Richard 153, 177, 224, 238, 239
    Cosima 224
Weber, Carl Maria von 212, 334
William Tell, overture (Rossini) 215
Witches Sabbath 181, 183
Wolf's Glen 212
Wood Winds Choir 27

Give the Gift of

Classical Music for Everybody

to Your Friends and Colleagues

CHECK YOUR LEADING BOOKSTORE OR ORDER HERE

❑ **YES**, I want _____ copies of *Classical Music for Everybody* at $16.95 each, plus $3 shipping per book (California residents please add $1.39 sales tax per book). Canadian orders must be accompanied by a postal money order in U.S. funds. Allow 15 days for delivery.

My check or money order for $_____ is enclosed.

Please charge my ❑ Visa   ❑ MasterCard

Name _____

Organization _____

Address _____

City/State/Zip _____

Card #_____Exp. Date _____

Signature _____

Phone _____

Please make your check payable and return to:

The Fitzwilliam Press
100 Monterey Lane
Sierra Madre, CA 91024

Call your credit card order to: 1-800-997-MUSIC (997-6874)

FREE Offer for readers of

Classical Music for Everybody

For those who don't quite know where to begin,
and for those who choose to deepen their present understanding

The Music Lover's Personal Library of Orchestral & Instrumental Music

This exclusive 12-page booklet has two very special lists of recorded performances on CD that extend the repertoire contained in this book. They are, of course, personal choices, but they carry the combined experience of close to a half century of listening. Great care has been exercised in the selection of the works that we felt should be included in a music lover's personal library. Much thought also went into the choice of the recordings. The music in the *Basic Library* is immediately appealing, and the performances evoke its mood and spirit in a way that a beginner is almost certain to enjoy and appreciate. The *Supplemental Collection* extends the basic libarary, and includes worthy alternatives or recordings of great historical performances. Recordings that make up our *Desert Island Collection* are highlighted by **boldfacing** - they are outstanding recorded performances whose magical quality make them a special treasure that is uniquely valuable, no matter the price.

To obtain your free copy, mail a card with your name and address to

**The Fitzwilliam Press
100 Monterey Lane
Sierra Madre, CA 91024**

**For fast service, call toll-free 1-800-997 MUSIC (997-6874)
Fax: 818 355 1296**